TURBOCHARGED TESTIMONIES

"☆☆☆☆☆ TurboCharged test drive results: 36 pounds in 5 weeks!"

"Success Story: Senior citizens can lose extra fat too!"

Mark Rubi, Extreme Weight Loss Research Examiner.com

"TurboCharged changed my life! I started at 54 years old, 134.8 pounds on my 5'3" body. Today I'm 110 pounds and keeping it off. My pants are falling off as I keep losing inches. My metabolic age is 12! My energy is phenomenal!"

Luci Hundley, TurboCharged Fan

"I have lost 110 pounds of FAT!! I should be the poster child for all that TurboCharged can accomplish."

Chuck Voelker, Facebook Fan

"With its straightforward advice, easy-to-follow food rules, and boundless encouragement, TurboCharged stands out from the rest of the diet and exercise guidebooks by digging deep into topics like body mass, metabolism, and eating habits. … With its numerous tips, real-life examples, well-articulated advice, and 'you can do it' encouragement, TurboCharged can help anyone get on track with diet and exercise."

Elizabeth Millard, ForeWord Reviews

"☆☆☆☆☆ There are very few body improvement books that can be recommended more highly than Turbo Charged. Even reading the book is addictive and to say much more about the book would be a disservice to those out there who are frustrated with fatty deposits in their bodies. Buy your own copy, keep your own copy for reference, and encourage your acquaintances with healthy outlooks who are struggling with expensive diets and special meals and memberships in programs to buy it too. This book works!"

Grady Harp, Vine Voice, Top 10 Amazon Reviewer

"One more pound to lose and I will have dropped 25 pounds in eight weeks…I've dropped my weight to a number I haven't seen since high school and I have abundant energy. Can't remember the last time I felt so good."

Danny Greenberg, Publisher, Los Angeles Sports & Fitness Magazine

"Rapid fat loss a breeze for TurboCharged challenge participants…Results for six weeks included fat loss between 8 and 29 pounds with fat loss averaging 12.9 pounds, muscle gain 3 pounds, and a loss of 8.8% of body fat."

Doni Luckutt, Reporter, Denver Post.com

TurboCharged
Recipes

Delicious Fuel for Your
Fabulous Fat Burning Machine

DIAN GRIESEL, Ph.D and TOM GRIESEL

THE BUSINESS SCHOOL OF HAPPINESS
CONNECTICUT

Turbocharged is a trademark of The Business School of Happiness, Inc.

For information contact:
The Business School of Happiness, Inc.
Attn: Permissions Dept.
P.O. Box 302
Washington Depot, CT 06794
860.619.0177

Published by The Business School of Happiness, Inc.
Interior Design by Carla Rood

The Business School of Happiness books and recordings are available through most bookstores as well as amazon.com. For further information, call 860.619.0177 or visit our websites at www.businessschoolofhappiness.com or www.turbocharged.us.com.

Substantial discounts on bulk quantities are available to corporations, professional associations and other organizations. For details and discount information, contact our special sales department.

PLEASE NOTE: The creators and publishers of this book are not and will not be responsible, in any way whatsoever, for the improper use made by anyone of the information contained in this book. All use of the aforementioned information must be made in accordance with what is permissible by law, and any damage liable to be caused as a result thereof will be the exclusive responsibility of the user. In addition, he or she must adhere strictly to the safety rules contained within the book, both in training and in actual implementation of the information presented herein. TurboCharged is a program for rapid body-fat loss. It makes no medical claims. It is the sole responsibility of every person planning to apply the techniques described in this book to consult a licensed physician in order to obtain complete medical information on his or her personal ability and limitations. The instructions and advice printed in this book are not in any way intended as a substitute for medical, mental or emotional counseling with a licensed physician or healthcare provider. Before beginning the TurboCharged program, we suggest that when you consult your physician you request a complete physical along with full blood-panel testing. These numbers will serve as an excellent baseline to measure your progress as you follow this program.

ISBN # 978-1-936705-07-8

Library of Congress # pending

DEDICATION
. . . .

To our Mom, Jane, who never failed to cook a tasty meal.

Dian: To Rory, Chamonix and Steel, who are mostly willing test subjects for recipes.

Tom: To Janet, who has cooked countless creative meals for years and keeps me filled and fulfilled in so many ways. And to Joe, who really knows how to make a killer salad.

CONTENTS

Dips & Dressings 40

Appetizers 56

Soups & Stews 70

8

Salads 96

Vegetarian 128

Eggs 166

Fish 178

Meats 200

Poultry 230

Desserts 248

Introduction

A TURBOCHARGED LIFESTYLE

Hopefully you are holding this book in your hands because you have read *Turbo-Charged: Accelerate Your Fat Burning Metabolism, Get Lean Fast and Leave Diet and Exercise Rules in the Dust*. Ideally you are now in your best shape ever and you seek to stay in Cruise Control, maintaining your new lean, fabulous, awe-inspiring physique.

If you haven't read *TurboCharged*, you can certainly use any of the recipes in this book and surely your health will benefit. However, we do recommend that you pick up and read *TurboCharged* first. The reason? The TurboCharged program is holistic. What we eat to keep our bodies fueled, using excess body fat for energy, is only one small part of the overall program. You can readily get a copy at amazon.com, on our website www.turbo-charged.us.com, or inquire at your local bookstore.

For discussion's sake, let's assume you have finished reading *TurboCharged*. Maybe you are relatively new to the program, maybe you have reached the Winner's Circle and now you have shifted into Cruise Control. Either way, you are a life-loving individual who likes to keep both your life in general, as well as what you eat, interesting. We understand. That's why we decided to share some tasty recipes that will help you stay on the Express-way or maintain your success in Cruise Control. For those who choose the SuperHighway, super-fast route to fat burning, we recommend that you stick with the basics outlined in *TurboCharged*. The simple route is the best route to getting to the lean physique you seek. However, occasional meals from any of these recipes are fine. Once you've reached your goal, knowing that as humans we like spice and variety, feel free to incorporate some of these recipes into your daily routine.

As a refresher to *TurboCharged*, all one has to do is commit to following these eight easy steps:

▶ Forget whatever you learned in the past about dieting.

▶ Measure your real success by tracking your body fat and your body composition.

▶ Fill your tank with water upon awakening, prior to eating and immediately when the first sign of thirst appears during or right upon completion of a meal. Also, Turbo-Chargers continue to fill up with 16 to 32 ounces of water in intervals no greater than two to three hours apart during the day.

▶ Rinse with a sorbitol-based mouthwash and/or brush your teeth after drinking and prior to eating. This will either help establish whether you are really hungry, or at least delay your meal since we all know food doesn't taste too good when accompanied by mouthwash or toothpaste.

▶ TurboChargers are active. We walk, play, clean our own homes, wrestle with children, park a little farther in the parking lot, pack our own groceries. We know that everyday activity helps to build flexibility and strength, and keeps our bodies in fat-burning mode.

▶ We incorporate Mini-Muscle workouts of one to three minutes, three to five or more times a day. These keep our brain focused on retaining muscles (while making us leaner and sexier)!

▶ We fuel our bodies with foods that are based on our evolutionary development and this keeps us burning excess body fat at all times. Our meals fall into one of six categories:

1. A meal with any amount of whole protein and/or fat alone or combined. This would include beef, fish, pork, venison, chicken, eggs, cheeses of all kinds and tofu.

2. A meal with any amount of fresh, whole fruits or vegetables. This includes baked potatoes, sweet potatoes, avocados and olives.

3. A meal of 90% whole protein and/or fat (as outlined in #1) along with no more than 10% vegetables. Think in terms of volume on a plate—not the calories of the food group.

4. A meal of 90% vegetables and/or fruits along with no more than 10% whole protein (as outlined in #1). Again, think in terms of volume on a plate—not calories of the food group. Use the "eyeball" rule.

5. A smoothie made with water (or ice) and a scoop of 100% whey, egg or pea protein powder that has no more than 3 grams of carbohydrate, about 25 grams of protein and approximately 100 calories per serving.

6. A smoothie made with water (or ice) and 1-2 whole fruits. A scoop of 100% whey, egg or pea protein is optional.

▶ We visualize our goal of a sleek, lean physique regularly at intervals throughout our day. (See *The TurboCharged Mind* book for more on this.)

TURBOCHARGED EATING FOR LIFE

TurboChargers know that "dieting" by any conventional standard other than the TurboCharged holistic program is not effective in controlling weight, has never worked and is destined to deliver failure coupled with plenty of depression and moodiness. We have experienced the benefits of TurboCharging and know that this program provides the map to get us permanently and once and for all to Leandom—the place we all want to live for the rest of our lives.

TurboCharging works because each of the Steps work together to eliminate hunger.

Prior to TurboCharging, most people likely would have been deriving the majority of their energy from a constant supply of sugar provided in countless forms by their diet. Because of this and the chronically elevated insulin levels this constant sugar consumption creates, the transition or "switch" to using body fat no longer works the way Nature intended it. TurboChargers know that a diet containing sugar, refined carbohydrates and grains will shut the fat-burning process down totally. The steps in TurboCharged retrain your body to easily source energy from your body fat (and fat from your diet) along with the natural sugars ingested from the fruits and vegetables we are now eating. Turbo-Charged foods healthfully and nutritiously satisfy all of your energy needs. You develop a true hybrid system, which will automatically and easily use all sources of available energy either from diet or body fat in a seamless fashion. When you follow the steps, during periods when you eat less, instead of converting lean body mass for energy, you will easily access your own body fat. This becomes obvious from the resulting lack of hunger and elevated feelings of well-being.

This said, TurboChargers do eat and we eat plenty of tasty and delicious foods.

We try to keep our meals as natural as possible and we always base them around the most power building, best-fueling foods available.

TURBOCHARGING RATIONALE

TurboChargers know that there are no miracle foods. We your authors, and other intelligent TurboChargers, never claim to know more than our Maker regarding the immensely complex aspects of creating and maintaining human life. We don't rely on fads, gimmicks or supplements. Rather we build our diets around the plethora of natural, fresh-as-possible foods so plentifully provided by nature.

As described in *TurboCharged*, when TurboChargers eat, we use a bit of evolutionary reasoning in our meal selections. The thought process works like this: "Our early ancestors were on the run, fighting for survival. Most likely they were subsisting on very few calories consisting of easy-to-find-and-eat fruits, vegetables, seeds and maybe nuts along with other basic vegetation. Considering the energy requirements of their day, this was probably pretty close to what TurboChargers would call "enlightened fasting." Good nutrition, but not a heck of a lot of calories. At other times, when they were really lucky, early humans were chowing down, sometimes for days at a time, on whatever wild beast they managed to catch. Since there was no refrigeration, along with the fact that meats and organs of the wild beast kind were high in both proteins and fats, this food source would spoil rapidly. It is likely that animal food was eaten as a sole meal source until it was gone or too rotten to eat. Our early relatives didn't have the luxury of refrigeration, leisurely sitting down to eat and mixing a variety of foods as we do today. It simply wasn't practical or possible.

This bit of ancestral history gives us two good pieces of information.

First, it is highly likely that the body's digestive system did not evolve to eat many different foods at the same time—particularly protein/fat foods along with carbohydrates. The idea of eating balanced meals may look good on paper, but in the real world, these meals put too much stress on our digestive systems, plus they are the cause of indigestion and GERD or acid reflux. Our digestive system is really amazing and will attempt to deal with anything we put in our tanks, but this doesn't make balanced meals a good idea. Digesting food is hard work for our bodies, and ideally we want to keep digestion time to a minimum if we want maximum efficiency and performance. Your digestion and energy levels will improve enormously by practicing the TurboCharged guidelines. Without getting too scientific, suffice it to say that different food groups each require different digestive processes. Mixing carbohydrates with fats and/or proteins will result in the meal lingering in your stomach too long. This then creates indigestion and makes overall digestion of these meals more difficult, burdensome or even incomplete. Once anyone tries TurboCharging for 10 days, they are convinced that our recommendations are correct.

Second, an interesting question arises if one compares this kind of eating to dieters of today. Think about it. Our ancestors were either practically starving OR they were pigging out on massive amounts of fatty meat before it spoiled. You might think they'd be fat—like a yo-yo dieter who consumes low calories one day and then binges on large quantities of foods and calories the next when their willpower is shot. But history proves this isn't the case. Our ancestors didn't diet and they were not fat. Instead, they were active and lean. They ate by separating their nutrients (because they really had no choice) . To get and stay lean, TurboChargers do the same.

TURBOPOWER FOODS

Taking this all into consideration, the recipes that follow are quite simple. They are loaded with taste, yet they involve very few ingredients. Fueling a TurboCharged body for optimum fast fat loss, involves eating whatever you want from the following sources but also by following the TurboCharging guidelines of macronutrient separation.

▶ *Fruits:* Fruits are visually attractive and naturally sweet. They are tasty, loaded with the water essential for transporting their plethora of nutrients, low in calories and high in natural fiber to keep things moving through your digestive system easily. Fruits deliver high-quality antioxidant-rich carotenoids and flavonoids, plus vitamins A and C, folate, manganese and potassium—just to name a few. Diets rich in fruits have been proven to reduce stroke, coronary artery heart disease and other cardiovascular diseases, reduce risk for type 2 diabetes, protect against cancers as well as help reduce bone loss. Fruits offer fast satiation, are low in calories per cup vs. most other foods and therefore are an ultimate TurboCharging food.

▶ *Green Vegetables:* Broccoli, cabbage, spinach and greens like kale, Swiss chard and escarole are rich in potassium, fiber, folate and vitamins A, E and C. These nutrients are linked to a reduced risk of heart disease and possibly some forms of cancer. Broccoli and spinach are especially potent tools against disease. Measured ounce for ounce, broccoli contains the same amount of calcium as a glass of milk and more

Introduction

vitamin C than an orange. Calcium is crucial to bone health, and vitamin C helps protect the body from toxins called free radicals that can damage cells and cause disease. Spinach is high in lutein, a compound that may help prevent macular degeneration (central vision loss). It's also an excellent source of folate, a B vitamin that helps prevent spina bifida in babies.

▶ *Orange, Yellow and Red Vegetables:* Bright orange vegetables like carrots, sweet potatoes and pumpkins are great sources of vitamin A in the form of carotenoids. Research shows a link between carotenoids and lower rates of heart disease and vision problems, such as cataracts and macular degeneration. Carotenoids act as strong antioxidants, compounds that protect the body from cell damage that can lead to disease. Sweet potatoes and carrots are especially high in beta carotene, a carotenoid that may help reduce the risk of certain cancers.

▶ *Eggs:* Eggs are simply egg-ceptional foods. Replete, prepackaged by Nature they contain optimal sources of carbohydrate, protein, fat and micronutrients. One whole egg contains 6 grams of high-quality protein, all 9 essential amino acids and about 68 calories. Their fat is the kind you want: An egg contains only 5 grams of fat and only 1.5 grams of this is saturated fat. New research dispels previous research about eggs having a negative impact on cholesterol. In fact, consuming two eggs a day does not affect a lipid profile adversely and may actually improve it. More important, eggs are a great source of choline with one egg yolk having about 300 micrograms. Choline is an important nutrient that helps regulate the brain, nervous and cardiovascular systems. Eggs are also one of the very few truly health-ful food sources that contain naturally occurring vitamin D. Eggs are an important natural protein source for TurboChargers.

▶ *Chicken:* Chicken is another source of protein with about 48 grams per 6-ounce serving. It can be a healthy food, depending on how it is prepared. Heavily coated with cornflakes for crispiness, you're defeating your TurboCharging efforts. When it comes to fat, the amount varies. Skinless chicken breast has about 3 grams of fat, and chicken breast with skin on it has about 14 grams per 6-ounce serving. Calorie counts also change depending on the skin or not with a skinless chicken breast hav-ing about 240 calories per 6-ounces and breast with skin having about 340 calories. Chicken is a source of calcium with 6-ounces of cooked chicken having about 21 milligrams. Potassium is another nutrient found in chicken with about 340 mg per 6 ounces. Chicken has no carbohydrates, but again, it is often accompanied by sauces (although none in this book!) that can alter the carb count.

▶ *Beef/Meats:* Calorie-for-calorie, beef is one of the most nutrient-rich foods to fuel an active and healthy TurboCharged lifestyle. A three-ounce serving of lean beef is an excellent source of protein, zinc, vitamin B12, selenium and phosphorus; and a good source of choline, niacin, vitamin B6, iron and riboflavin. TurboChargers aim to get these essential vitamins and minerals from the source—not from a pill—as we know they are essential for developing and maintaining cognitive ability, keep-ing muscles rich with oxygen while metabolism stays high, and keeping our energy high for activity and action. Substantial evidence shows protein will help a body get and stay lean, while fueling muscle efficiently for physical activity.

▶ *Fish:* Fish is low-fat and is a good quality protein. It is filled with vitamins like riboflavin (Vitamin B2), which aids the body in the metabolism of amino acids, fatty acids, and carbohydrates; and Vitamin D, which aids calcium absorption to help prevent osteoporosis. Fish is also rich in calcium and phosphorus and a great source of minerals, such as iron, zinc, potassium (a mineral needed for muscles, nerves, and fluid balance in the body), iodine, and magnesium. Fish that are rich in Omega-3-s—such as salmon, tuna, trout, herring and sardines—are the best sources of this type of essential fatty acid that may reduce the risk of blood clots and help stabilize heart rhythms. Maybe there is truth to the old wives' tale that fish is brain food—particularly the fattier species. Research has shown that these fatty acids may also play a role in preventing depression and Alzheimer's disease. They also have an anti-inflammatory effect that may benefit people with degenerative diseases such as rheumatoid arthritis.

> NOTE: The FDA cautions pregnant women to eat no more than 12 ounces of fish per week, to limit possible fetal exposure to methylmercury.

▶ *Nuts:* Nuts, including almonds, brazil nuts, cashews, hazelnuts, macadamia nuts, pecans, pine nuts, pistachios, walnuts and peanuts, are nutrient-dense—with many nutritional benefits including protein, fiber, micronutrients, plant sterols, gamma-tocopherol and other phytochemical compounds, like flavonoids and phenolic compounds. Most nuts contain many minerals, including magnesium. Population studies indicate that individuals who regularly consume nuts have reduced risk for cardiovascular disease and diabetes. In clinical trials, nuts appear to have a neutral effect on glucose and insulin, and a beneficial effect on lipid profile. All this is good news for individuals with diabetes or those at risk for diabetes, providing overall caloric intake is regulated to maintain a healthy body weight. They are also a great source of monounsaturated fat, as well as the antioxidant vitamin E and the amino acid arginine, which may help lower abnormally elevated cholesterol. Eating a one-ounce serving of nuts regularly, about five times a week, has been shown to reduce the risk of heart disease. Eat a variety of nuts, but be mindful of portions since they are high in calories.

▶ *Beans:* Can beans make you happy? Maybe. Beans are an excellent source of folate, a type of B vitamin. Some studies indicate that low folate levels may contribute to depression. Beans are also an excellent source of fiber and protein. Research at Tulane University has shown that people who eat beans and other legumes regularly, four or more times a week, had lower cholesterol. Although beans were likely not a regular food of our ancestors and they are very dense calorically, we include them because they provide some added nutrition and energy for those who prefer a vegetarian way of eating. Children will often eat them without objections and they add some more natural fiber to the diet.

▶ *Cheese:* Cheese is a common staple that is produced throughout the world. It can be found in a wide range of flavors, textures and forms. In general, cheese supplies a great deal of protein, fat, calcium, phosphorus, zinc, vitamin A, riboflavin and vitamin B12. A shade larger than a one-ounce serving of cheddar cheese contains about 7 grams of protein and 200 milligrams of calcium. Cheese has a low lactose

Introduction

content—which is important to TurboChargers because lactose is the sugar naturally found in milk. It is also a sugar that is harmful to teeth. Cheese, on the other hand, due to its high calcium content, is great for bones and teeth. For those who are beginning TurboChargers, those who might still have high blood pressure, the important considerations when choosing a cheese would initially be its sodium content and fat percentage. There are low-sodium cheeses and choosing these would be advisable. The content of B vitamins in cheese is too important to overlook, and the bit of fat they provide in moderation can be helpful to keeping you on track with your life-long goals of leanosity. This said, for those traveling the SuperHighway to their ultimate destination of a lean, fabulous physique—we'd probably have to recommend that you go light on the cheese. It is simply too tasty, making it a food that is easy to overindulge on. A cube or two is fine—but keep in mind, cheese is an excellent food for gaining weight. All said, for children, we highly recommend plenty of whole-fat cheese—and we are not talking about the processed kind that comes in spray cans, jars or prepackaged between crackers. Choose quality cheese for increased health.

▶ *Red Wine and Grapes:* We simply cannot leave a discussion regarding power foods and ignore red wine. If you like wine, drink it. However, beware that your body will become immensely more efficient in processing anything you eat—so the alcohol in wine will get to your cells that much more quickly. As such, we recommend no more than two glasses daily, and be sure to alternate those with a big glass of water. Grape skins, used in making red wine, contain high levels of resveratrol, an antioxidant that has been shown to decrease the risk of heart disease, prevent changes in the blood that contribute to atherosclerosis, and help prevent the development of certain cancers. However, we'd be remiss if we didn't point out that simply eating grapes will provide the same benefits—without the alcohol.

▶ *Tea and Coffee:* The next time you're sipping a cup of tea or coffee, drink to your health. Studies show that red, black and green teas (green tea is simply less processed than red or black tea) contain compounds called polyphenols—antioxidants that help protect cells from damage, reduce risk of certain types of cancer, prevent blood clotting and lower cholesterol levels. The antioxidants in coffee appear to lower the risk of diabetes and heart disease. If drinking caffeinated versions, limit yourself to no more than two normal size cups daily. More than that and you will likely end up with jitters that can trigger a crash. Also, remember, TurboChargers drink their teas or coffee black or only use no more than two tablespoons of half and half—not skim, 1%, 2% or whole milk and no artificial creamers. We drink these without added sweeteners or use an artificial one if we really insist.

A note on tofu: We are not including tofu as a TurboCharging power food. Also, you will not find any recipes in this book that use tofu or any soy-based products. Although in TurboCharged we acknowledged tofu as a vegetarian option, we are not fans of this highly processed, denatured food. Please see Turbocharged.us.com for more information and links to sites that are filled with information elaborating on this perspective and the detrimental effects of eating tofu and other soy products.

NO SUPPLEMENTS NECESSARY — JUST EAT SMART

TurboCharging power foods—offering significant health effects that go beyond basic nutritional needs—are a topic of great interest among researchers today.

These carefully chosen power foods are high in antioxidants, which are those compounds that block cell damage caused by toxic substances called free radicals.

Plant-based foods, which TurboChargers eat in unlimited quantities, are also high in phytochemicals—naturally occurring substances produced by plants that may prevent disease and help slow the aging process in both the body and brain.

All this said, we offer one caveat—supplements don't provide the same protective benefits as whole foods. The combination of natural substances found in whole foods works synergistically to promote health. So TurboChargers go to the market (or maybe their own gardens); they find these ingredients; and they eat for their good health. We don't believe gimmicks, supplements or magic potions will accelerate our health, and instead accept that they could possibly cause a crash.

TURBOCHARGING YOUR CHILDREN

Childhood obesity is a serious health problem. About one in four U.S. kids are classified as being overweight. Lack of physical activity is one of the culprits. Current guidelines recommend that kids strive for at least 30 minutes of moderate activity per day. Parents shouldn't face this problem sitting down. Turn off the TV and computer and try these tips to motivate "couch potato" kids. TurboCharging your children starts with being a good role model.

▶ Play with your kids in the park, bike around the neighborhood or take an after-dinner stroll.

▶ Encourage your kids to try an organized sport or activity and make sure you show your commitment, too. If you can't coach, be a score keeper, transport kids to and from games, volunteer for the "healthy" snack committee, and always cheer on your team.

▶ Emphasize the fun of playing rather than the thrill of winning. Kids who feel a lot of competitive pressure tend to burn out on sports at an early age.

▶ Help your kids find something they like to do—dancing, skiing, roller skating, skateboarding, snowboarding, cycling, shooting baskets, jumping rope, or anything that gets them moving.

▶ Check out neighborhood recreation centers or Town Hall activities. Go to family swim nights or purchase a fun kid-exercise video for home for winter days, but above all encourage outdoor activities.

▶ Lead by example. Find extra ways to stimulate exercise. Walk, don't drive, and take the stairs rather than the elevator. Plan family activities that incorporate fitness.

Introduction

Take a walk at a zoo or museum. Try skating or bowling rather than a movie.

▶ TurboChargers often use pedometers as a fun, simple way to measure activity. Kids love these gadgets. Set individual goals and keep a chart to track progress. At the end of the week, let the "winner" pick an activity that the whole family can enjoy. And most importantly, remember to have fun! Swimming, sleigh riding, frolicking and just good old play or a game of tag all count as perfect TurboCharging activities.

PSYCH YOUR KIDS INTO HEALTHY EATING

Getting kids to eat properly involves more than just preparing the right foods. To regenerate the TurboChargers in your children, leading to greater odds of a lifetime of health in a lean body, try some of these ideas…

▶ Let kids eat when they are hungry so they get used to being able to interpret signals from their body.

▶ Get your kids involved in the entire meal-planning process, from clipping coupons to shopping for foods to meal preparation and cooking.

▶ Serve kid-size portions, using kid-size plates, which are less overwhelming. Make them ask for seconds.

▶ Put healthy foods within easy reach of little hands. Keep them on the lower shelves in the pantry and refrigerator.

▶ Don't give up on serving healthy foods too quickly. Research has shown that it takes 10 to 15 exposures for a child to accept a new food.

▶ Look for creative ways to add veggies to favorite foods. Serve spinach pizza or add shredded veggies to tomato sauce or meat loaf.

▶ Don't use high-fat or sugary desserts as rewards. It makes sweets seem more valuable than the rest of the meal. Don't forbid them either, just serve in moderation.

▶ Eat meals as a family whenever possible and set a good;example by eating well yourself.

▶ Don't worry if they can't finish. However, upon their declaration of being "full", insist on drinking a 4-6 ounce glass of water. This will truly fill the belly and get those satiation hormones triggered in addition to setting the stage for a good life-long TurboCharging practice.

▶ After the evening meal is complete, if your child is seeking a snack, make sure to have plenty of fresh fruit available. The habit of eating fruit as an evening snack is a life-extender.

▶ Encourage dessert choices from the menus within this book. They are delicious, tasty and provide the fat for energy that kids require.

FLAVORING WITH HERBS & SPICES

TurboChargers stick with TurboCharging fruits, vegetables, nuts, seeds, fish, chicken, meats and cheeses. But that doesn't mean we always eat them plain. Variety is the spice of life. Here are a few spices to consider trying and the foods they best blend with taste-wise.

▶ Basil: Aromatic and sweet flavor. Can be used as whole leaves, chopped, minced or ground. Goes beautifully with mild cheeses like mozzarella, lamb, fish, roasts, stews, ground beef, vegetables, and eggs.

▶ Bay Leaves: Pungent air. Use a whole leaf—but be sure to remove it before serving. Good for vegetables, seafood and beef stews.

▶ Caraway: Spicy and aromatic. This is the seed that you used to eat on rye bread. Can add a nice touch when sprinkled into soups or onto soft cheeses.

▶ Chives: Sweet, mild flavor similar to an onion. Delish when finely chopped in salads, over fish or a steaming cracked-open baked potato and as a finishing touch to an omelet. Also great in soups.

▶ Cilantro: Fresh is best. We cannot get enough cilantro into our homemade guacamole. Excellent with salads, fish, chicken, beans, and with avocados, tomatoes and onions.

▶ Curry Powder: A strong character folks seem to love or hate. Curry is actually a stable of blended spices combined to give flavor to meat, poultry, fish or vegetables. We'd recommend going lightly on this until you establish your personal preference.

▶ Dill: Both dill seeds and fresh dill will add big bursts of flavor. Don't get confused by the fine lacey leaves. A little fresh dill packs a punch. Leaves can be used as a garnish or cooked with soup, fish, potatoes or beans.

▶ Fennel: A sweet and distinct flavor. Think licorice. Both seed and leaves are good, but fresh fennel bulbs thinly sliced are delectably delicious. Great sliced in salads or cooked with fish for a kick.

▶ Ginger: A pungent, strong root. This spice is available ground, but fresh thin slices are our favorite. Add as a side to meat dishes or slice up to make a soup zing! Also, very tasty to add a few fresh slices in seltzer or hot water for a natural ginger-ale.

▶ Marjoram: Dried is typically available. Nice with fish, poultry, omelets, lamb and stew.

▶ Mint: Cool and full of scent. Fabulous for beverages. Mint can be added to green tea, black or the tea of your choice. Mint in cold water makes a perfect special summer drink. Fish, lamb, cheese, soups, peas and carrots are also complemented beautifully with a little fresh mint accent. Mint adds a colorful and flavorful touch when torn and sprinkled in tiny pieces over a fresh fruit salad.

▶ Oregano: Strong and aromatic. Fresh or ground, use sparingly at first until you establish your preference. Delicious with tomatoes, fish, eggs, omelets, stews, poultry and vegetable. A very versatile spice that will give you that "made in Italy" feeling.

▶ Paprika: This is that bright red pepper that you might think of more as a decoration than a spice. It is, however, both. Adds a nice touch to meat, vegetables or soups and does add a colorful garnish to potatoes, salads or eggs.

▶ Parsley: Fresh is best! Try whole sprigs, coarsely or finely chopped on fish, omelets, soups and meat. Also, chopped it will add an entirely new dimension to a salad.

▶ Rosemary: Nothing in the world is as flavorfully aromatic as fresh rosemary. Can be used to season fish, beef, lamb, poultry, onions, eggs and potatoes.

▶ Saffron: An orangy-yellow spice used to both flavor and color foods. Common for soups and chicken.

▶ Sage: Fresh or dried, although this is exceptional fresh. The flowers can be used in salads. Add to fish, omelets, beef, poultry and cheeses. Single leaves dropped in hot oil and quickly fried will make a delectable addition to a few slices of cheese. A little goes a long way.

▶ Tarragon: This is a pungent hot spice. Use to flavor salads, fish, poultry, tomatoes, eggs, green beans and carrots.

▶ Thyme: Sprinkle leaves on fish or poultry before broiling or baking and the entire house will be looking forward to dinner. Throw sprigs directly on coals if you are grilling for an aromatic smokiness for your meat.

SEASONINGS CHECKLIST FOR VEGETABLES

▶ Beets: Marjoram, Mint, Savory, Thyme.

▶ Broccoli: Caraway Seed, Dill, Mustard Seed, Tarragon.

▶ Brussels Sprouts: Basil, Caraway Seed, Dill, Mint, Nutmeg, Savory, Tarragon.

▶ Carrots: Allspice, Bay Leaves, Caraway Seed, Dill, Ginger, Mace, Marjoram, Mint, Nutmeg, Thyme.

▶ Cauliflower: Caraway Seed, Dill, Mace, Rosemary, Tarragon.

▶ Cucumbers: Basil, Dill, Mint, Tarragon

▶ Eggplant: Marjoram, Oregano

▶ Onions: Caraway Seed, Mustard Seed, Nutmeg, Oregano, Sage, Thyme.

▶ Peas: Basil, Dill, Marjoram, Mint, Oregano, Sage, Rosemary, Savory.

▶ Potatoes: Basil, Bay Leaves, Caraway Seed, Dill, Chives, Celery Seed, Mustard Seed, Oregano, Poppy Seed, Thyme.

▶ Spinach: Basil, Mace, Marjoram, Nutmeg, Oregano.

▶ Squash: Allspice, Basil, Cinnamon, Cloves, Ginger, Mustard Seed, Nutmeg, Rosemary.

▶ Sweet Potatoes: Allspice, Cardamon, Cinnamon, Cloves, Nutmeg.

▶ Tomatoes: Basil, Bay Leaves, Celery Seed, Oregano, Sage, Sesame Seed, Tarragon, Thyme.

A MIXTURE FOR THE SALT SHAKER

- ▶ 4 tsp onion powder
- ▶ 2 tsp paprika
- ▶ 4 tsp garlic powder
- ▶ 3 tsp pepper

TO GO ORGANIC OR NOT?

In the short run organic foods are usually more expensive. However, if we calculate the incalculable—the cost on our long-term health—they might be a bargain. According to the Environmental Working Group (EWG), which bases its finding from thousands of government tests, you can reduce your toxic pesticide exposure by a whopping 80% when you buy organic versions of just a few foods. An entire cart of all organic foods might be nice, but it is an unnecessary expense.

To enjoy healthier and safer meals by minimizing your exposure to pesticides and other toxins and hormones, start with focusing on these foods first.

Invest in These Organic Foods:

- ▶ Celery
- ▶ Peaches and Nectarines
- ▶ Strawberries and Blueberries
- ▶ Apples, Apple Juice and Dried Apples
- ▶ Sweet Red, Green and Yellow Bell Peppers
- ▶ Kale, Spinach, Collard Greens, Lettuce and most other green leafy vegetables
- ▶ Cherries
- ▶ Carrots
- ▶ Pears
- ▶ Eggs

To meet USDA "organic" labeling requirements, the meat and poultry must come only from animals that are fed organic feed, given no hormones or antibiotics and generally allowed to eat on the free range.

When buying beef, organic is good, but free range is better—if you must make a choice. Cows naturally eat grass. They have evolved for eons eating grass. When cows are pent up and fed corn meal and who knows what else, even if it is "organic," this does not produce health-promoting meat. If you can get organic and free range-beef—that would be ideal. Also, fat stores many pesticides, hormones, steroids, etc. So, choose fattier meats only when organic and/or grass fed, and if not, abstain from eating the fat.

Introduction

Eggs are an organic must, or skip them. According to Fred Pescatore, MD in his excellent book *Feed Your Kids Well*, he states: "Organic eggs contain omega-3 and omega-6 fatty acids in the beneficial ratio of one-to-one. Commercial eggs, on the other hand, contain up to 19 times more omega-6 than omega-3 fatty acids, making them a very unhealthy product." Enough said.

The EWG says the following are the fruits and veggies that test out at the lowest pesticide levels. So save your money with these and don't worry about whether or not they are organic.

- ▶ Watermelon
- ▶ Cantaloupe
- ▶ Pineapples
- ▶ Grapefruit
- ▶ Tomatoes
- ▶ Avocado
- ▶ Kiwi
- ▶ Papaya
- ▶ Mango
- ▶ Onions
- ▶ Broccoli
- ▶ Eggplant
- ▶ Cabbage
- ▶ Asparagus
- ▶ Sweet Peas
- ▶ Sweet Onions
- ▶ Sweet Potatoes

SPOTTING SUGAR

TurboChargers always try to cook with fresh, whole ingredients whenever possible. However, there will be times you want to pull out a pre-made salsa or some other food to get a meal ready more quickly. That said, it is of utmost importance to read labels. You want to watch for hidden sugars or carbohydrates within foods. Obviously the words flour or sugar are…obvious! But sugars and carbohydrates go by many other names. Since we don't want any of them in our bodies, it's helpful to know what to look for on a food label.

All of the following ingredients are sugars (carbohydrates). When perusing a product label, check to see if any of these appear on it. If they do, lookt o see whether they're one of the first ingredients (which means it's a main ingredient). Remember too that manufacturers are allowed a 10% margin of error in label claims. You can be assured the error is in their favor—not in favor of your goals of a lean physique.

- ▶ Agave
- ▶ Brown Rice Syrup
- ▶ Cane Syrup
- ▶ Corn Starch
- ▶ Corn Syrup
- ▶ Dextrose
- ▶ Fructose
- ▶ Golden Syrup
- ▶ High-Fructose Corn Syrup
- ▶ Honey Invert Sugar
- ▶ Jaggery
- ▶ Lactose
- ▶ Maple Syrup
- ▶ Milk
- ▶ Molasses
- ▶ Pulled Sugar
- ▶ Rock Sugar
- ▶ Sorghum
- ▶ Sucrose
- ▶ Treacle

> **TURBOTIPS:**
> You won't need to add sugar in your tea if you choose a flavorful kind like jasmine or oolong. Remember that you can always add ice, too. You can also spice up a tea by adding some cinnamon, cloves, fresh mint sprigs or orange or lemon peels.

WATCH OUT FOR HIDDEN MSG

The following information is an excerpt from the Mayo Clinic website at: http://www.mayoclinic.com/health/monosodium-glutamate/AN01251

Monosodium glutamate (MSG) is a flavor enhancer commonly added to Chinese food, canned vegetables, soups and processed meats. Although the Food and Drug Administration (FDA) has classified MSG as a food ingredient that's "generally recognized as safe," the use of MSG remains controversial. For this reason, when MSG is added to food, the FDA requires that it be listed on the label.

MSG has been used as a food additive for decades. Over the years, the FDA has received many anecdotal reports of adverse reactions to foods containing MSG. These reactions—known as MSG symptom complex—include:

- ▶ Headache
- ▶ Migraines
- ▶ Flushing

Introduction

- ▶ Sweating
- ▶ Facial pressure or tightness
- ▶ Numbness, tingling or burning in face, neck and other areas
- ▶ Rapid, fluttering heartbeats (heart palpitations)
- ▶ Chest pain
- ▶ Nausea
- ▶ Weakness
- ▶ Hyperactivity in children

However, researchers have found no definitive evidence of a link between MSG and these symptoms. Researchers acknowledge, though, that a small percentage of people may have short-term reactions to MSG. Symptoms are usually mild and don't require treatment. The only way to prevent a reaction is to avoid foods containing MSG.

If you see "hydrolyzed" in an ingredient list, the product contains MSG. Watch for the following terms, which also signal MSG.

- ▶ Autolyzed Yeast
- ▶ Calcium Caseinate
- ▶ Gelatin
- ▶ Glutamate
- ▶ Glutamic Acid
- ▶ Hydrolyzed Corn Gluten
- ▶ Monopotassium Glutamate
- ▶ Sodium Caseinate
- ▶ Textured Protein
- ▶ Hydrolyzed Protein, such as wheat, soy or vegetable protein.

POPULAR LOW-CALORIE FOODS

- ▶ Fresh Apricots
- ▶ Lemon
- ▶ Artichokes
- ▶ Mustard Greens
- ▶ Asparagus
- ▶ Okra Green Beans
- ▶ Oysters (Except Smoked)
- ▶ Beet Greens

▶ Peas

▶ Red Beets

▶ Fresh Pears

▶ Broccoli

▶ Pickles

▶ Brussels Sprouts

▶ Pineapple

▶ Cauliflower

▶ Celery

▶ Radishes

▶ Eggplant

▶ Red Snapper

▶ Fresh Cherries

▶ Sauerkraut

▶ Chicory Greens

▶ Squash

▶ Tangerines

▶ Cucumbers

▶ Brook Trout

▶ Escarole

▶ Turnips

▶ Flounder

▶ Turnip Greens

▶ Grapes

▶ Vegetable Juice (Fresh With Pulp)

▶ Grouper

▶ Watercress

▶ Halibut

▶ Watermelon

Introduction

Introduction

LOW-CALORIE BEVERAGES

- ▶ WATER!
- ▶ Plain Tea
- ▶ Dry Wines
- ▶ Black Coffee
- ▶ Vermouth
- ▶ Brandy (42 proof)
- ▶ Diet Sodas (although not recommended)
- ▶ Light Beer
- ▶ Mineral Water
- ▶ Tomato Juice
- ▶ Seltzer Water

TURBOTIPS:
Seltzer water is calorie-free, as is plain tap water. Add a slice or two of ginger for a sugar-free, natural ginger-ale, or try a slice of lemon for your own version of lemon soda. Other condiments like sprigs of mint, cucumbers, sticks of ginger, slices of oranges—all make natural "vitamin" water.

NOTES
· · · · · · ·

Beverages

GREEN TEA LEMONADE

- ▶ 4 cups freshly brewed green tea (made with 4 teabags), chilled
- ▶ 3 cups prepared sugar-free lemonade
- ▶ 4 lemon slices
- ▶ 4 sprigs fresh mint

1. Shake or stir together green tea and lemonade; pour over ice.
2. Garnish with lemon slices and mint.

ICED MINT TEA

- ▶ 3 decaffeinated black tea bags
- ▶ 1 cup tightly packed fresh mint leaves
- ▶ 2 cups boiling water
- ▶ 4 cups cold water
- ▶ Sugar substitute (optional)

1. Place teas bags and mint in a teapot.
2. Pour in boiling water.
3. Let tea steep 20 minutes.
4. Strain tea into a pitcher.
5. Add 4 cups cold water; mix well.
6. Sweeten to taste with sugar substitute, if desired.

FRESH GINGER TEA

- ▶ Piece of fresh ginger root
- ▶ Water

1. Cut root into 1/2"-1" pieces.
2. Boil in pot on stove.
3. Add more water to pot and reboil to make more.

TOMATO JUICE COCKTAIL

Serves 4

- ▶ 1/2 cup low-sodium tomato juice
- ▶ 1 Tbsp fresh lemon juice
- ▶ Pinch of freshly ground black pepper
- ▶ Pinch of elery salt
- ▶ Celery stick

1. In tall glass, combine tomato juice, lemon juice, black pepper and celery salt; add enough ice cubes to fill glass.
2. Serve with celery stick stirrer.

CLOVED ICED TEA

Serves 4

- ▶ 1 quart boiling water
- ▶ 4 tsps tea in metal ball or 4 tea bags
- ▶ 1/2 lime (or lemon)
- ▶ 8 cloves
- ▶ Stevia to taste

1. To boiling water in heavy pitcher or other container, add tea, entire squeezed 1/2 lime (including peel) and cloves.
2. Let stand for about an hour until cooled.
3. Remove squeezed tea bags or tea ball.
4. Chill in refrigerator.
5. Each individual may add artificial sweetener to taste if desired.

COFFEE-EGG BREAKFAST COCKTAIL

Serves 2

- ▶ 2 cups strong black coffee
- ▶ 1 egg yoke
- ▶ 2 pinches of cinnamon
- ▶ 1 pinch of paprika
- ▶ 1 pinch ground ginger
- ▶ 1/4 tsp lemon juice

1. Place all ingredients in a blender and process at low speed until completely combined.
2. Chill.
3. Stir briskly before serving.

Dips & Dressings

KNOW YOUR DRESSING

The following salad dressings and dips provide delicious healthful variations from the usual options. They are all made from wholesome, natural fruits, vegetables, nuts, seeds and spices.

All of these recipes are:

▶ Chemical Free
▶ Preservative Free
▶ Salt Free
▶ Refined Sugar Free

Any recipe that follows is a perfect addition to a TurboCharged meal. You have the option of enjoying a super dressing atop a large healthy salad or you have a great dip that only needs a pile of crudité vegetables or you can try stuffing some celery stalks or scooped-out cucumbers with any of the dips.

To make a dressing into a dip, use less liquid or add more solid food.

To make a dip into a dressing, use more liquid.

If any recipe calls for use of a nut butter, it is very easy to make your own healthy version.

Simply buy some fresh, raw nuts of choice, put desired amount into a high-powered blender or food processor, when nuts get to a fine powdery nature, keep blending and add a few drops of water for added moisture.

BEWARE OF COMMERCIAL SALAD DRESSINGS

Salad dressings are known for sabotaging the best TurboCharging intentions. A typical bottled dressing incorporates ingredients that will trigger a crash.

Here's a list of the stuff found in a generic bottle of Thousand Island dressing: *partially hydrogenated soybean oil,* sugar, water, whole tomatoes, vinegar, chopped pickle, egg yolk, *high-fructose corn syrup, salt, xantham gum,* spices, garlic powder, *sorbic acid,* dehydrated onions, *artificial coloring, natural flavoring (another way of saying MSG), calcium disodium, EDTA.* Plus a sodium content of 160 mg and a calorie content of 100 calories per Tbsp.

Follow this simple rule: If you are reading an ingredient list, put it down the minute you see a word you do not immediately recognize and know its definition and physical impact. (Note the italic words above as an example.) And of course if the product lists any kind of sugar as an ingredient, put it down and skip it.

CREAMY CUCUMBER DRESSING

Serves 4

- ▶ Juice from 1/2 pink grapefruit
- ▶ 1 medium cucumber, peeled and chopped
- ▶ 1/2 cup walnuts

1. Combine all ingredients in an electric blender until smooth.

CLASSIC PESTO

Serves 4

- ▶ 2 cups lightly packed fresh basil
- ▶ 1 cup grated Parmesan cheese
- ▶ 1/2 -2/3 cup extra-virgin olive oil
- ▶ 1-2 cloves garlic, optional

1. Whirl basil, Parmesan, half the oil, and if desired, garlic in a blender or food processor until smooth.
2. Add more oil, if needed.
3. If you're not ready to use the pesto immediately, cover and refrigerate it for up to 5 days.
4. Or freeze if you want to store it longer.
5. Serve over your favorite cooked pasta, or on bruschetta.

COCKTAIL SAUCE

Serves 4

- ▶ 8-oz can tomato sauce
- ▶ 1 Tbsp horseradish
- ▶ 1 tsp Worcestershire sauce
- ▶ 1 tsp lemon juice

1. Mix all ingredients.
2. Chill thoroughly.
3. Serve with steamed, warm or chilled shrimp.

TURBOTIPS:
If you've never tried a "warm" shrimp cocktail—you are in for a treat!

VARIETY DRESSING

Serves 4

- 1/2 cup tomato juice
- 1/2 tsp dry mustard
- 1/2 tsp salt
- 1/4 tsp black pepper
- 1/4 tsp paprika
- 1 Tbsp grated onion
- 2 Tbsps minced parsley
- 2 tsps chopped green pepper
- Dash cayenne

1. Place all ingredients in a jar and shake together vigorously until thoroughly blended.
2. Cover and refrigerate when not in use.

CAVIAR FOR COWBOYS

Serves 8

- 15-oz can black beans, rinsed and drained
- 4-oz can chopped ripe olives, drained
- 1 small onion, finely chopped (about 1/4 cup)
- 1 clove garlic, finely chopped
- 2 Tbsps vegetable oil
- 2 Tbsps lime juice
- 1/4 tsp salt
- 1/4 tsp crushed red pepper
- 1/4 tsp ground cumin
- 1/8 tsp pepper
- 8-oz package cream cheese, softened
- 2 hard-cooked eggs, peeled and chopped
- 1 green onion with top, sliced

1. Mix all ingredients except cream cheese, eggs and green onion.
2. Cover and refrigerate at least 2 hours.
3. Spread cream cheese on serving plate.
4. Spoon bean mixture evenly over cream cheese.
5. Arrange eggs on bean mixture in ring around edge of plate; sprinkle with green onions.
6. Serve with Romaine or Endive leaves for scooping.

MUSTARD SALAD DRESSING

Serves 4

- 1/2 cup whole fat Greek-style yogurt
- 1 tsp prepared mustard
- 1 tsp parsley
- 1 tsp dried onion flakes
- 1/4 tsp each paprika, pepper and dill weed

1. Combine all ingredients in an electric blender until smooth.

VINAIGRETTE SAUCE

Serves 4

- ▶ 2 Tbsps white wine vinegar
- ▶ 1 Tbsp water
- ▶ 1/2 tsp vegetable oil
- ▶ Dashes of salt, pepper, thyme
- ▶ 1 Tbsp finely chopped shallots (or onions)

1. Mix all ingredients thoroughly, and chill in refrigerator.
2. Stir or shake well before using.

ALL-PURPOSE BALSAMIC MARINADE

Serves 4

- ▶ 2/3 cup regular or white balsamic vinegar
- ▶ 1/3 cup olive oil
- ▶ 2 Tbsps finely chopped fresh rosemary leaves
- ▶ 4 cloves garlic, finely sliced
- ▶ 2 tsps kosher sea salt
- ▶ 1 tsp freshly ground pepper

1. Mix all ingredients together.

MEXICAN JET FUEL DRESSING

Serves 6

- ▶ 1/2 cup red-wine vinegar
- ▶ 1 1/2 Tbsps lemon juice
- ▶ 1 Tbsp Dijon mustard
- ▶ 1 Tbsp fructose (granulated or syrup) or honey
- ▶ 2 tsps Worcestershire sauce
- ▶ 1 tsp minced garlic or 1/2 tsp garlic powder
- ▶ 1/2 tsp ground cumin
- ▶ 1/2 tsp salt
- ▶ 1/2 tsp pepper
- ▶ 1 cup water

1. Put all ingredients except water in a jar with a tight-fitting lid; shake well.
2. Add water and shake again until blended.
3. Store in refrigerator.
4. Shake well before using.

TURBOTIPS:
This dressing is better if it is made a day ahead.

To vary the flavor, try substituting 1 Tbsp dried tarragon for the cumin.

Dips & Dressings

AVOCADO GRAPEFRUIT DRESSING

Serves 4

- ▶ Juice from 1/2 pink grapefruit
- ▶ 1/2 medium-size cucumber, chopped
- ▶ 1 avocado, peeled, pitted, quartered

1. Combine all ingredients in an electric blender until smooth.

CREAMY CUCUMBER DRESSING

Serves 4

- ▶ Juice from 1/2 pink grapefruit
- ▶ 1 medium cucumber, peeled, chopped
- ▶ 1/2 cup walnuts

1. Combine all ingredients in an electric blender until smooth.

CREAMY CELERY DRESSING

Serves 4

- ▶ 3/4 cup chopped tender center of celery
- ▶ 1/2 medium cucumber, peeled, chopped
- ▶ 1/8 cup walnuts
- ▶ 3 Tbsps Bragg's Liquid Amino Acids

1. Combine all ingredients in an electric blender until smooth.

FRUIT SALSA

Serves 8

- ▶ 3 pieces of whole fresh fruit (peaches, pears, apples, apricots, kiwi, strawberries, mangoes, papaya, pineapple, or a combination of fruits), chopped
- ▶ 1 Vidalia onion, chopped
- ▶ 2 4-oz cans chopped chilies, or your choice of fresh chilies, seeds removed and chopped

1. Stir ingredients together gently until well mixed.
2. Let stand for at least four hours and up to 1 day to develop the flavors.

CREAMY TOMATO DRESSING

Serves 4

- ▶ 2 cups chopped tomatoes
- ▶ 1/2 cup walnuts

1. Combine all ingredients in an electric blender until smooth.

CASHEW MAYONNAISE
DRESSING

Serves 4

- ▶ Cashew butter
- ▶ Distilled water
- ▶ Lime juice

1. Mix to taste and consistency desired using an electric blender.

TOMATO DRESSING

Serves 4

- ▶ 6-oz can V-8 juice (low sodium)
- ▶ 1/8 head lettuce
- ▶ 1/4 small onion
- ▶ 1/4 tsp each dill weed, pepper, lemon juice and paprika
- ▶ Lemon juice and paprika

1. Blend all ingredients in blender.

FRENCHY FRENCH DRESSING

Serves 4

- ▶ 1 cup unsalted tomato juice
- ▶ 2 tbsps rice vinegar
- ▶ 1 tsp onion flakes
- ▶ 1/8 tsp sweet basil
- ▶ 1/8 tsp dry mustard
- ▶ 1/8 tsp garlic powder
- ▶ 1/8 tsp pepper

1. Combine and chill.
2. Mix before using.

FRESH TOMATO SALSA #1

Serves 4

- ▶ 2 cups finely chopped tomato
- ▶ 1/4 cup chopped green onions
- ▶ 1 Tbsp finely chopped fresh cilantro
- ▶ 1 Tbsp fresh lime juice
- ▶ 1 tsp minced fresh jalapeno pepper
- ▶ 1/4 tsp salt
- ▶ Fresh cilantro sprigs (optional)
- ▶ Fresh jalapeno pepper (optional)

1. Combine first 6 ingredients in medium bowl; stir well.
2. Cover and chill at least 2 hours.
3. Serve with sliced pepper or endive leaves for dipping.
4. If desired, garnish with cilantro sprigs and a jalapeno pepper.

FRESH SALSA #2

Serves 8

- ▶ 3 tomatoes, finely chopped
- ▶ 1 small onion, finely chopped
- ▶ 1/2 tsp salt
- ▶ 1 Tbsp lime juice
- ▶ 1Tbsp fresh cilantro, finely chopped
- ▶ 1 jalapeno pepper, minced
- ▶ 2 Tbsps parsley, finely chopped
- ▶ 1 garlic clove, minced
- ▶ 1 tsp macadamia, olive or avocado oil
- ▶ 8-oz canned tomato sauce
- ▶ 5 dashes of Tabasco

1. Combine all ingredients in a bowl and mix well.
2. Cover and chill for at least 3 hours.
3. Serve at room temperature.

GUACAMOLE

Serves 6

- ▶ 4 ripe avocados
- ▶ 2 plum tomatoes, peeled, seeded and chopped
- ▶ 1 Tbsp onions, finely chopped
- ▶ 4 chopped chili peppers
- ▶ 2 Tbsps fresh lemon juice
- ▶ 1 Tbsp Worcestershire sauce
- ▶ 1 tsp chopped garlic
- ▶ 1 tsp salt
- ▶ 1/4 tsp cayenne pepper
- ▶ 4 dashes Tabasco

1. Mash avocados.
2. Coarsely chop tomatoes and chili peppers in food processor.
3. Add avocados and all other ingredients to processor and blend until smooth.
4. Refrigerate in covered container.
5. Put the avocado seed in container to prevent darkening of guacamole.

STILTON CHEESE BALL

Serves 6

- ▶ 8 ounces extra sharp Cheddar cheese, room temperature
- ▶ 8 ounces cream cheese, room temperature
- ▶ 3 ounces Stilton cheese, room temperature
- ▶ 1 small clove garlic, crushed
- ▶ 1 Tbsp Worcestershire sauce
- ▶ 3/4 cup pecans, finely chopped
- ▶ 1/2 cup fresh parsley, finely chopped
- ▶ 1/4 tsp Tabasco

1. Break the cheese into pieces.
2. Add the Worcestershire sauce, Tabasco, and crushed garlic.
3. Thoroughly mix to a creamy consistency with an electric blender.
4. Stir in 1/2 cup pecans and refrigerate until firm enough to shape into a ball.
5. Roll the cheese ball with parsley and remaining pecans until covered.
6. Refrigerate for 24 hours before serving.
7. Drop onto Endive or Radicchio leaves and enjoy!

FRESH LEMON DRESSING

Serves 4

- ▶ 1 tsp dry mustard
- ▶ Artificial sweetener equal to 1/2 tsp of sugar (if desired)
- ▶ Juice of 2 lemons
- ▶ Pinch of seasoned salt
- ▶ Dash black pepper 1 tsp paprika

1. Shake all ingredients together vigorously in a covered jar until well blended.
2. Refrigerate when not in use.

GORGONZOLA SPREAD
WITH WALNUTS

Serves 8

- ▶ 1 lb cream cheese, room temperature
- ▶ 6 ounces Gorgonzola cheese, room temperature
- ▶ 12 walnut halves
- ▶ 1 bunch chives, finely chopped
- ▶ Salt and pepper to taste

1. In a food processor grate the walnuts and set aside.
2. Combine the cream cheese and Gorgonzola with a little salt and pepper.
3. Mash until smooth and add walnuts and chives.
4. Mix again until well blended.
5. Serve immediately.
6. Spoon into endive leaves.

Dips & Dressings

CRUNCHY GUACAMOLE

Serves 8

- ▶ 2 ripe California avocadoes, peeled and diced
- ▶ 1 1/2 Tbsp lemon juice, preferably fresh
- ▶ 1-2 cloves garlic, minced
- ▶ 1 tsp dried leaf basil, crushed
- ▶ 1/2 cup red pepper, finely diced
- ▶ 2 Tbsps of your favorite salsa
- ▶ 1 1/2 Tbsp slivered almonds, coarsely chopped
- ▶ 2 Tbsps thinly sliced green onion
- ▶ Dollop sour cream garnish
- ▶ 1/2 tsp salt (optional)
- ▶ 1 Tbsp minced cilantro (optional)

1. Peel and mash 1 avocado, mix with lemon juice, cilantro, garlic, basil and salt.
2. Dice remaining avocado, fold into mixture with red pepper, salsa, green onion, and chopped almonds.
3. Garnish with sour cream.
4. Serve 1" sliced red, yellow, orange & green peppers, leaves of Romaine, or favorite firm lettuce leaves of choice.

OLIVE SPREAD

Serves 12

- ▶ 2 8-oz packages cream cheese, softened
- ▶ 16-oz can black olives, finely chopped
- ▶ 1/2 cup green olives, finely chopped
- ▶ 1-2 cloves garlic, minced
- ▶ 2 Tbsps lemon juice
- ▶ 3/4 cup chopped parsley, optional

1. In a large mixing bowl, blend all ingredients together.
2. Push into ball shape in the bowl, cover, and refrigerate.
3. When firm, shape with your hands into balls.
4. If you wish, roll in chopped parsley.
5. Wrap and refrigerate until serving.
6. Serve with cut-up fresh vegetables.

FAST GUACAMOLE & "CHIPS"

Serves 6

- ▶ 2 ripe avocados
- ▶ 1/2 cup restaurant-style chunky salsa (sugar free)
- ▶ 1/4 tsp hot pepper sauce (optional)
- ▶ 1/2 seedless cucumber, sliced into 1/8-inch rounds

1. Cut avocados in half; remove and discard pits.
2. Scoop flesh into medium blow.
3. Mash with fork.
4. Add salsa and hot pepper sauce, if desired; mix well.
5. Transfer guacamole to serving bowl; surround with cucumber "chips".

Dips & Dressings

SHRIMP PATE

Serves 12

- ▶ 1/2 lb cooked peeled shrimp
- ▶ 1/4 cup (1/2 stick) unsalted butter, cut in chunks
- ▶ 2 tsps dry vermouth or chicken broth
- ▶ 1 tsp lemon juice
- ▶ 1 tsp Dijon mustard
- ▶ 1/4 tsp ground mace
- ▶ 1/4 tsp salt
- ▶ 1/8 tsp ground red pepper
- ▶ 1/8 tsp freshly ground black pepper
- ▶ 1/2 cup chopped pistachio nuts
- ▶ 2 large heads Belgian endive

1. Combine shrimp, butter, vermouth, lemon juice, mustard, mace, salt, ground red pepper and black pepper in blender or food processor.
2. Blend to a puree.
3. If mixture is too soft to handle, refrigerate 1 hour.
4. Spread pistachio nuts on sheet of waxed paper.
5. Gently form mixture into an 8" log.
6. Roll in nuts to coat.
7. Chill 1 to 3 hours.
8. Separate endive into individual leaves and serve with shrimp log.

> **TURBOTIPS:**
> Variation: Spoon shrimp pate into serving bowl and sprinkle with pistachio nuts.

BLACK BEAN SALSA

Serves 6

- ▶ 1 can black beans, rinsed and drained
- ▶ 1 cup frozen corn, thawed
- ▶ 1 large tomato, chopped
- ▶ 1/4 cup chopped green onions
- ▶ 2 Tbsps chopped fresh cilantro
- ▶ 2 Tbsps lemon juice
- ▶ 1 Tbsp vegetable oil
- ▶ 1 tsp chili powder
- ▶ 1/4 tsp salt

1. Combine beans, corn, tomato, green onions, cilantro, lemon juice, oil, chili powder and salt in medium bowl; mix well.
2. Garnish with lemon wedges and additional fresh cilantro, if desired.

> **TURBOTIPS:**
> This salsa is great served on a bed of lettuce and eaten as a salad.

SUPER EASY AVOCADO

Serves 4

- ▶ 1 avocado
- ▶ 1/4 onion, finely chopped
- ▶ 1/4 cup chopped sweet pepper
- ▶ Herbal or vegetable seasoning

1. Mash avocado with onion, pepper and seasoning.
2. Spread into recesses of celery stalks and serve.

Dips & Dressings

TOMATO-CUCUMBER

Serves
4

GUACAMOLE

- 1 pint cherry or grape tomatoes, halved or 2 medium tomatoes, coarsely chopped
- 2 medium cucumbers or 1 large English cucumber, peeled and coarsely chopped
  - 2 Haas avocados, coarsely chopped
  - 1/2 cup chopped red onion
  - 1 1/2 Tbsps lime juice
  - 1 tsp grated lime rind
  - 1/2 tsp ground cumin
  - Salt and pepper

1. In a bowl, toss tomatoes, cucumber, avocado, onion, lime juice, ride and cumin.
2. Add salt and pepper to taste.
3. Serve with Boston lettuce leaves and make "wraps" or use as a dip with wedges of celery, or 1" slices of assorted colors of peppers.

TURBOTIPS:
To keep this dish bright and colorful, serve immediately after preparing.

SPINACH ARTICHOKE DIP

Serves
8

- 10-oz package frozen chopped spinach, thawed
- 1 can artichoke bottoms
- 2 cloves garlic
  - 8 ounces cream cheese
  - 1 cup grated Parmesan cheese
  - 1/4 tsp pepper

1. Heat oven to 350°F.
2. Grease a 1-quart ovenproof pan.
3. In a food processor, process spinach, artichokes, garlic, cream cheese, Parmesan and pepper until well combined.
4. Scrape down sides of processor, as needed.
5. Spread spinach mixture in prepared pan.
6. Bake until warmed through, about 30 minutes.
7. Serve hot with cut-up vegetables.

TURBOTIPS:
Canned artichoke bottoms are prefered because they have a deeper flavor than frozen artichoke hearts.

This can be kept refrigerated for up to five days.

EGGPLANT PATE

Serves
4

- ▶ 1 medium eggplant
- ▶ 3/4 cup raw sesame seeds, ground
- ▶ 1/4-1/2 of the juice from a lemon
- ▶ 1/2 cup parsley, chopped

1. Pierce the eggplant with a fork in 7 or 8 places to allow the steam to escape when it bakes.
2. Place the eggplant on a baking sheet and bake it at 350°F for 30 minutes.
3. After baking, allow the eggplant to cool.
4. While the eggplant is cooling, place the sesame seeds in a nut grinder.
5. Grind the seeds as fine as possible.
6. When the eggplant is cool, remove the skin.
7. Mash the pulp until it is smooth.
8. Combine the pulp, sesame seeds, lemon juice and parsley.
9. Mix these pate ingredients until they are even distributed.
10. Serve as a spread or a dip with a variety of crudité vegetables.

> **TURBOTIPS:**
> Variations: Add 1 clove garlic, minced.
> For a richer pate, use more sesame seeds.

GARBANZO SPREAD

Serves
4

- ▶ 2 cups mashed beans
- ▶ 2 Tbsps onion
- ▶ 1 tsp basil
- ▶ 1 tsp oregano
- ▶ 1 tsp cumin
- ▶ 1 tsp cumin
- ▶ 1 tsp garlic powder (or 1 minced clove of garlic)
- ▶ 1 Tbsp parsley
- ▶ 1 Tbsp lemon juice or apple cider vinegar
- ▶ 1 Tbsp ground sesame seeds

1. Blend all the ingredients together in a food processor with the "s" blade or blender until they make a smooth spread.
2. Serve with cucumber slices or endive leaves.

Dips & Dressings

BLACK BEAN DIP

Serves
4

- ▶ 4-oz black beans, drained and rinsed
- ▶ 1/2 cup sugar-free salsa, hot or mild
- ▶ 2 Tbsps lime juice
- ▶ 1/4 tsp cumin
- ▶ Salt and pepper to taste

1. In a food processor, combine black beans, salsa, lime juice and cumin.
2. Process until smooth.
3. Season with salt and pepper.
4. Transfer to small bowl to serve.
5. Garnish with cilantro, sliced green onions, and chopped sweet peppers, if you wish.
6. Serve with endive leaves.

CREAMY PEANUT GINGER DIP

Serves
4

TURBOTIPS:
If you prefer a milder less "vinegary" taste, reduce the vinegar to 2 Tbsps, or to taste.

- ▶ 1 cup creamy peanut butter
- ▶ 1/4 cup soy sauce
- ▶ 6 Tbsps apple cider
- ▶ 1" cube peeled ginger, chopped
- ▶ 1/2 cup fresh cilantro, chopped
- ▶ 1/4 cup hot water

1. Combine everything but the water in a blender.
2. Pulse until smooth, about 20 seconds, while gradually adding the hot water.
3. Serve with fresh veggies.

PARTY BEAN DIP

Serves
12

- ▶ 16-oz can refried beans
- ▶ 8-oz package cream cheese
- ▶ 12-oz jar salsa, divided
- ▶ Slices of jalapeno peppers, optional

1. Preheat oven to 350°F.
2. Spread beans into bottom of a greased 9" pie pan or oven-safe dish.
3. Beat cream cheese until creamy in a medium-sized mixing bowl.
4. Add 2/3 cup salsa and beat until smooth.
5. Spread creamy cheese over beans.
6. Bake 20 minutes.
7. Let cool 5 minutes.
8. Spread remaining salsa over hot dip and garnish with jalapeno slices, if you wish.
9. Serve with pepper wedges.

Dips & Dressings

TACO DIP

Serves
8

- 16-oz can refried beans
- 1 cup sour cream
- 1 cup salsa
- 1 cup shredded mozzarella, or cheddar cheese

1. Layer first 4 ingredients in 9" pie pan or casserole dish in the order listed.
2. Bake at 350°F until cheese is melted and heated through about 15 minutes.
3. Serve sliced green peppers for dipping.

GARLIC & HERB CHEESE SPREAD

Serves
12

- 2 8-oz packages of cream cheese, softened
- 8-oz package feta cheese, crumbled
- 2-3 cloves garlic, peeled and minced
- 2 Tbsps chopped fresh dill, or 2 tsps dried dill

1. In a medium bowl, thoroughly blend ingredients with electric mixer.
2. Cover and chill for at least 4 hours.
3. Serve in dish alongside firm, raw veggies.
4. After mixing the ingredients together, chill them thoroughly, and then shape into a cheese ball before serving.

CHEESY PIZZA DIP

Serves
12

- 2 8-oz packages cream cheese, softened
- 2 tsps dried Italian seasoning
- 2 cups shredded mozzarella cheese
- 1 1/2 cups shredded Parmesan cheese
- 12-oz jar salsa

1. Preheat oven to 350°F.
2. In a medium-sized mixing bowl, combine cream cheese and seasoning.
3. Spread into bottom of a greased 9" pie plate.
4. In the bowl, combine mozzarella & Parmesan cheeses.
5. Sprinkle half over cream cheese mixture.
6. Spread salsa over cheeses.
7. Top with remaining cheeses.
8. Bake 18-20 minutes, or until bubbly.
9. Serve with raw vegetables.
10. Substitute 1 1/2 cups of pizza sauce for the salsa.

TURBOTIPS:
Instead of baking the Dip, place it into a microwave-safe pie plate or dish, and then microwave on High for 3 minutes, or until cheese melts.

Substitute 1 1/2 cups of pizza sauce for salsa.

SALSA DIP

Serves
12

- 8-oz package cream cheese
- 1/2 cup sour cream
- 1 cup sugar-free salsa
- 3/4 cup grated mozzarella cheese

1. In a medium-sized mixing bowl, beat cream cheese until soft and creamy.
2. Fold in sour cream.
3. Spread mixture in a 9" pie plate.
4. Spoon salsa over top.
5. Sprinkle with mozzarella cheese.
6. Cover and refrigerate until serving.
7. Serve with vegetable crudité.

SPICY GUACAMOLE

Serves
8

- 2 avocados
- 1/2 cup chopped red onion
- 1/2 cup cubed tomatoes
- Salt and pepper to taste
- 1 tsp lime juice

1. Cut the avocados in half, remove the pit, and spoon out into a bowl.
2. Mash the avocados with a fork.
3. Stir in remaining ingredients gently.
4. Serve with sliced fresh vegetables.

CARIBBEAN SALSA

Serves
6

- 2 cups chopped fresh or canned pine-apple
  - 2 yellow or red bell peppers, seeded and chopped
  - 3 kiwifruit, peeled and chopped
  - 1 small red onion, finely chopped
  - 1 cup chopped peeled mango
  - 1/4 cup finely chopped fresh cilantro
  - l2 tsp chopped seeded jalapeño pepper*
- Juice of 1 lime

1. Combine pineapple, bell peppers, kiwi, onion, mango, cilantro, jalapeño and lime juice.
2. Cover and chill 2 hours.
3. Serve with fish or chicken.

TURBOTIPS:
*Use caution when handling hot peppers.

Wear disposable gloves or wash hands thoroughy in hot, soapy water afterward.

SMOKED SALMON DIP

Serves 6

- ▶ 2 6-oz cans smoked salmon
- ▶ 8-oz package cream cheese, softened
- ▶ 1/3 cup ground walnuts or parsley, optional

1. Mix salmon and cream cheese with fork in a medium-sized mixing bowl.
2. Chill for an hour or so until mixture becomes stiff enough to handle.
3. Shape into a ball.
4. Return to mixing bowl and fridge.
5. Let stand for another hour or so to blend flavors.
6. Just before serving, roll in ground nuts or finely chopped parsley, if you wish.
7. Serve with sliced sweet red pepper slices or spoon onto endive leaves and serve.

BLACK BEAN SALSA

Serves 8

- ▶ 2 15-oz cans black beans, rinsed
- ▶ 1 cup corn (if canned, drain)
- ▶ 1 large tomato, diced
- ▶ 8 stems cilantro, chopped
- ▶ 4 Tbsps lime juice
- ▶ Salt and pepper to taste, optional
- ▶ Chopped garlic and/or sliced scallions, optional

1. Gently toss all ingredients together in a large mixing bowl.
2. Cover and let marinate in the refrigerator overnight.
3. Serve with endive leaves, cucumber "chips" or pepper wedges.

TURBOTIPS:
Garnish with sliced black olives or jalapeno peppers.

HUMMUS

Serves 6

- ▶ 2 15-oz cans chick peas (garbanzos), one drained, one with liquid
- ▶ 1/4 cup raw sesame seeds
- ▶ 1 Tbsp olive oil
- ▶ 1/4 cup (60ml) lemon juice
- ▶ 1 garlic clove, peeled
- ▶ 1 tsp cumin
- ▶ Salt

1. Place all ingredients, except salt, into a blender container in the order listed and secure lid.
2. Blend about 3 minutes, starting at a lower speed and gradually increasing.
3. Stop and scrape sides of container as necessary and continue blending.
4. Season to taste with salt.

Appetizers

CALIFORNIA DEVILED EGGS

Serves 12

- ▶ 2 ripe California avocados
- ▶ 1 Tbsp fresh lemon juice
- ▶ 1/4 tsp garlic powder
- ▶ 2 Tbsps finely chopped shallots or green onions
- ▶ 2 tsps capers, drained and mashed
- ▶ 12 hard-cooked eggs, peeled, cut in half, and yolks discarded or set aside for another use
- ▶ Slivers of red, yellow or green bell pepper for garnish

1. Cut the avocadoes in half, remove the pits, peel and cut into cubes.
2. Place in medium-size bowl, add the lemon juice and garlic powder, and mash to blend.
3. Stir in the shallots and capers, if using.
4. Fill the whites evenly with the avocado mixture and garnish each egg half with bell pepper slivers.

ROSEMARY-SCENTED NUT MIX

Serves 32

- ▶ 1/4 tsp red pepper flakes
- ▶ 2 Tbsps unsalted butter
- ▶ 2 cups pecan halves
- ▶ 1 cup unsalted macadamia nuts
- ▶ 1 cup walnuts
- ▶ 1 tsp dried rosemary, crushed
- ▶ 1/2 tsp salt

1. Preheat oven to 300°F.
2. Melt butter in large saucepan on low.
3. Add pecans, macadamia nuts and walnuts; mix well.
4. Add rosemary, salt and red pepper flakes; cook and stir 1 minute.
5. Pour mixture onto nonstick jelly-roll pan.
6. Bake 15 minutes, shaking pan occasionally.

TOMATO & MOZZARELLA CHEESE

- ▶ 3/4 lb Mozzarella cheese, thinly sliced
- ▶ 4 tomatoes, thinly sliced
- ▶ 1 Tbsp capers, rinsed
- ▶ 8 black olives, pitted
- ▶ 4 anchovy fillets, finely chopped
- ▶ Salt and pepper to taste

1. Arrange the tomato and mozzarella slices on a serving dish, alternating the slices.
2. Decorate the plate with capers, olives, and anchovy pieces.
3. Sprinkle to taste with salt and pepper.

EGG-STUFFED TOMATOES

- ▶ 4 ripe tomatoes
- ▶ 1 tsp Dijon mustard
- ▶ Salt and pepper to taste
- ▶ 1/4 cup extra-virgin olive oil
- ▶ 1 tsp fresh parsley, finely chopped
- ▶ 1 tsp fresh mint, finely chopped
- ▶ 1 tsp fresh basil, finely chopped
- ▶ 4 chopped anchovy fillets
- ▶ 3 hard-boiled eggs, coarsely chopped
- ▶ 12 capers

1. Slice each tomato in half.
2. Scoop out the pulp and seeds.
3. Salt and pepper the insides of the tomatoes.
4. Mix the mustard with the salt and pepper to taste.
5. Add the oil and mix with the parsley, mint, basil, anchovies, capers, and eggs.
6. Fill each tomato with 1/4 of the mixture.
7. Serve immediately.

WATER CHESTNUTS

- ▶ 1 lb water chestnuts
- ▶ Bay leaf

1. With a sharp knife, cut a slit across the pointed end of chestnuts.
2. Cover with water in sauce pan.
3. Add bay leaf and simmer for 20 minutes.
4. Drain.

TURBOTIPS:
These are tasty, crunchy and only 10 calories each.

Appetizers

BEEF & SPINACH ROLLS

Serves
4

- ▶ 9 ounces lean boneless beef sirloin
- ▶ 3 cups packed trimmed washed and dried fresh spinach leaves
- ▶ 1/4 tsp salt
- ▶ Pinch freshly ground black pepper
- ▶ 1/4 ounce freshly grated Parmesan cheese

1. Preheat oven to 350°F.
2. Slice beef horizontally almost all the way through; spread open butterfly-fashion.
3. Place beef between 2 sheets of wax paper; with meat mallet or bottom of heavy saucepan; gently pound until very thin.
4. Remove and discard wax paper; set beef aside.
5. In large nonstick skillet, heat 2 Tbsps water; add spinach.
6. Cook over medium-high heat, stirring occasionally, until wilted.
7. Drain, discarding liquid; set spinach aside to cool.
8. Sprinkle beef on both sides with salt and pepper; place onto work surface.
9. Sprinkle beef evenly with cheese; top with cooled spinach.
10. Starting from shortest end, roll beef to enclose filling.
11. Place medium cast-iron skillet over medium–high heat; add beef roll, seam-side down.
12. Cook, turning as needed, 1 minute, until browned on all sides.
13. Transfer skillet to oven; bake 15 minutes, until cooked through.
14. Remove from oven; let stand 5 minutes.
15. Slice beef roll crosswise into 12 equal pieces, arrange on serving platter.

Appetizers

SOUTHERN DEVILED EGGS

Serves
12

- ▶ 1/2 cup mayonnaise
- ▶ 1 tsp Dijon mustard
- ▶ 1/4 cup chopped pimientos
- ▶ 6 slices cooked bacon, crumbled or 1/4 cup toasted slivered almonds
- ▶ 2 Tbsps chopped flat-leaf parsley
- ▶ 1/2 tsp each salt and pepper
- ▶ 12 large hard-cooked eggs, halved lengthwise
- ▶ Italian parsley leaves, for garnish

1. In a small bowl, mix mayonnaise, mustard, pimientos, bacon or almonds, parsley, salt, pepper and egg yolks.
2. Spoon mixture into each halved egg white.
3. Garnish each with a whole parsley leaf.

FRESH TACO "WRAPS"

Serves
4

Cilantro-Cashew "Cheeze"(makes 1 cup)
- ▶ 1 1/2 tsps garlic (about 2 cloves)
- ▶ 1/2 tsp sea salt
- ▶ 1 cup raw cashews
- ▶ 2 1/2 Tbsps fresh lemon juice (1 lemon)
- ▶ 1/4 cup packed fresh cilantro leaves
- ▶ 1/4 cup filtered water

Ground Walnut Meat (makes 1 cup)
- ▶ 1 cup raw walnuts
- ▶ 1 1/2 tsps ground cumin
- ▶ 1 1/2 tsps ground coriander
- ▶ 1/2 tsp liquid aminos, such as Bragg's Essential Amino Acids or soy sauce
- ▶ Pinch of sea salt, to taste

- ▶ 8 small-to-medium romaine leaves
- ▶ 1/2 cup low-sodium salsa, any flavor
- ▶ 1 avocado, pitted and sliced

To make "cheeze":
1. Place garlic in a food processor; process into small pieces.
2. Add cashews and process into a paste.
3. Add lemon juice, cilantro, and water; process to mix well.
4. Set aside.

To make walnut meat:
1. Place walnuts, cumin, coriander, liquid aminos, and salt in a food processor.
2. Process into small pieces until the mixture looks like ground meat; be careful not to over-process into a butter.
3. Spread 2 Tbsps cheese down the inside spine of each romaine leaf.
4. Sprinkle with 2 Tbsps walnut meat.
5. Add salsa and avocado slices.
6. Wrap and serve.

TURBOTIPS:

The "cheeze" keeps for three or four days in the fridge and the meat for up to a week.

For the "wrap," use the biggest lettuce leaves you can find.

Another option is to scoop the cashew mixture on top of a salad, or serve as a dip with carrots or cucumbers.

Make sure you have "filled your tank" with plenty of fresh water prior to eating this as it is so tasty, it is easy to over indulge.

Relax and eat slowly; you will fill up fast on this meal.

Appetizers

MOZZARELLA SKEWERS

Serves
6

- ▶ 1 lb fresh mozzarella
- ▶ 24 basil leaves
- ▶ 3 oranges, peeled and segmented
- ▶ 1/4 cup olive oil
- ▶ Sea salt
- ▶ 12 small skewers

1. Thread mozzarella cubes, basil leaves, and orange segments alternately, roughly 2-3 of each, per skewer.
2. Drizzle them with olive oil and then top with a little crunchy sea salt.

CILANTRO SHRIMP

Serves
4

- ▶ 1 bunch finely chopped cilantro
- ▶ 3 fresh-juiced limes
- ▶ 1 lb cooked, peeled and deveined shrimp
- ▶ 1 clove finely chopped garlic
- ▶ Salt to taste
- ▶ 1/4 cup olive oil

1. In large bowl combine all ingredients and toss.
2. Place bowl tightly covered in the refrigerator for at least 3 hours.
3. Serve cold with your favorite white wine or chilled beverage.

ORIENTAL BEEF IN

Serves
4

LETTUCE WRAPPERS

- ▶ 1/4 cup rice wine vinegar
- ▶ 1 Tbsp reduced-sodium soy sauce
- ▶ 2 tsps minced fresh mint leaves
  - ▶ 1 tsp minced pared fresh ginger root
  - ▶ 1 tsp grated orange zest
  - ▶ 1 tsp oriental sesame oil
  - ▶ 8 large iceberg lettuce leaves
  - ▶ 8 ounces cooked lean boneless roast beef, cut into 1/4 strips
  - ▶ 1 cup bean sprouts
  - ▶ 1 cup shredded seeded pared cucumber

1. In medium bowl, combine vinegar, soy sauce, minced mint leaves, ginger, zest and oil; set aside.
2. Place lettuce leaves on work surface; top center of each leaf with 1 ounce beef strips, 2 Tbsps bean sprouts, 2 Tbsps cucumber and 1 mint leaf.
3. Fold sides of each lettuce leaf over filling; starting from shortest end, roll leaves to enclose.
4. Place 2 rolls on each of 4 plates, seam-side down; serve with vinegar mixture for dipping.

TURBOTIPS:
The dipping sauce may be made up to three days ahead and refrigerated; prepare extra to use as a dipping sauce for cut-up raw vegetables.

BASIC DEVILED EGGS

Serves
6

- 6 hard-cooked eggs, peeled, cut in half, and yolks mashed in a bowl
- 2 Tbsps + 2 tsps mayonnaise
- 1 Tbsp prepared yellow mustard
- 2 tsps distilled white vinegar
- 1/4 tsp salt, or to taste
- 1/4 tsp black pepper, or to taste
- Paprika for garnish

1. Combine the thoroughly mashed yolks and mayonnaise, then stir in the mustard and vinegar.
2. Stir in the salt and pepper, then taste and adjust if necessary.
3. Stir well with a spoon to achieve a creamy texture.
4. Fill the whites evenly with the mixture and garnish each egg half with paprika.

HERBED DEVILED EGGS

Serves
6

- 6 hard-cooked eggs, peeled, cut in half and yolks mashed in a bowl
- 1/4 cup mayonnaise
- 1 1/2 tsps fresh lemon juice
- 1 Tbsp finely chopped fresh Italian parsley
- 1/2 tsp finely chopped fresh dill
- 2 tsps finely chopped fresh chives
- Salt and black pepper to taste
- Fresh Italian parsley leaves for garnish

1. Combine the thoroughly mashed yolks with mayonnaise and lemon juice.
2. Stir in the finely chopped herbs.
3. Taste, then season with salt and pepper.
4. Fill the whites evenly with the mixture and garnish each egg half with a whole parsley leaf.

SHRIMP COCKTAIL

Serves
4

- 10-12 large shrimp
- Salsa
- Sprig of parsley or cilantro
- Lemon wedges

1. Follow recipe for boiled shrimp (above).
2. Chill shrimp in their shells.
3. Peel and devein before serving.
4. Fill cocktail glasses to half with salsa.
5. Hang shrimp over the edges of the glass.
6. Top with a sprig of parsley or cilantro and a lemon wedge.

Appetizers

GREEN CREPES

Serves
4

Avocado Mix:
- ▶ Soften avocado
- ▶ Lemon juice
- ▶ Fresh corn
- ▶ Diced banana pepper
- ▶ Diced pimientos
- ▶ Kelp

Cucumber Mix:
- ▶ Dice cucumbers, very fine
- ▶ Fresh young peas
- ▶ Finely diced tomatoes
- ▶ Dill seeds

Zucchini Mix:
- ▶ Finely shredded zucchini
- ▶ Finely shredded carrots
- ▶ Chopped scallions
- ▶ Fresh sweet basil

Alfalfa Sprouts Mix:
- ▶ Minced alfalfa sprouts
- ▶ Chopped kohlrabi or fennel,
- ▶ Grated radishes
- ▶ Minced chives

Parsnip Mix:
- ▶ Finely grated parsnips
- ▶ Chopped fennel
- ▶ Nuts
- ▶ Grated carrots
- ▶ Ginger

1. Put spoonfuls of the mixture onto the lettuce leaves.
2. Carefully roll them up and spear with a cocktail stick.
3. Garnish with a black or stuffed green olive.

MUSHROOMS ITALIANO

Serves 4

- ▶ 1 lb fresh mushrooms
- ▶ 10-oz can unsalted tomato juice
- ▶ 2 Tbsps herb vinegar
- ▶ 1 tsp dehydrated onion flakes
- ▶ 1/8 tsp garlic powder
- ▶ 1/2 tsp dried salad herbs
- ▶ 1/8 tsp oregano
- ▶ 1/4 tsp tarragon
- ▶ 2 Tbsps apple juice (frozen concentrate)

1. Wash mushrooms; remove stems.
2. Set aside in a large mixing bowl.
3. Mix rest of ingredients well.
4. Add mushrooms to marinate overnight, stirring occasionally.
5. Serve with toothpicks.

SCALLOPS/SHRIMP STUFFED AVOCADOS

Serves 4

- ▶ 12 ounces bay scallops or tiny shrimp
- ▶ 1/3 cup fresh lime juice
- ▶ 1 1/2 tsp dried oregano
- ▶ 1 Tbsp fresh minced cilantro
- ▶ 1/2 cup olive oil
- ▶ Sea salt
- ▶ Freshly ground black pepper
- ▶ 3 large ripe avocados
- ▶ Minced chili Serrano

1. Put the shrimp or scallops in a bowl and add lime juice, oregano, cilantro and oil.
2. Season and let stand for 15-20 minutes.
3. Mixture will become opaque.
4. Slice all the way around each avocado to split it in half the long way.
5. When you have sliced all the way around, hold the avocado sideways with the bottom half held firmly.
6. Twist the top half on the bottom half and they will separate easily.
7. With the tip of a sharp knife, stab the pit and remove it.
8. Scoop out the pulp in little balls, preserving the shells.
9. Mix the balls of pulp with the shrimp or scallops.
10. Fill the shells with the mixture.
11. Top with minced Serrano.

Appetizers

BEEF ASIAN LETTUCE WRAPS

Serves 4

- ▶ 16 Boston Bibb or butter lettuce leaves
- ▶ 1 lb ground beef
- ▶ 1 Tbsp olive oil
- ▶ 1 large onion, chopped
- ▶ 2 cloves fresh garlic, minced
- ▶ 1 Tbsp soy sauce
- ▶ 1/4 cup Thai peanut sauce
- ▶ 2 tsps minced pickled ginger
- ▶ 1 Tbsp rice wine vinegar
- ▶ Asian chile pepper sauce (optional)
- ▶ 8-oz can water chestnuts, drained and finely chopped
- ▶ 1 bunch green onions, chopped
- ▶ 2 tsps Asian (dark) sesame oil

1. Rinse whole lettuce leaves and pat dry, being careful not to tear them.
2. Set aside.
3. In a medium skillet over high heat, cook the ground beef in 1 Tbsp of olive oil, stirring often and reducing the heat to medium, if necessary.
4. Drain, and set aside to cool.
5. Cook the onion in the same pan, stirring frequently.
6. Add the garlic, soy sauce, peanut sauce, ginger, vinegar and chile pepper sauce to the onions and stir.
7. Stir in chopped water chestnuts, green onions and sesame oil and continue cooking until the onions just begin to wilt.
8. Arrange lettuce leaves around the outer edge of a large serving platter and pile meat mixture in the center.

> TURBOTIPS:
> For a vegetarian option: Substitute 1 1/2 cups of cooked lentils for the ground chopped beef.

DEVILED-SALMON EGGS

Serves 6

- ▶ 6 hard-cooked eggs
- ▶ 3 Tbsps mayonnaise
- ▶ 1/2 cup boned and flaked salmon, canned or smoked
- ▶ 1/2 tsp lemon juice
- ▶ 1 tsp prepared mustard
- ▶ 1 tsp Worcestershire sauce
- ▶ 1/2 tsp salt
- ▶ Dash of pepper

1. Cut eggs in half lengthwise.
2. Remove yolks, reserving whites.
3. Mash yolks and mayonnaise together until smooth.
4. Add remaining ingredients (reserve enough salmon for garnish) and mix well.
5. Spoon mixture into egg whites.
6. Garnish with piece of salmon.

SPICY CALAMARI

Serves 4

- ▶ 1 lb squid (calamari)
- ▶ 2 Tbsps olive oil
- ▶ 2 large garlic cloves, sliced
- ▶ 1/2 tsp red pepper flakes
- ▶ 14.5-oz can diced tomatoes
- ▶ 1 tsp dried basil leaves
- ▶ 1/2 tsp dried oregano
- ▶ Dash sugar substitute
- ▶ Freshly ground pepper

1. Clean squid under running water.
2. Remove and discard hard clear pieces in centers.
3. Cut squid into 1/2" rings; halve tentacles.
4. In a medium saucepan over medium heat, cook olive oil, garlic, and red pepper flakes 1 to 2 minutes or until garlic is lightly golden.
5. Remove garlic with a slotted spoon and reserve.
6. Add tomatoes, basil, oregano and sugar substitute to saucepan.
7. Bring to boil; add squid.
8. Reduce heat to low and cook 20 to 25 minutes or until squid is tender, stirring occasionally.
9. Season to taste with salt and pepper.
10. Transfer to a serving dish and scatter reserved garlic over top.
11. Serve on small plates as an appetizer followed by a hearty salad.

LACY PARMESAN CHIPS

Serves 4

- ▶ 3-oz piece Parmesan cheese, grated

1. Put oven rack in middle position and preheat oven to 375°F.
2. Line non-stick baking sheet with greased tinfoil or Silpat.
3. Arrange mounds (approximately 1 Tbsp rounded) of cheese 3 inches apart.
4. Flatten each mound lightly to form a 3-inch round.
5. Bake until golden, 7-10 minutes.
6. Transfer with spatula to rack.
7. Cool 5 minutes before serving or storing.

Appetizers

GARLIC SHRIMP WITH
AVOCADO DIP

Serves
8

- ▶ 8 12" skewers
- ▶ 2 medium ripe Haas avocados, pitted and peeled
- ▶ 3 Tbsps jalapeno hot sauce
- ▶ 1/2 tsp salt
- ▶ 24 peeled and deveined jumbo shrimp
- ▶ 1 Tbsp olive oil
- ▶ 1 large garlic clove, pushed through a press
- ▶ Pinch cayenne pepper

1. Cut up avocados and place them directly into a food processor.
2. Puree with hot sauce and salt until smooth.
3. Set aside.
4. Heat grill to medium-high heat.
5. In a bowl, rub shrimp with oil, garlic and cayenne.
6. Thread 3 shrimp onto each of 8 skewers, leaving small spaces between shrimp.
7. (If using wooden skewers, soak in water for 1 hour before using so they won't burn.) Grill shrimp covered, about 2 1/2 minutes per side, until golden and just cooked through.
8. Serve with avocado dip.

SHRIMP & MUSHROOMS

Serves
4

- ▶ 1 lb firm white mushrooms
- ▶ 1/4 cup olive oil
- ▶ 1/2 tsp lemon juice
- ▶ 1/8 tsp freshly ground black pepper
- ▶ 1/8 tsp minced garlic
- ▶ 1 lb cleaned shrimp, cooked
- ▶ 1 1/4 tsps salt
- ▶ 2 Tbsps minced parsley

1. Wash and dry mushrooms.
2. Remove stems and use for another purpose.
3. Slice caps paper thin; add oil, lemon juice, pepper, and garlic to caps.
4. Marinate in refrigerator for 2 hours, mixing frequently.
5. Thirty minutes before serving, mix in shrimp and salt.
6. Season to taste.
7. Sprinkle with parsley.

FINGER HAM & EGG BALLS

Serves 4

- ▶ 3 eggs, hard-cooked and shelled
- ▶ 1 tsp minced chives
- ▶ 2 Tbsps mayonnaise
- ▶ Pinch of paprika
- ▶ Salt to taste
- ▶ 1/4 tsp white horseradish
- ▶ 1/4 lb boiled ham

1. Separate yolks and whites of eggs.
2. Mash yolks with fork.
3. Add chives, mayonnaise, paprika, and salt.
4. Put egg whites in blender with horseradish and ham.
5. Blend until smooth.
6. Mix two mixtures together.
7. Shape into 1" balls.
8. Refrigerate.

FRESH TOMATO SALAD

Serves 4

- ▶ 5 ripe large tomatoes, cut into 1/3 inch thick rounds
- ▶ 1 small red onion, thinly sliced
- ▶ 1/4 cup extra virgin olive oil
- ▶ 4 ounces feta cheese, crumbled
- ▶ 1 Tbsp balsamic vinegar
- ▶ 1/4 cup kalamata olives
- ▶ 1 tsp chopped fresh parsley

1. Arrange tomatoes on platter.
2. Top with onion slices.
3. Drizzle oil and vinegar over top.
4. Sprinkle with salt and pepper.
5. Let stand a little while.
6. When ready to serve top with crumbled feta cheese, olives and chopped parsley.

CURRIED DEVILED EGGS

Serves 4

- ▶ 4 hard-boiled eggs
- ▶ 1/8 tsp sea salt
- ▶ 1 Tbsp mayonnaise
- ▶ 1/8 cayenne pepper
- ▶ 1/2 tsp prepared mustard
- ▶ Paprika
- ▶ 1/2 tsp curry powder

1. Remove eggs from shells carefully.
2. Slice in half lengthwise.
3. Remove yolks with a spoon.
4. Mash yolks with other ingredients to form a paste.
5. Refill hollows of egg white with paste.
6. Sprinkle with paprika for color.
7. Use other seasoning as desired.

Appetizers

BOILED SHRIMP

Serves 4

- ▶ 1 1/2 lbs shrimp in shell
- ▶ 2 ribs celery, cut into 2" pieces
- ▶ 1 clove garlic, unpeeled
- ▶ 2 slices onion
- ▶ Juice of 1 lemon
- ▶ 1 bay leaf
- ▶ 8-12 black peppercorns
- ▶ 4 sprigs fresh parsley

1. In a large saucepan, heat 2 quarts of water with all the ingredients except the shrimp.
2. Boil water for 5 minutes.
3. Add shrimp and bring to a boil again.
4. Remove shrimp when they turn pink (just a few minutes).
5. Flush with cool water.
6. Discard vegetables and herbs.
7. If to be served cold, chill and serve shrimp in their shells.
8. If to be used in a recipe, shell and devein at once.
9. Remove quickly from water when pink.

STUFFED PIQUILLO PEPPERS

Serves 4

- ▶ 2 Tbsps finely diced shallots
- ▶ 1 scallion (white part only), thinly sliced
- ▶ 1 1/2 tsp aged Spanish sherry vinegar
- ▶ 1 can piquillo peppers, drained, rinsed and dried
- ▶ 3 ounces soft goat cheese
- ▶ Olive oil cooking spray
- ▶ 1 tsp chopped fresh parsley
- ▶ 1/2 tsp chopped fresh thyme

1. Whisk shallots, scallion and vinegar in a bowl.
2. Season with salt and pepper.
3. Slice open the top of each pepper to create a pocket.
4. Spoon cheese into peppers, dividing it equally among them.
5. Heat a large frying pan over medium heat; coat with cooking spray.
6. Cook peppers, flipping once, until cheese begins to melt, about 30 seconds each side.
7. Transfer to a platter.
8. Sprinkle with parsley and thyme.
9. Drizzle dressing over peppers and serve.

NOTES
· · · · · · ·

Soups & Stews

SPICY BLACK BEAN STEW

Serves
4

- ▶ 2 tsps olive oil
- ▶ 2 medium red onions, cut into 1" chunks
- ▶ 1 medium pickled jalapeno pepper, seeded and minced
- ▶ 1 Tbsp minced pared fresh ginger root
- ▶ 4 garlic cloves, minced
- ▶ 1 cup diced seeded poblano chilies
- ▶ 2 cups diced butternut squash
- ▶ 1 lb drained cooked black beans
- ▶ 2 cups stewed tomatoes (no salt added), chopped
- ▶ 1 cup thawed frozen corn kernels
- ▶ 1/3 cup minced fresh cilantro

1. In large saucepan or Dutch oven, heat oil; add onions, pepper, ginger and garlic.
2. Cook over medium-high heat, stirring frequently, 5 minutes, until onions are softened.
3. Add chilies; cook, stirring frequently, 5 minutes, until chilies are softened.
4. Add squash; cook, stirring frequently, 5 minutes, until squash is softened.
5. Add beans, tomatoes and 3/4 cup water to vegetable mixture; bring to a boil.
6. Reduce heat to low; simmer, covered, 30 minutes, until vegetables are tender and mixture is slightly thickened.
7. Stir in corn, cilantro and salt; cook, stirring constantly, 2 minutes, until mixture is heated through.

QUICK BROCCOLI BISQUE

Serves
2

- ▶ 2 cups cooked broccoli
- ▶ 1 cup low-sodium chicken broth

1. In food processor, combine broccoli and chicken broth; puree until smooth.
2. Transfer to saucepan; cook until heated.

CHILLED BEET SOUP

Serves 8

- ▶ 1 cup peeled, coarsely chopped baking potato
- ▶ 1 cup coarsely chopped parsnip
- ▶ 1 cup coarsely chopped onion
- ▶ 2 15-oz cans sliced beets, undrained
- ▶ 2 10.5-oz cans low-sodium chicken broth
- ▶ 1/4 cup water
- ▶ 1 Tbsp lemon juice
- ▶ 1 Tbsp red wine vinegar
- ▶ 1/2 tsp prepared horseradish
- ▶ 1/4 tsp ground white pepper
- ▶ 1/2 cup shredded cucumber

1. Arrange first 3 ingredients in a steamer basket over boiling water.
2. Cover and steam 6 to 8 minutes or until crisp-tender.
3. Position blade in food processor bowl; add potato mixture and beets.
4. Process 1 1/2 minutes or until smooth.
5. Transfer beet mixture to a Dutch oven; add chicken broth and next 6 ingredients, stirring well.
6. Bring mixture to a boil.
7. Reduce heat, and simmer, uncovered, 5 minutes or until thoroughly heated.
8. Transfer to a large bowl; cover and chill.
9. To serve, ladle soup into individual goblets.
10. Top each serving with 1 Tbsp shredded cucumber.

TURBOTIPS:
This tasty soup can be served hot or cold.

SUMMER GAZPACHO

Serves 4

- ▶ 10.5–oz can low-sodium tomato soup
- ▶ 1 3/4 cup no-salt-added tomato juice
- ▶ 2/3 cup peeled, seeded, and finely chopped cucumber
- ▶ 1/2 cup finely chopped green pepper
- ▶ 1/2 cup finely chopped tomato
- ▶ 1/3 cup finely chopped onion
- ▶ 2 Tbsps red wine vinegar
- ▶ 1 Tbsp lemon juice
- ▶ 1 clove garlic, minced
- ▶ 1/2 tsp pepper
- ▶ 1/4 tsp salt
- ▶ 1/4 tsp hot sauce
- ▶ Thinly sliced cucumber (optional)

1. Combine first 12 ingredients in a large bowl; stir well.
2. Cover and chill at least 8 hours.
3. To serve, ladle soup into individual bowls, and garnish with cucumber slices if desired.

Soups & Stews

FRENCH ONION SOUP

Serves
8

- Vegetable cooking spray
- 2 medium onions, sliced and separated into rings
- 3 cups canned no-salt-add beef broth, undiluted
- 1 Tbsp low-sodium Worcestershire sauce
- 1/4 tsp salt
- 1/4 tsp pepper
- 1/4 cup shredded Gruyere cheese

1. Coat a large saucepan with cooking spray; place over medium-high heat until hot.
2. Add onion, and sauté 2 minutes or until tender.
3. Add beef broth and next 3 ingredients; bring to a boil.
4. Reduce heat, and simmer, uncovered, 15 minutes.
5. Ladle soup into 4 soup bowls; sprinkle cheese on top and broil for 1 minute until evenly browned and cheese melts.

Microwave Instructions: Coat a 2-quart casserole with cooking spray. Add onion and microwave, uncovered, at HIGH 4 to 6 minutes or until onion is crisp-tender, stirring every 2 minutes. Add beef broth and next 3 ingredients. Microwave, uncovered, at HIGH 6 to 8 minutes or until boiling.

LAYERED VEGETABLE STEW

Serves
8

- 14.5–oz can no-salt-added whole tomatoes, drained and coarsely chopped
- 2 cups sliced leeks
- 2 cups sliced zucchini
- 5 cups shredded romaine lettuce
- 1 clove garlic, minced
- 9-oz package frozen artichoke hearts, thawed
- 1/4 cup minced fresh parsley
- 1 tsp pepper
- 1/2 tsp salt
- 10-oz package frozen chicken broth
- 1/2 cup grated Romano cheese

1. Layer first 10 ingredients in a Dutch oven, beginning with tomato.
2. Pour chicken broth over vegetables (do not stir).
3. Bring mixture to a boil.
4. Cover, reduce heat, and simmer, covered, 10 minutes.
5. Lightly stir vegetable mixture, and cook, covered, 20 additional minutes or until vegetables are tender, stirring often.
6. To serve, ladle stew into individual bowls, and sprinkle each with 1 Tbsp cheese.

MEXICAN BLACK BEAN SOUP

Serves 8

- ► 2 Tbsps water
- ► 1 cup chopped onion
- ► 1/2 cup chopped green pepper
- ► 1/2 cup sliced carrot
- ► 1/4 cup chopped celery
- ► 2 15-oz cans black beans, rinsed and drained
- ► 14.5-oz can no-salt-added tomatoes, undrained and chopped
- ► 10-oz can tomatoes with chilies, undrained and chopped
- ► 1 cup water
- ► 1/2 cup low-sodium beef broth, undiluted
- ► 1/2 tsp ground cumin
- ► 1/2 tsp pepper
- ► 1/4 tsp garlic powder

1. Heat water in a large saucepan over medium-high heat.
2. Add onion, green pepper, carrot, and celery; sauté until tender.
3. Add beans and remaining ingredients to vegetable mixture.
4. Bring mixture to a boil.
5. Cover, reduce heat, and simmer 30 minutes, stirring occasionally

VEGETABLE CHILI

Serves 8

- ► 2 cups chopped onion
- ► 1 cup chopped green pepper
- ► 14.25-oz can no-salt-added beef broth
- ► 2 lb eggplant, cubed
- ► 2 15-oz cans kidney beans, drained
- ► 2 10.75–oz can low-sodium tomato soup
- ► 1/4 cup sliced ripe olives
- ► 2 Tbsps chili powder
- ► 1 tsp ground coriander
- ► 1 tsp dried oregano
- ► 1 tsp pepper
- ► 1/2 cup finely shredded reduced-fat sharp Cheddar cheese.

1. Combine first 3 ingredients in a Dutch oven.
2. Bring to a boil; cover, reduce heat, and simmer, 15 minutes.
3. Add eggplant and next 7 ingredients; cover and cook 50 minutes or until vegetables are tender, stirring occasionally.
4. To serve, ladle chili into individual bowls.
5. Sprinkle 1 Tbsp cheese over each serving.

Soups & Stews

VEGETABLE-BEEF SOUP

Serves 5

- ▶ Vegetable cooking spray
- ▶ 1/2 lb ground chuck
- ▶ 2 1/3 cups chopped cabbage
- ▶ 2 cups chopped celery
- ▶ 1 1/3 cups frozen sliced carrot, thawed
- ▶ 1 cup frozen chopped onion, thawed
- ▶ 1/2 cup frozen chopped green pepper, thawed
- ▶ 4 cups canned no-salt-added beef broth, undiluted
- ▶ 2 14.5-oz cans no-salt-added whole tomatoes, undrained and chopped
- ▶ 11-oz can no-salt-added whole kernel corn, drained
  - ▶ 1 tsp dried oregano
  - ▶ 1/2 tsp dried thyme
  - ▶ 1/2 tsp pepper
  - ▶ 1/4 tsp salt

TURBOTIPS:
This recipe makes enough for two meals. Measure out the needed portions, and freeze the rest of the soup (up to two months) to serve at another time.

1. Coat Dutch oven with cooking spray; place over medium-high heat until hot.
2. Add ground chuck; cook until meat is browned, stirring until it crumbles.
3. Remove from Dutch oven; drain and pat dry with paper towels.
4. Wipe drippings from pan with a paper towel.
5. Coat Dutch oven with cooking spray; place over medium-high heat until hot.
6. Add cabbage and next 4 ingredients; sauté 5 minutes or until tender.
7. Return meat to Dutch oven.
8. Add broth and remaining ingredients.
9. Bring to a boil; cover, reduce heat, and simmer 20 to 25 minutes or until vegetables are tender.

HOME ON THE RANGE BEANS

Serves 8

- ▶ Vegetable cooking spray
- ▶ 1/4 cup chopped onion
- ▶ 16-oz can light red kidney beans
- ▶ 15.8-oz can Great Northern beans
- ▶ 8-oz can no-salt-added tomato sauce
- ▶ 3 Tbsps no- salt-added tomato juice
- ▶ 1 Tbsp prepared mustard
- ▶ 1/4 tsp garlic powder
- ▶ 1/8 tsp pepper

1. Coat a medium saucepan with cooking spray; place over medium-high heat until hot.
2. Add onion; sauté until tender.
3. Add kidney beans and remaining ingredients.
4. Cook over medium heat, uncovered, 20 minutes.

TURKEY VEGETABLE STEW

Serves 8

- ▶ 1 1/4 cups sliced carrot
- ▶ 1 cup sliced celery
- ▶ 3/4 cup chopped onion
- ▶ 3/4 cup water
- ▶ 1 Tbsp chopped fresh basil
- ▶ 2 Tbsps no-added-tomato paste
- ▶ 2 10.5-oz cans low-sodium chicken broth
- ▶ 14.5-oz can no-salt-added whole
- ▶ Tomatoes, undrained and chopped
- ▶ 1/4 tsp pepper
- ▶ 1/4 tsp hot sauce
- ▶ 2 cloves garlic, minced
- ▶ 2 1/2 cups chopped cooked turkey breast (skinned before cooking and cooked without salt)
- ▶ 10-oz package frozen English peas, thawed
- ▶ 10-oz package frozen okra, thawed

1. Combine first 8 ingredients in a large Dutch oven.
2. Add next 3 ingredients, stirring well to combine.
3. Bring to a boil; cover, reduce heat, and simmer 30 minutes.
4. Stir in turkey, peas, and okra; simmer, uncovered, 10 minutes or until thoroughly heated.

GAZPACHO DELIGHT

Serves 6

- ▶ 2 cups cold beef, chicken broth or vegetable stock
- ▶ 2 medium cucumbers, peeled seeded, and finely chopped
- ▶ 1 bunch scallions, finely chopped
- ▶ 1 medium green pepper, finely chopped
- ▶ 2 tomatoes, finely chopped
- ▶ 2 garlic cloves, minced
- ▶ 1 cup tomato sauce
- ▶ 1/2 cup water
- ▶ 1 Tbsp red wine vinegar
- ▶ 1/2 tsp Tabasco
- ▶ 2 tsps Worcestershire sauce
- ▶ 1 tsp fresh parsley, finely chopped
- ▶ Salt and black pepper to taste

1. Pour the beef broth, chicken broth or vegetable stock into a large bowl, then add the cucumbers, scallions, green pepper, tomatoes, garlic, tomato sauce, water, red wine vinegar, and Tabasco.
2. Stir until the ingredients are well combined and season with salt and pepper.
3. Chill in the refrigerator for at least 4 hours, then add the Worcestershire and parsley.
4. Serve the gazpacho in chilled bowls.

TURBOTIPS:
For a variation of this popular soup, lump crabmeat or chopped shrimp may be added.

Soups & Stews

SQUASH & ZUCCHINI SOUP

Serves
6

- ▶ 1 large chopped onion
- ▶ 3 cups water
- ▶ 2 chopped yellow squash
- ▶ 2 chopped large ripe tomatoes
- ▶ 1 chopped sweet red pepper
- ▶ 1 chopped sweet yellow pepper
- ▶ 1 chopped zucchini
- ▶ 3 large cloves garlic, minced
- ▶ 1 1/2 tsp salt
- ▶ 1/2 tsp fennel seeds
- ▶ 1/4 tsp ground black pepper
- ▶ 1/2 cup grated Parmesan cheese

1. In a large sauce pan, over medium heat, add the onion; sauté until softened for 5 minutes.
2. Add the water, yellow squash, tomatoes, red and yellow peppers, zucchini, garlic, salt, fennel seeds and black pepper.
3. Bring to a boil then reduce heat and simmer until vegetables are tender about 15 minutes.
4. In a food processor, purée 2 1/2 cups of the soup.
5. Then return purée to the pan with the remaining soup.
6. Heat through, sprinkle with Parmesan cheese and serve immediately.

CHICKEN SOUP

Serves
10

- ▶ 7-8 lb hen
- ▶ 2 bunches parsley
- ▶ 2 bunches celery
  - ▶ 2 large onions
  - ▶ 5 quart water
  - ▶ Salt and pepper to taste

1. In a large pot, place all ingredients.
2. Bring to a boil and skim residue.
3. Lower fire to a slow boil and cook for 2 hours.
4. Take out hen; strain vegetables.
5. Chop parsley and cut celery into 1" pieces.
6. Add parsley and celery back to soup.

TURBOTIPS:
Hen may be cut into bite-size pieces and also added to soup or may be used for chicken salad.

ELISA'S SOUP

Serves
4

- ▶ 3 crowns broccoli
- ▶ 5 cloves garlic
- ▶ 2 onions
- ▶ 2 stalks celery
- ▶ 3 cup vegetable or chicken stock (if homemade, remove all fat)

1. Throw all in pot, simmer 20 minutes.
2. Put all veggies in blender with half of liquid puree and add black pepper.
3. Killer soup all veggie.

CREAM OF MUSHROOM SOUP

Serves
4

- ▶ 1 lb fresh white mushrooms
- ▶ 1oz dried Morel mushrooms
- ▶ 2 chopped shallots
- ▶ 1 clove garlic, minced
- ▶ 1 quart hot beef broth or stock
- ▶ 1/2 tsp dried thyme
- ▶ Chopped fresh parsley for garnish

1. Soak dried Morel mushrooms in about 1 cup warm water for about 20 minutes, then drain and reserve liquid to add extra flavor to soup.
2. Chop the fresh white mushrooms and the Morel mushrooms.
3. Sauté in a large pan the shallots and garlic.
4. Cook until softened about 5 minutes.
5. Add both types of mushrooms and stir over moderate heat for about 5 minutes.
6. Add beef broth or stock and morel soaking liquid and bring to a boil, stirring.
7. Add the thyme and salt and pepper.
8. Cover and simmer for 30 minutes.
9. In a food processor, blend about 3/4 of the mixture until smooth.
10. Pour back into pan, add cream and season to taste.
11. Reheat, serve immediately, and garnish with parsley.

LENTIL & HAM SOUP

Serves
8

- ▶ 1 lb lentils
- ▶ 6 cups beef broth or stock
- ▶ 2 cups water
- ▶ 1 lb ham, cut into bite-size pieces
- ▶ 1 cup chopped celery
- ▶ 1 cup chopped green onions
- ▶ 2/3 cup chopped onion
- ▶ 2 Tbsps chopped fresh parsley
- ▶ 1 clove garlic, minced
- ▶ 1 bay leaf
- ▶ 1/2 tsp thyme
- ▶ 1/4 cup dry white wine (optional)
- ▶ Salt and pepper to taste
- ▶ Tabasco

1. In a large pot, place lentils, beef broth or stock, and water.
2. Cover and simmer for 1 hour.
3. In a skillet, sauté ham and add to the lentils.
4. In the ham drippings, sauté vegetable until tender then add to the lentils.
5. Add bay leaf and thyme.
6. Cover and simmer for 1 hour.
7. Stir occasionally and add water if necessary for desired consistency.
8. Add wine, salt, pepper and Tabasco
9. Remove bay leaf and serve immediately.

VEGETABLE STOCK

Serves 8

- ▶ 3/4 lb mixed vegetable and trimmings, chopped turnips, celery, leeks, scallions
- ▶ Parsley
- ▶ 2 1/2 quarts, parsley
- ▶ 1 chopped onion
- ▶ 2 bay leaves, torn
- ▶ Salt and pepper to taste

1. Put all ingredients in a large pot.
2. Add water and bring to a boil.
3. Simmer, uncovered, for 1 hour, then drain.

BEEF & VEGETABLE SOUP

Serves 6

- ▶ 2 tsps butter
- ▶ 1 cup diced onions
- ▶ 1 cup diced celery
- ▶ 1 cup diced carrot
- ▶ 10 ounces lean boneless beef loin, cut into 1/2 cubes
- ▶ 1 cup low-sodium beef broth
- ▶ 1 cup coarsely chopped green beans
- ▶ 1 cup thawed frozen corn kernels
- ▶ 1/4 cup chopped scallions
- ▶ 1/4 cup minced fresh flat-leaf parsley
- ▶ 1/4 tsp freshly ground black pepper

1. In large saucepan, melt butter; add onions, celery and carrot.
2. Cook over medium-high heat, stirring frequently, 5 minutes, until vegetables are softened.
3. Add beef, broth green beans, corn, scallions, parsley, pepper and 2 cups water to vegetable mixture; bring liquid to a boil.
4. Reduce heat to low; simmer, stirring occasionally 20 minutes, until beef is cooked through and vegetables are tender.

FAST & EASY GAZPACHO

Serves 4

- ▶ 1 cup chopped tomato
- ▶ 1/2 cup chopped green bell pepper
- ▶ 1/2 cup chopped onion
- ▶ 1/2 cup chopped celery
- ▶ 1 Tbsp fresh cilantro
- ▶ 2 tsps fresh lemon juice
- ▶ 1/2 tsp celery seeds
- ▶ Black pepper to taste
- ▶ 2 Tbsps sour cream

1. In food processor, combine tomato, green bell pepper, onion, celery, 1 Tbsp fresh cilantro and 2 tsps fresh lemon juice; puree.
2. Stir in 1/2 tsp celery seeds and freshly ground black pepper, to taste; refrigerate covered, until chilled.
3. Serve topped with sour cream.

COUNTRY BEEF STEW

Serves 4

- ▶ 2 tsps olive oil
- ▶ 1 cup chopped onions
- ▶ 1 garlic clove, minced
- ▶ 1/2 tsp freshly ground black pepper
- ▶ 10 ounces lean boneless beef loin, cut into 2" cubes
- ▶ 10 ounces small red potatoes, quartered
- ▶ 1 cup small whole white mushrooms, woody ends removed
- ▶ 1 cup pearl onions
- ▶ 1 cup baby carrots
- ▶ 2 cups low-sodium beef broth
- ▶ 1/4 cup red wine vinegar
- ▶ 1 Tbsp tomato paste (no salt added)
- ▶ 1/4 tsp dried thyme leaves
- ▶ 1/4 tsp dried tarragon leaves
- ▶ 1 bay leaf
- ▶ 2 Tbsps minced fresh flat-leafed parsley

1. In large saucepan, heat oil; add chopped onions and garlic.
2. Cook over medium-high heat, stirring frequently 5 minutes, until onions are softened.
3. On sheet of wax paper or paper plate, sprinkle 1/4 tsp of the pepper; add beef, turning to coat evenly.
4. Add beef to onion mixture; cook, stirring frequently, 4 minutes, until beef is browned on all sides.
5. Add potatoes, mushrooms, pearl onions and carrots; cook, stirring frequently, 2 minutes.
6. Add broth, vinegar, tomato paste, thyme, tarragon, bay leaf, remaining 1/4 tsp pepper and 5 cups water to beef mixture; bring liquid to a boil.
7. Reduce heat to low; simmer, cover, 40 minutes, until beef is cooked through and vegetable are tender.
8. Stir in parsley; discard bay leaf.

EASY ARTICHOKE SOUP

Serves 4

- ▶ 1 cup low-sodium chicken broth
- ▶ 1/2 cup drained canned artichoke hearts
- ▶ 2 Tbsps minced fresh flat-leaf parsley
- ▶ 1 Tbsp fresh lemon juice

1. In food processor or blender, combine chicken broth, canned artichoke hearts, parsley and lemon juice; puree until smooth.
2. Transfer to small saucepan; heat.

GROUND-BEEF CHILI

Serves 8

- ► 1 tsp olive oil
- ► 1 1/2 cups cubed green bell peppers
- ► 1 cup chopped onions
- ► 2 garlic cloves, minced
- ► 1 Tbsp + 1 tsp mild or hot chili powder
- ► 1 tsp ground cumin
- ► 1/4 tsp cinnamon
- ► 1/4 tsp ground red pepper
- ► 10 ounces lean ground beef (10% or less fat)
- ► 2 cups canned whole Italian tomatoes (no salt added), drained and chopped
- ► 1 bay leaf
- ► 1 tsp dried oregano leaves

1. In large saucepan or Dutch oven, heat oil; add bell peppers and onions.
2. Cook over medium-high heat, stirring frequently, 5 minutes, until onions are softened.
3. Add garlic; cook, stirring frequently, 1 minute.
4. Add chili powder cumin, cinnamon and ground red pepper; cook, stirring constantly, 30 seconds, until vegetables are well coated.
5. Add beef to vegetable mixture; cook, stirring to break up meat, 4-5 minutes until no longer pink.
6. Add tomatoes, bay leaf and oregano; bring mixture to a boil.
7. Reduce heat to low; simmer, covered, 1 1/2 hours, until mixture is thickened.
8. Remove and discard bay leaf.

MEDITERRANEAN LAMB STEW

Serves 4

- ► 1/4 tsp salt
- ► 1/4 tsp freshly ground black pepper
- ► 10 ounces lean boneless loin of lamb, cut into 1" cubes
- ► 1 Tbsp + 1 tsp vegetable oil
- ► 1 cup chopped onions
- ► 2 cups quartered white mushrooms
- ► 1 Tbsp minced fresh oregano leaves or 1/2 tsp dried
- ► 1 tsp grated lemon zest
- ► 1 garlic clove, minced
- ► 1 cup pearl onions
- ► 1 cup frozen cut okra
- ► 1 cup cubed eggplant
- ► 1 cup tomato sauce (no salt added)
- ► 1/2 cup low-sodium beef broth
- ► 2 Tbsps minced fresh flat-leaf parsley

1. In large saucepan, heat oil; add lamb.
2. Cook over medium-high heat, stirring frequently, 4 minutes, until lamb is browned on all sides.
3. Add chopped onions; cook, stirring frequently, 5 minutes, until onions are softened.
4. Reduce heat to medium-low; add mushrooms, oregano, zest and garlic.
5. Cook, stirring constantly, 1 minute, until mushrooms begin to release their liquid.
6. Add pearl onions, okra, eggplant, tomato sauce and broth; cook, covered, stirring occasionally, 40 minutes, until lamb is cooked through and tender.
7. Stir in parsley.

CHICKPEA & ROOT VEGETABLE STEW

Serves 4

- 1 cup diced well-washed leeks
- 5 ounces all-purpose potato, pared and cut into 1/2" pieces
- 4 ounces sweet potato, pared and cut into 1/2" pieces
- 1 cup carrot chunks (1" pieces)
- 1 cup parsnip chunks (1" pieces)
- 1 cup diced turnips (1/2" pieces)
- 1/2 tsp ground dried sage
- 1/2 tsp salt
- 1/4 tsp freshly ground black pepper
- 1 cup apple cider
- 1/4 cup tomato paste (no salt added)
- 2 Tbsps cider vinegar
- 8 ounces drained cooked chick peas
- 1/2 cup minced fresh flat-leaf parsley

1. In large nonstick skillet, add leeks.
2. Cook over medium-high heat, stirring frequently 5 minutes, until softened.
3. Add all-purpose and sweet potatoes, carrots, parsnip and turnips; stir to coat.
4. Sprinkle with sage, salt and pepper, stir to combine.
5. Add cider, tomato paste and vinegar to vegetable mixture; bring liquid to a boil.
6. Reduce heat to low; simmer, covered.
7. 20 minutes, until potatoes are softened.
8. Stir chickpeas into potato mixure; return liquid to a boil.
9. Reduce heat to low; simmer, covered until vegetables are softened and mixture is heated through.
10. Stir in parsley.

SALSA GAZPACHO

Serves 4

- 2 1/2 cups tomato juice
- 1 cup coarsely chopped, peeled, firm ripe tomato
- 3/4 cup coarsely chopped red and/or green bell pepper
- 3/4 cup finely chopped onion
- 1/2 cup coarsely chopped, peeled cucumber
- 2 Tbsps freshly squeezed lemon juice
- 1/2 tsp garlic powder
- 1/4 tsp Worcestershire sauce
- 1/4 tsp pepper
- For garnish: snipped fresh chives or green onion tops

1. In large bowl mix all ingredients except garnish until blended.
2. Cover and chill at least 4 hours or overnight.
3. Serve in chilled bowls; sprinkle with chives.

TURBOTIPS:
This recipe is also good as a sauce (salsa) for a wide variety of salads, vegetables and entrées.

It's best prepared a day ahead so the flavors blend.

Soups & Stews

Soups & Stews

SPINACH & WHITE BEAN SOUP

Serves 8

- ▶ 2 garlic cloves, minced
- ▶ 1/2 tsp dried rosemary leaves
- ▶ 1/4 tsp crushed red pepper flakes
- ▶ 8 ounces drained cooked white beans
- ▶ 1/2 cup half & half
- ▶ 2 Tbsps tomato paste (no salt added)
- ▶ 1/2 tsp salt
- ▶ 2 cups water
- ▶ 1/4 tsp freshly ground black pepper
- ▶ 1/2 cup finely diced carrot
- ▶ 2 cups shredded well-washed trimmed spinach leaves
- ▶ 1/2 cup drained roasted red bell peppers, cut into strips

1. In large saucepan, add garlic, rosemary and red pepper flakes.
2. Cook over low heat, stirring occasionally, 4 minutes, until garlic is softened.
3. Stir beans, half & half, tomato paste, salt, black pepper and water into garlic mixture; bring to a boil.
4. Reduce heat to low; simmer, stirring occasionally, 3 minutes, until mixture is heated through and flavors are blended.
5. Transfer bean mixture to blender or food processor and puree until smooth.
6. Return bean mixture to saucepan; bring to a boil.
7. Add carrot; cook, stirring occasionally, 4 minutes, until carrot is softened.
8. Stir in spinach and roasted peppers; cook, stirring occasionally, 3 minutes, until spinach is softened and mixture is heated through.

ONION SOUP

Serves 4

- ▶ 1 1/4 cups sliced onions
- ▶ 1 tsp butter
- ▶ 1 quart beef bouillon
- ▶ Salt to taste
- ▶ 1/8 tsp black pepper
- ▶ 1/8 tsp herb seasoning
- ▶ Grated Parmesan cheese

1. Sauté onions lightly in butter.
2. Drain off butter thoroughly.
3. Combine onions in pot with bouillon, salt, black pepper and herb seasoning.
4. Bring to boil then simmer 30 minutes.
5. Serve with Parmesan cheese; sprinkle sparingly.

MIXED-BEAN CHILI

Serves 4

- ▶ 2 tsps olive oil
- ▶ 1 cup minced scallions
- ▶ 1 cup diced green bell pepper
- ▶ 2 tsps mild or hot chili powder
- ▶ 1 tsp ground cumin
- ▶ 1 tsp ground coriander
- ▶ 1/2 tsp dried oregano leaves
- ▶ 8 ounces sweet potatoes, pared and cut into 1/2" chunks
- ▶ 1 1/2 cups stewed tomatoes (no salted added), chopped
- ▶ 8 ounces drained cooked black beans
- ▶ 8 ounces drained cooked red beans

1. In large saucepan or Dutch oven, heat oil; add scallions.
2. Cook over medium-high heat, stirring frequently, 4 minutes, until softened.
3. Add bell pepper; cook, stirring frequently, 5 minutes, until pepper is softened.
4. Add chili powder, cumin, coriander and oregano; stir to combine.
5. Add sweet potatoes and 1 cup water to vegetable mixture; bring liquid to a boil, Reduce heat to low; simmer covered, 15 minutes, until potatoes are tender.
6. Stir in tomatoes, black and red beans and salt; return mixture to a boil.
7. Reduce heat to low; simmer, stirring occasionally, until vegetables are very tender and mixture is thickened.

15-MINUTE GARDEN
VEGETABLE SOUP

Serves 6

- ▶ 1 Tbsp olive oil
- ▶ 2 Tbsps each of pre-chopped onion, celery and bell pepper
- ▶ 1 cup shredded carrots
- ▶ 1 cup fresh broccoli or cauliflower florets
- ▶ 1 cup sliced fresh mushrooms
- ▶ 1 3/4 cups organic chicken or vegetable broth
- ▶ 1/2 tsp dried basil
- ▶ 1/4 tsp each minced garlic and ground black pepper
- ▶ 1 cup baby spinach leaves

1. Heat oil in Dutch oven over medium heat.
2. Add onion, celery and bell pepper; cook and stir 2 minutes.
3. Add carrots, broccoli and mushrooms.
4. Cook and stir 5 minutes.
5. Stir in 1 1/2 cups water, chicken broth, basil, garlic and black pepper.
6. Bring to boiling.
7. Reduce heat; cover and simmer 5 minutes.
8. Stir in spinach to wilt.
9. Serve immediately.

Soups & Stews

MOROCCAN LENTIL & VEGETABLE SOUP

Serves 6

- ▶ 1 Tbsp olive oil
- ▶ 1 cup chopped onion
- ▶ 4 medium cloves garlic, minced
- ▶ 1/2 cup dried lentils, rinsed and drained
- ▶ 1 1/2 tsps ground coriander
- ▶ 1 1/2 tsps ground cumin
- ▶ 1/2 tsp black pepper
- ▶ 1/2 tsp ground cinnamon
- ▶ 3 3/4 cups fat-free reduced sodium chicken or vegetable broth
- ▶ 1/2 cup chopped celery
- ▶ 1/2 cup chopped sun-dried tomatoes (not packed in oil)
- ▶ 1 medium yellow summer squash, chopped
- ▶ 1/2 cup chopped green bell pepper
- ▶ 1/2 cup chopped fresh parsley
- ▶ 1 cup chopped plum tomatoes
- ▶ 1/4 chopped fresh cilantro or basil

1. Heat oil in medium saucepan over medium heat.
2. Add onion and garlic; cook 4 minutes or until onion is tender, stirring occasionally.
3. Stir in lentils, coriander, cumin, black pepper and cinnamon; cook 2 minutes.
4. Add chicken broth, celery and sun-dried tomatoes; bring to a boil over high heat.
5. Reduce heat to low; simmer, covered, 25 minutes.
6. Stir in squash, bell pepper and parsley.
7. Continue cooking, covered, 10 minutes or until lentils are tender.
8. Top with plum tomatoes and cilantro just before serving.

RATATOUILLE

Serves 8

- ▶ 1-2 eggplants, in chunks, stems removed (no need to peel)
- ▶ 1-2 onions, sliced, optional
    - ▶ 1 or 2 peppers, seeded and sliced, optional
    - ▶ Basil to taste
    - ▶ 2-3 zucchini, cut in chunks
    - ▶ 4-6 fresh tomatoes, chunked, or one 28-oz can tomatoes, any type
- ▶ 1-2 cloves fresh garlic, pressed

1. Begin heating tomatoes in a deep pan or Dutch oven (no oil necessary).
2. Add onions, eggplants and squash.
3. Simmer over low heat for about one hour, covered.
4. Add basil halfway through.
5. Garnish with black olives or capers and serve with Parmesan cheese sprinkled on top.
6. Serve over rice or alone as a side dish.

TURBOTIPS:
Ingredients can be varied to use whatever is available.

Make enough to last several days as it improves over time and also freezes well.

SWEET POTATO-COCONUT SOUP

Spicy Relish
- ▶ 1 Tbsp olive oil
- ▶ 1 Tbsp unsalted butter
- ▶ Pinch of red-pepper flakes
- ▶ 1/2 small sweet potato, peeled and cut into small dices
- ▶ Salt and fresh black pepper
- ▶ 1/4 cup finely chopped fresh flat-leaf parsley

Sweet Potato-Coconut Soup
- ▶ 1 1/2 Tbsp olive oil
- ▶ 1 small red onion, chopped
- ▶ 2" piece of fresh ginger, grated
- ▶ Pinch of red-pepper flakes
- ▶ 3 cups homemade chicken stock
- ▶ 1/2 cup water
- ▶ 1 1/2 lbs sweet potatoes, peeled and cut into large dice
- ▶ 1 1/2 cups unsweetened coconut milk
- ▶ 1 Tbsp clover honey
- ▶ Large pinch of ground cinnamon

For relish:
1. Heat oil and butter over medium heat.
2. Add red-pepper flakes; heat for 10 seconds.
3. Add the diced sweet potato, salt and pepper.
4. Cook, covered, stirring occasionally, until softened, 15 minutes.
5. Uncover, increase heat to high, and cook until diced potatoes are gold brown, 5 to 7 minutes.
6. Transfer to a bowl; stir in the parsley.

For soup:
1. Heat oil in a saucepan over medium heat.
2. Add onion and ginger; cook until soft, 5 minutes.
3. Add red-pepper flakes and cook for 30 seconds.
4. Add stock and water; bring to a boil.
5. Add sweet potatoes; bring to a simmer.
6. Cook until potatoes are soft, 20 to 30 minutes.
7. Cool for 10 minutes.
8. Transfer mixture to a blender and process until smooth.
9. Return to saucepan; simmer over low heat.
10. Whisk in coconut milk, honey, and cinnamon.
11. Cook until thickened and warmed through.
12. Season with salt and pepper.
13. Ladle into bowls; top with a spoonful of the spicy relish.

Soups & Stews

ARCTIC CHAR CHOWDER

Serves 8

- ▶ 1 1/2 lbs Arctic Char (or wild salmon).
- ▶ Thicker fillets are easier to cut into cubes
- ▶ 1/4 cup butter
- ▶ 1/2 cup chopped onion
- ▶ 1/2 cup chopped carrots
- ▶ 1/2 cup chopped celery
- ▶ 1-2 cups vegetable broth
- ▶ 28-oz can crushed tomato (no salt added)
- ▶ 1/2 tsp thyme
- ▶ 1 whole bay leaf
- ▶ Salt and pepper to taste
- ▶ 1/2 cup heavy cream (optional)

1. Make sure all bones are removed from the fish and typically for chowder, it's best to also remove the skin.
2. You can do this by using the tip of a sharp knife to separate the meat from the skin, or ask to have it done for you when you buy the fish.
3. Cut the fish into 3/4-inch cubes and salt and pepper lightly.
4. Melt butter in a heavy pot over medium heat.
5. Add the onion, celery and carrots and cook for 5 minutes.
6. Add the broth, tomatoes, thyme and bay leaf.
7. Cover and let simmer for 15 minutes.
8. Add the fish and cream.
9. Mix to incorporate cream and then simmer, covered or uncovered, for another 10-15 minutes, stirring occasionally.
10. Remove the bay leaf.
11. Adjust the seasoning if needed and if you have any fresh herbs on hand (tarragon or thyme are especially good) add a bit for flavor.

CHICKEN STOCK

Serves 4

- ▶ 1 medium stewing chicken, cut into pieces, remove skin
  - ▶ 1 large onion
  - ▶ 2 carrots
  - ▶ 1/2 cup lemon juice
  - ▶ 1/4 tsp each pepper, paprika, basil, tarragon
  - ▶ 1/2 cup chopped parsley
  - ▶ 2 stalks celery

1. Wash chicken and place in deep pot.
2. Cover with water.
3. Add vegetables.
4. Cover.
5. Bring to boil.
6. Lower heat and simmer for 2 hours.
7. Strain, reserving chicken and vegetables for another use.

TURBOTIPS:

This stock may be used in place of oil to sauté meat, vegetables, etc..

May be frozen for later use.

BEEF VEGETABLE SOUP

Serves 8

- ▶ 1 lb stewing beef with bone
- ▶ 1/2 cup diced celery
- ▶ 1/2 cup diced onion
- ▶ 2 Tbsps dried parsley
- ▶ 1 tsp thyme
- ▶ Pinch ground cloves
- ▶ 16-oz can tomatoes, undrained, chopped
- ▶ Bay leaf
- ▶ Salt and pepper
- ▶ 2 family-sized packages of frozen vegetables

1. Brown meat well in large soup kettle.
2. Add cold water, about 4 quarts, and when fat comes to surface of water, skim it off with slotted spoon or paper towel.
3. Add remaining ingredients, except vegetables, and cook for about 2 1/2 hours, covered.
4. Remove meat, set aside and allow to cool.
5. Add 2 large family-size packages of frozen mixed vegetables.
6. Cook gently for several hours.
7. Remove meat from bone, dice and add to soup.
8. Remove bay leaf.
9. Cool and refrigerate.

> TURBOTIPS:
> It will taste even better the next day! Divide into one-meal portions and freeze.

SEAFOOD STEW

Serves 8

- ▶ 2 lb fish (turbot, sole or perch)
- ▶ 1 large onion, chopped
- ▶ 1/4 tsp garlic powder
- ▶ 3 cup water
- ▶ 1 large can tomatoes (salt free) or 8 fresh tomatoes, peeled
- ▶ 2 carrots, sliced
- ▶ 1/4 head green cabbage
- ▶ 1/4 head red cabbage
- ▶ 1 cup fresh or frozen peas (uncooked)
- ▶ 1 cup frozen corn (uncooked)
- ▶ 1 small bell pepper, chopped
- ▶ 1 29-oz can tomato puree
- ▶ 1/2 cup red or white wine
- ▶ 1 tsp basil
- ▶ 1 tsp parsley flakes
- ▶ 1/8 tsp pepper
- ▶ 3 stalks celery, diced

1. Sauté onions and garlic powder in 1/4 cup water until golden brown.
2. Add the rest of the vegetables with 1/2 cup water and mix.
3. Simmer 1/2 hour.
4. Add tomato puree, 2 cups water, wine and spices.
5. Mix thoroughly.
6. Simmer for 1 hour.
7. Cut fish into bite size pieces and add to vegetables.
8. Mix again.
9. Simmer for 1 hour, adding a little water if necessary.

Soups & Stews

CHILI CON CARNE

Serves
6

- ▶ 1 lb ground meat (beef, venison, buffalo, chicken, turkey, pork combos)
- ▶ 1 cup chopped onion
- ▶ 1-2 Tbsp olive oil
- ▶ 2-4 cloves minced garlic
- ▶ 1-2 carrots diced
- ▶ 1 cup chopped green peppers
- ▶ 1 stalk celery, diced
- ▶ 2 Tbsps chili powder
- ▶ 1 tsp cumin
- ▶ 1 bay leaf
- ▶ 1/2 tsp sea salt
- ▶ Freshly ground black pepper
- ▶ 1 can chopped Italian tomatoes with liquids
- ▶ 1 cup beef broth and or red wine
- ▶ 2 Tbsps tomato paste
- ▶ 2 dried chili peppers, crumbled

1. Use a Dutch oven or crockpot.
2. Sauté chopped onions in 1 Tbsp of olive oil.
3. Add the ground meat combination and brown throughout on medium heat.
4. The meat and onions can be browned without oil in an non-stick skillet and transferred to the Dutch oven.
5. Add tomatoes, garlic, carrots, celery, green peppers, spices and broth and bring to a simmer over medium heat.
6. Reduce heat to very low and simmer with lid tightly closed for 30 minutes.
7. Stir occasionally to prevent meat from scorching and sticking to bottom of the pot.
8. Add tomato paste and chili peppers.
9. Cook another 30 minutes before serving.

PARTY CHILI

Serves
4

- ▶ 4 Tbsps olive oil
- ▶ 1/2 cup sliced onion
- ▶ 2 cloves garlic, minced
- ▶ 3 lbs hamburger
- ▶ 2 8-oz cans tomato sauce
- ▶ 2 tsps chili powder
- ▶ 1 tsp cumin
- ▶ 1 1/2 tsp salt

1. Heat oil in skillet.
2. Sauté onion for about 3 minutes.
3. Add garlic and sauté until light brown.
4. Push onion and garlic to side of pan.
5. Add hamburger in one piece, and as it browns break it up slowly.
6. (This is done to allow meat to retain its juices.) When hamburger is slightly browned, add tomato sauce, chili powder, cumin, and salt.
7. Simmer for 15 minutes.

BUTTERNUT SQUASH SOUP

Serves
4

- ▶ 1 small butternut squash (about 1 1/4 lbs), peeled, seeded and cut into 1 inch pieces
- ▶ 2 Tbsps olive oil, divided
- ▶ 1/2 tsp salt, divided
- ▶ 1/4 tsp pepper, divided
- ▶ 2 yellow squash (about 1 1/4 lbs), cut into 1 inch pieces
- ▶ 1/4 cup finely chopped onion
- ▶ 1 1/2 tsps pumpkin pie spice (see tip below)
- ▶ 1 Tbsp tomato paste
- ▶ 2 14.5-oz cans vegetable or chicken broth
- ▶ 1/2 cup heavy cream
- ▶ Pumpkin seeds (optional)
- ▶ Sour cream (optional)

1. Heat oven to 450°F.
2. Toss butternut squash with 1 Tbsp olive oil, 1/4 tsp salt, & 1/8 tsp pepper.
3. Arrange in a single layer on a baking sheet.
4. Roast 15 minutes, turning once.
5. Toss yellow squash and onion with remaining oil, salt and pepper.
6. Add to baking sheet with squash.
7. Continue roasting 20 minutes, until all vegetables are tender.
8. In a large saucepan over medium heat, cook pumpkin pie spice, stirring constantly, 1 minute or until fragrant.
9. Stir in tomato paste and cook 1 minute more.
10. Add roasted vegetables and broth.
11. Bring to a boil, reduce heat to low and simmer 20 minutes.
12. Stir in cream.
13. Remove from heat.
14. Puree soup with an immersion blender.
15. Heat gently to warm through.
16. Add salt and pepper to taste.
17. To serve, divide soup in bowls and garnish with toasted pumpkin seeds, and sour cream if desired.

TURBOTIPS:
To make your own pumpkin spice mixture, combine 1 tsp cinnamon, 1/4 tsp ginger, 1/8 tsp of allspice and nutmeg and a pinch of ground cloves.

An immersion blender makes quick work of cream soups and involves much less cleaning than regular blenders.

KALE, TOMATO & BEAN STEW

Serves 4

- ► 2 Tbsps olive oil
- ► 4 garlic cloves, thinly sliced
- ► 1/2 tsp dried rosemary
- ► 2 lbs kale, tough stems removed, leaves washed and cut into 2-inch pieces
- ► 1 cup water
- ► 1 cup crushed tomatoes, preferably fire roasted
- ► 1/2 tsp salt
- ► 1/4 tsp pepper
- ► 1 cup canned white beans, rinsed and drained
- ► Parmesan cheese (optional)

1. In large saucepan over medium-high heat, heat olive oil until it shimmers.
2. Add garlic and rosemary.
3. Cook, stirring, about 1 minute, until garlic turns golden brown.
4. Add kale and 1 cup water.
5. Cover the pan and cook 5 minutes, stirring occasionally, until kale has reduced to about 2 cups and is tender.
6. Stir in tomatoes, salt, pepper and beans.
7. Reduce heat to low and cook 15 minutes for flavors to blend.
8. Serve with shavings of Parmesan cheese if desired.

SPAGHETTI SQUASH

Serves 4

- ► 1 Tbsp olive oil
- ► 1 cup chopped onion
- ► 4 medium cloves garlic, minced
- ► 1/2 cup dried lentils, rinsed & drained
- ► 1 1/2 tsps ground coriander
- ► 1 1/2 tsps ground cumin
- ► 1/2 tsp black pepper
- ► 1/2 tsp ground cinnamon
- ► 3 3/4 cups fat-free reduced sodium chicken or vegetable broth
- ► 1/2 cup chopped celery
- ► 1/2 cup chopped sun-dried tomatoes (not packed in oil)
- ► 1 medium yellow summer squash, chopped
- ► 1/2 cup chopped green bell pepper
- ► 1/2 cup chopped fresh parsley
- ► 1 cup chopped plum tomatoes
- ► 1/4 chopped fresh cilantro or basil

1. Mix all ingredients together except spaghetti squash in a large bowl.
2. Let stand 20 minutes.

Spaghetti Squash:
1. Slice squash in half from top to bottom.
2. Place in deep baking pan with 1" of water.
3. Use a fork and puncture the skin side of the squash several times.
4. Bake in 350°F oven for 20-30 minutes.
5. Test for tenderness.
6. Squash is done when it easily shreds into spaghetti "strips" when raked with a fork.
7. Scoop out and toss with other mixed ingredients.

VEGETARIAN MINESTRONE

Serves 4

- 1 Tbsp olive oil
- 1 large onion, chopped
- 2 ribs celery, sliced
- 1 tsp dried thyme
- 1 tsp dried basil
- 1/4 tsp dried oregano
- 2 cloves crushed garlic
- 1/4 tsp pepper
- 2 cup water
- 2 13.75-oz cans vegetable broth
- 16-oz can chopped tomatoes with juice
- 1 large red potato, chopped
- 10-oz box frozen chopped spinach, thawed
- 10-oz box frozen mixed vegetable, thawed
- 16-oz can red kidney beans, drained
- 1/4 cup grated Parmesan cheese

1. Heat oil in large sauce pan over medium-high heat.
2. Add onion and celery, cook for about 6-8 minutes, stirring occasionally.
3. Stir in thyme, basil, oregano, garlic and pepper.
4. Cook for about 2 minutes.
5. Add water, vegetable broth and tomatoes with juice, bring to a boil over high heat.
6. Stir in potato.
7. Reduce heat to medium-low, simmer uncovered for about 10 minutes.
8. Stir in spinach, vegetables and kidney beans, simmer 5-10 minutes until heated through.
9. Sprinkle with Parmesan cheese before serving.

WINTER SQUASH SOUP

Serves 4

- 3 cup cubed winter squash
- 1 diced onion
- 1/2 cup sliced celery
- 4 cup chicken or vegetable broth
- 1/4 tsp Cajun seasoning

1. Steam whole squash for 1/2 hour on a rack over water either on the stove in a covered pot or in the oven over a roasted pan.
2. Remove squash, let cool enough to work with.
3. Peel and remove seeds.
4. Cut into 1" cubes (prepare ahead).
5. Place squash, onion and celery in stock and simmer over low flame for 1/2 hour.
6. Remove vegetables, saving soup.
7. Mash vegetables or process lightly in food processor or blender.
8. Return mixture to soup.
9. Season; simmer 5-10 minutes longer.

Soups & Stews

HOMEMADE CHICKEN SOUP

Serves 4

- ▶ 2 lbs chicken wings, all possible skin and fat removed
- ▶ 2 quarts water
- ▶ 1 large carrot cut into 1" rounds
- ▶ 1 onion in thick slices
- ▶ 1 large rib celery cut into 1" pieces
- ▶ 4 tsps chopped parsley
- ▶ 1 Tbsp chopped dill
- ▶ 2 tsps salt
- ▶ 1/2 tsp savory

1. In a heavy saucepan with tight cover place all ingredients including chicken.
2. Bring to a strong boil, then cover tightly and simmer for about an hour or until chicken is fully tender to the fork.
3. Remove chicken pieces and take off all meat.
4. Strain out all vegetables to produce clear soup.
5. Let soup cool, remove fat from top.
6. Combine chicken meat and clear soup, heat until close to a boil, then serve.

FAMILY BEEF STEW

Serves 6

- ▶ 1 1/2 lbs boneless stew meat, all visible fat trimmed off, then cut in 1 to 1 1/2" cubes
- ▶ 1 1/2 cups water
- ▶ 1 Tbsp onion flakes
- ▶ 1 Tbsp parsley flakes
- ▶ 1/2 tsp salt
- ▶ 1/4 tsp paprika
- ▶ 1 package frozen mixed vegetables

1. Brown the beef cubes in a pan under the broiler for a few more minutes, turning to brown all sides.
2. Combine the water and all other ingredients except the vegetables, and cook with meat in a tightly covered skillet over slow to moderate heat for about 2 hours (check several times and add a little water if needed).
3. Add the vegetables and cook for 20 to 30 minutes longer until meat and vegetable are done, tender to the fork.

EGG DROP SOUP

Serves 4

- ▶ 1 medium size egg
- ▶ 1 cup clear soup (broth, bouillon, or consommé)

1. Beat the egg lightly with a fork and drop into broth when at the simmering point (don't boil), stirring constantly.
2. When egg has thickened slightly, serve.
3. Season to taste with celery salt.

NEW ENGLAND BEEF STEW

Serves 4

- ▶ 1 1/4 lbs very lean beef, all visible fat removed
- ▶ 8-oz can tomato sauce
- ▶ 1 cup water
- ▶ 1/2 bay leaf
- ▶ 1/8 tsp thyme
- ▶ 10 small onions
- ▶ 6 medium carrots, scraped and cut in 1" pieces
- ▶ 8-oz can peas, drained

1. Cut meat into 1 inch cubes and place in shallow no-stick pan in broiler, 2 1/2" from heat, turning until all sides are brown.
2. Transfer to saucepan and add tomato sauce and water, salt, bay leaf, and thyme.
3. Simmer, covered, for 1 1/4 hours.
4. If liquid dries out, add a little more water.
5. Meat should be almost tender.
6. Add onions and carrots, cook another 1/2 hour, or until vegetables are done.
7. Add peas.
8. Cook a few moments longer until peas are heated through.
9. Add more salt if desired.

OUR FAVORITE VEGETABLE SOUP

Serves 4

- ▶ 1/4 medium head of cabbage, shredded
- ▶ 4 ribs celery, cut up small
- ▶ 1 green pepper, diced
- ▶ 1 package frozen French-style green beans
- ▶ 1 1/2 cups tomato juice
- ▶ 2 low sodium chicken or beef bouillon cubes
- ▶ 4 cups water
- ▶ 1 bay leaf
- ▶ 1 can mushrooms (butter, if any, removed), drained
- ▶ 1 can water chestnuts, drained, sliced

1. Cook together until vegetables are tender, cabbage, celery, pepper, green beans, tomato juice, bouillon cubes, water, and bay leaf (about 20 minutes).
2. Remove bay leaf.
3. Drain, reserving liquid.
4. Process cooked vegetables in blender at medium speed until pulverized.
5. Add to liquid, mixing thoroughly, mushrooms and water chestnuts.
6. Serve piping hot, with lemon slices or watercress as garnish if you like.

SPANISH COLD SOUP

Serves
6

- ▶ 3 medium onions, quartered
- ▶ 8 medium tomatoes, peeled, quartered
- ▶ 2 Tbsps red wine
- ▶ 1/2 tsp garlic salt (or more, to taste)
- ▶ Black pepper
- ▶ 1 Tbsp paprika
- ▶ 1 Tbsp olive oil
- ▶ 10 ripe olives, sliced
- ▶ 1 large cucumber, peeled, diced
- ▶ 2 Tbsps chopped parsley

1. Process half the onions, tomatoes, wine, salt, and pepper in blender at medium speed until smooth.
2. Pour into saucepan and repeat with other half of the onions, tomatoes, wine and salt.
3. Add paprika and oil, simmer all together 10 minutes.
4. Chill.
5. Add olives and cucumber, sprinkle parsley over the top and chill.

THICK VEGETABLE BLENDER SOUP

Serves
4

- ▶ 1/2 cup French-cut green beans, cooked
- ▶ 1 can green asparagus, with juice
- ▶ 2 sprigs parsley, cut up
- ▶ 1/8 tsp paprika
- ▶ 1/2 tsp onion flakes
- ▶ 1/4 tsp seasoned salt
- ▶ 1/2 can bean sprouts, drained
- ▶ 1 small can mushrooms, drained

1. Process all ingredients except last two in blender at low speed.
2. Pour into saucepan, add bean sprouts and mushrooms, and heat thoroughly before serving.
3. Salt and pepper to taste.

EASY BOUILLABAISSE

Serves
2

- ▶ 1/4 lb any fish of your choice (perch, turbot, sole)
- ▶ 1/4 lb cooking shrimp
- ▶ 1 medium size onion, chopped
- ▶ 1 lb can tomato puree (salt free)
- ▶ 1 Tbsp lemon juice
- ▶ 1/4 tsp dry mustard
- ▶ 1/4 tsp crushed bay leaf
- ▶ Dash of pepper
- ▶ 1/4 cup dry red or white wine

1. Wash fish and cut into small pieces.
2. Brown onion and bell pepper in a little water.
3. Add more water as necessary.
4. Add tomato puree.
5. Add all the rest of the ingredients.
6. Add shrimp and fish last.
7. Simmer 1/2 hour.

Soups & Stews

STRACCIATELLA SOUP

Serves
4

- ▶ 1 lb fresh spinach or 2 frozen packages
- ▶ 2 Tbsps butter
- ▶ 1 1/4 tsps salt
- ▶ 1/4 tsp white pepper
- ▶ 1/8 tsp nutmeg
- ▶ 4 egg yolks
- ▶ 1/4 cup grated Parmesan cheese
- ▶ 6 cups boiling chicken broth

1. Cook spinach for 4 minutes.
2. Drain thoroughly.
3. Purée in electric blender or force through sieve.
4. Melt butter in saucepan; add spinach, salt, pepper and nutmeg.
5. Cook over low heat for 2 minutes, stirring constantly.
6. Beat egg yolks and Parmesan cheese.
7. Pour into boiling broth and mix with fork.
8. Add spinach mixture.
9. Simmer for 5 minutes.

ITALIAN GARLIC SOUP

Serves
4

- ▶ 6 large garlic cloves
- ▶ 2 quarts water
- ▶ 2 tsps seasoned salt
- ▶ 1/4 tsp thyme
- ▶ 1/4 tsp sage
- ▶ 1 bay leaf
- ▶ 2 cloves
- ▶ Pinch of saffron
- ▶ 4 egg yolks
- ▶ 1/4 cup olive oil
- ▶ Parsley sprigs

1. Chop garlic and place in boiling water.
2. Add salt, thyme, sage, bay leaf, cloves and saffron.
3. Boil for 30 minutes.
4. Beat egg yolks with wire whisk.
5. Once creamy, add olive oil 1 tsp at a time; beat well after each tsp added.
6. Add egg yolks to soup and beat with wire whisk.
7. Garnish with parsley.

SPEEDY INTERNATIONAL STEW

Serves
4

- ▶ 2 14.5-oz cans stewed tomatoes (Italian, Mexican, or Cajun)
- ▶ 15-oz can black beans, drained, rinsed
- ▶ 16-oz can corn kernels, drained, rinsed

1. Place all ingredients in a medium saucepan.
2. Cover and cook over medium heat for 5-10 minutes, stirring occasionally

Salads

SALAD ANYTIME, ANY WAY YOU LIKE

Salads are suitable for any main meals—breakfast, lunch and/or dinner.

Super TurboChargers have been known to drink a salad for breakfast by simply placing all the ingredients in a blender, whipping them up and drinking away.

Try a salad topped with any of the dressings in this book, or you might be surprised to find they are quite tasty plain and undressed as well.

Salads are not only enjoyable taste sensations when the ingredients are ripe and fresh, but also they are packed with nutritious ingredients. When making a salad, be inventive.

There are great vegetables and lettuces that you can include that make a plain salad an event. Don't skip…

- ▶ Arugula
- ▶ Radicchio
- ▶ Endive
- ▶ Red Leaf, Boston
- ▶ Chicory
- ▶ Mache
- ▶ Watercress
- ▶ Baby Lettuces
- ▶ Artichoke Hearts
- ▶ Hearts Of Palm
- ▶ Chickpeas
- ▶ Red, Green, Yellow and Orange Peppers
- ▶ Grated Red Cabbage
- ▶ Grated Carrots
- ▶ Cucumbers
- ▶ Sprinklings of Raw Nuts or Seeds
- ▶ And of course any other vegetables that strike your tastebuds…

FRUITED GREEN SALAD

Serves 4

- 1 1/2 cups torn Boston lettuce
- 1 1/2 cups torn red leaf lettuce
- 1/2 lb jicama, peeled and cut into very thin strips
- 1 1/2 cups sliced celery
- 1 large pink grapefruit, peeled and sectioned
- 2 medium kiwifruit, peeled and sliced
- 1 small purple onion, thinly sliced
- 1/4 cup sliced green onions
- 2 Tbsps lime juice
- 1/4 tsp salt
- 1/4 tsp pepper

1. Combine first 8 ingredients in a large bowl and toss well.
2. Combine lime juice and next 3 ingredients in a bowl.
3. Stir with a wire whisk to combine.
4. Pour over lettuce mixture, tossing gently.

TEX-MEX SALAD

Serves 2

- 15-oz can no-salt-added black beans, drained and rinsed
- 1/4 cup chopped green onions
- 1/4 cup whole kernel corn, thawed
- 1/2 cup salsa
- 2 cups shredded romaine lettuce

1. Combine first 3 ingredients and stir.
2. Spoon mixture over shredded lettuce.

BACON & EGG SALAD

Serves 4

- 9 hard-cooked eggs
- 9 slices bacon, cooked crisp
- 1/2 tsp seasoned salt
- 1/4 tsp dry mustard
- 1/4 cup mayonnaise

1. Chop eggs and bacon together in wooden chopping bowl.
2. Add salt and mustard.
3. Fold in mayonnaise and mix well.

Salads

BLACK & WHITE BEAN SALAD

Serves
5

- ▶ 15-oz can great Northern beans, rinsed and drained
- ▶ 15-oz can black beans, rinsed and drained
- ▶ 1 1/4 cups peeled, seeded and chopped tomato
- ▶ 3/4 cup diced sweet red pepper
- ▶ 3/4 cup diced sweet yellow pepper
- ▶ 3/4 cup thinly sliced green onions
- ▶ 1/2 cup commercial salsa (no sugar added)
- ▶ 1/4 cup red wine vinegar
- ▶ 2 Tbsps chopped fresh cilantro
- ▶ 1/4 tsp salt
- ▶ 1/8 tsp freshly ground pepper
- ▶ 10 cups finely shredded romaine lettuce (about 1 head)

1. Combine beans and chopped tomato in a large bowl, tossing gently.
2. Add red pepper, yellow pepper and green onions, tossing to combine.
3. Combine salsa and next 4 ingredients; stir with a wire whisk until well blended.
4. Pour over bean mixture and toss gently.
5. Line a large serving bowl with shredded lettuce; top with bean mixture.

QUICK GREEK SALAD

Serves
4

- ▶ 3-4 tomatoes
- ▶ 1-2 cucumbers
- ▶ 4-oz package feta cheese, crumbled
- ▶ Drizzle of olive oil
- ▶ Pepper

1. Chop tomatoes and cucumbers.
2. Place in large bowl.
3. Toss with crumbled feta cheese.
4. Drizzle with olive oil.
5. Season with pepper.
6. Toss again and serve immediately.

SPINACH SALAD CAPRESE

Serves
4

- ▶ 6 cups fresh spinach
- ▶ 12 cherry tomatoes, halved
- ▶ 1/2 cup chopped fresh basil
- ▶ 4 ounces fresh mozzarella cheese, cubed
- ▶ 1/4 cup light olive oil

1. Gently combine all ingredients.
2. Toss to mix.
3. Serve immediately.

SEAFOOD & AVOCADO SALAD

Serves 4

- ▶ 1 large avocado, pitted, peeled, and cubed
- ▶ 1 1/2 lbs crabmeat or tuna fish
- ▶ 2 stalks celery, chopped
- ▶ 6 radishes, sliced
- ▶ 4 Tbsps lemon juice
- ▶ 4 Tbsps tarragon vinegar
- ▶ 1/2 small onion, chopped
- ▶ 1/4 tsp cayenne pepper
- ▶ Seasoned salt to taste

1. Toss all ingredients together well.
2. Serve with Thousand Island Dressing.

SIMPLE COLESLAW

Serves 4

- ▶ 1/4 cup Dijon mustard
- ▶ 1/4 cup mayonnaise
- ▶ 1/2 tsp-equivalent sugar substitute
- ▶ 1 Tbsp lemon juice
- ▶ 1/2 tsp salt
- ▶ 3 cups shredded cabbage

1. Mix mustard, mayonnaise, sugar substitute, lemon juice and salt.
2. Add cabbage and toss well.

COLORFUL CORN SALAD

Serves 8

- ▶ 2 cups of frozen corn
- ▶ 1/3 cup canned no-salt-added chicken broth, undiluted
- ▶ 3/4 cup chopped green pepper
- ▶ 1/2 cup chopped purple onion
- ▶ 2 Tbsps chopped fresh cilantro
- ▶ 2 Tbsps rice wine vinegar
- ▶ 2 tsps lime juice
- ▶ 1/4 tsp salt
- ▶ 1/4 tsp garlic powder
- ▶ 1/4 tsp ground red pepper
- ▶ 4-oz jar diced pimiento, drained lettuce leaves (optional)

1. Combine corn and broth in a large nonstick skillet; cook over medium-high heat 3 to 5 minutes or until liquid evaporates.
2. Remove from heat; add green pepper and next 8 ingredients, stirring well.
3. If desired, serve corn mixture in a lettuce-lined bowl.

Salads

JICAMA SALAD

Serves 4

- ▶ 1 1/2 lb jicama peeled and cut into 1/2" cubes
- ▶ 2 tsp extra-virgin olive oil
- ▶ 3 Tbsps fresh lime juice
- ▶ 3/4 tsp chipotle chile powder (or 1 1/2 tsp ancho chile powder)
- ▶ 1/2 tsp salt
- ▶ 25 fresh mint leaves cut into thin strips
- ▶ 2 Tbsps queso añejo (or feta or goat cheese)

1. Combine jicama and oil in a bowl and toss well.
2. Add lime juice, chile powder and salt.
3. Toss to coat.
4. Divide salad among 4 bowls, then sprinkle each with 1/4 mint and cheese right before serving.

CAULIFLOWER SALAD

Serves 4

- ▶ 1 cauliflower, cut into flowerets
- ▶ 1 carrot, thinly sliced
- ▶ 1 green pepper, diced
- ▶ 1/2 cup lemon juice (or juice of 1 lemon)
- ▶ 1 clove garlic, minced (optional)
- ▶ 1/2 bunch parsley, minced
- ▶ 3 green onions, thinly sliced

1. Blanch the cauliflower, carrots and peppers about 2 to 3 minutes.
2. Drain and rinse the vegetables under cold water.
3. Then transfer them to a salad bowl.
4. Combine the lemon juice (or vinegar), the garlic, parsley and green onions.
5. Pour over the vegetables, tossing gently to distribute dressing.
6. Chill and serve.

How to blanch vegetables:
1. Boil about 4 inches of water in a 3-quart pot.
2. Add the vegetables to be blanched to the boiling water.
3. Boil 1 to 3 minutes, depending on the fragility of the vegetable.
4. Drain the vegetables, then place them in ice water just long enough to cool.
5. Remove the vegetables from the water and drain them well.

CHINESE CABBAGE SALAD

- ▶ 8 leaves Chinese cabbage
- ▶ 2 red bell peppers
- ▶ 2 avocados
- ▶ 1 pint cherry tomatoes (or 3 regular tomatoes, diced)
- ▶ 1 grapefruit

1. Wash and dry the Chinese cabbage.
2. Cut up four of the leaves and place them in a large mixing bowl.
3. Place the remaining four leaves on two dinner plates.
4. Dice the red bell peppers.
5. Quarter, peel and dice the avocadoes (or half the avocados and scoop out the flesh with a tsp).
6. Place the diced peppers and avocados, along with all the tomatoes, into the mixing bowl with the cut-up cabbage.
7. Juice the grapefruit and pour the salad.
8. Stir well and place a dollop of salad on each of the four Chinese cabbage leaves on the dinner plates.

FAST & EASY VEGETABLE SALAD

- ▶ 1 clove garlic
- ▶ 4 heads Bibb lettuce, broken into bite-size pieces
- ▶ 1 bunch watercress, stems trimmed
- ▶ 8 leaves celery cabbage, broken into bite-size pieces
- ▶ 12 cherry tomatoes

Dressing:
- ▶ 1 tsp dry mustard
- ▶ 1 tsp vegetable oil
- ▶ 2 Tbsps wine vinegar
- ▶ 1 tsp salt
- ▶ 1/2 tsp oregano
- ▶ 1 tsp tarragon
- ▶ 1 tsp minced chives
- ▶ 1 tsp minced parsley

1. Rub salad bowl with garlic.
2. Place chilled greens in bowl.
3. Mash mustard into oil until smooth and combine in screw-top jar with rest of dressing ingredients.
4. Shake vigorously and pour over greens at serving time.
5. Toss well and serve immediately.

Salads

SUMMER SALAD WITH RED ONIONS

Serves
4

- ▶ 1 head Boston lettuce
- ▶ 1 head Romaine lettuce
- ▶ 1 medium cucumber, sliced very thin (skin on)
- ▶ 1 medium red onion, cut in very thin rings
- ▶ 2 small zucchini, sliced very thin (skin on)
- ▶ 2 raw mushrooms, sliced through tops and stems
- ▶ 2 sprigs parsley, minced
- ▶ 1 tsp vegetable oil
- ▶ 1 tsp seasoned salt
- ▶ Pepper to taste
- ▶ 2 Tbsps wine vinegar
- ▶ 8 red radishes, trimmed, cut into rosettes, and crisped in ice water

1. Wash vegetables and keep very cold before using for crispness.
2. Cut lettuce into salad bowl in 1" strips.
3. Add other vegetables.
4. Beat together vegetable oil, salt, pepper, and vinegar, pour over salad and toss lightly but thoroughly.
5. Top with whole radishes.
6. Serve immediately.

ENDIVE & ARTICHOKE SALAD

Serves
4

- ▶ 4 large or 6 small whole Belgian endive, chilled
- ▶ 12 artichoke hearts in brine, drained
- ▶ 1 roast pimento, cut in strips
- ▶ 1 1/2 Tbsps vegetable oil
- ▶ 1 Tbsp tarragon vinegar
- ▶ Black pepper
- ▶ 1/2 tsp garlic salt
- ▶ Capers

1. Wash and dry endive, cut off ends, cut in bite-size pieces, either crosswise or lengthwise, into salad bowl.
2. Drain and quarter hearts of artichoke and add to endive, together with pimento strips.
3. Pour oil over top of salad and toss well to coat all surfaces.
4. Add vinegar, pepper, garlic salt, and capers, toss again and serve immediately (do not add dressing until just before serving).

CUCUMBER-TOMATO DELITE

Serves
4

- ▶ 4 medium tomatoes
- ▶ 2 small-to-medium cucumbers
- ▶ 1/4 cup wine vinegar
- ▶ 1 Tbsp dill, preferably fresh
- ▶ 1/2 tsp mixed herbs
- ▶ 1/2 tsp tarragon
- ▶ Artificial sweetener equal to 1 tsp sugar, only if desired
- ▶ Small onion, chopped (optional)
- ▶ Salt, pepper to taste
- ▶ Lettuce

1. Cut tops off tomatoes, removing pulp and placing in bowl; chop pulp.
2. Set tomato shells aside in refrigerator.
3. Cut cucumbers into very thin slices and add to chopped tomato pulp.
4. Combine all remaining ingredients except lettuce in a cup, stir well, and pour over cucumbers and chopped tomato.
5. Stir with a fork to combine well.
6. Marinate for an hour or more in refrigerator.
7. Salt and pepper tomato shells to taste, and place on lettuce on individual serving plates.
8. Drain marinated mixture and spoon into tomato shells, spooning any excess on lettuce around the tomato shells.
9. Top with a little chopped parsley if desired.

SNOW PEA SALAD

Serves
2

- ▶ 2 Tbsps rice wine vinegar
- ▶ 1 Tbsp low-sodium soy sauce
- ▶ 1/4 tsp ground ginger
- ▶ 1/4 tsp garlic powder
- ▶ 1 cup fresh snow pea pods, trimmed
- ▶ 8-oz can sliced water chestnuts, drained
- ▶ 1 Tbsp chopped fresh parsley
- ▶ Green onion fans (optional)

1. Combine first 4 ingredients in a jar; cover tightly, and shake vigorously.
2. Wash snow peas arrange in a steamer basket over boiling water.
3. Cover and steam 3 minutes; drain and rinse with cold water.
4. Combine snow peas, water chestnuts and parsley in a small bowl.
5. Pour vinegar mixture over snow pea mixture and toss lightly.
6. Garnish with green onion fans if desired.

Salads

POTATO-VEGETABLE SALAD

Serves 8

- 1 lb round red potatoes, quartered
- 10-oz package frozen Brussels sprouts, thawed
- 1 1/2 cups cherry tomatoes, halved
- 1/3 cup white wine vinegar
- 1 Tbsp olive oil
- 1/2 tsp granulated sugar substitute
- 1/4 tsp onion powder
- 1/4 tsp dried dillweed
- 1/8 tsp salt

1. Cook potatoes in boiling water to cover 12 minutes.
2. Drain.
3. Set aside; keep warm.
4. Cut Brussels sprouts in half lengthwise.
5. Cook according to package directions.
6. Combine potatoes, sprouts and tomatoes.
7. Combine vinegar and remaining 5 ingredients.
8. Add to potato mixture; toss.
9. Serve warm.

MEXICAN TURKEY & BEAN SALAD

Serves 5

- 1/4 cup + 2 Tbsps salsa
- 1/4 cup + 2 Tbsps vinegar
- Vegetable cooking spray
- 1/2 lb freshly ground raw turkey
- 1/2 tsp chili powder
- 1/4 tsp dried oregano
- 1/8 tsp pepper
- 15-oz can dark red kidney beans, drained
- 1/3 cup thinly sliced green onions
- 1/3 cup chopped sweet yellow pepper
- 8 cherry tomatoes, quartered
- 3 cups torn iceberg lettuce
- 3 cups torn curly endive
- 1 cup frozen green beans, thawed and drained

1. Combine salsa and vinegar in a small jar; cover tightly and shake vigorously.
2. Set aside.
3. Coat a skillet with cooking spray; place over medium heat until hot.
4. Add turkey and next 3 ingredients; cook until turkey is browned, stirring until it crumbles.
5. Drain, if necessary.
6. Combine turkey mixture, kidney beans, and next 3 ingredients in a large bowl; toss lightly.
7. Add 1/3 cup salsa mixture, and toss.
8. Place lettuce and endive in a large bowl; spoon turkey mixture over lettuce mixture.
9. Top with green beans, and drizzle with remaining salsa mixture.

TURBOTIPS:
Serve this main-dish salad with a plush mixed-lettuce salad.

SALMON & JULIENNE VEGETABLES
 Serves 4

- ▶ 4 5-oz center-cut salmon fillets, poached

Salad:
- ▶ 2 large portabello mushroom caps
- ▶ 2 Tbsps red wine vinegar
- ▶ Salt and freshly ground pepper to taste
- ▶ 10-oz bag baby spinach
- ▶ 1 cup seeded plum tomatoes, cut in matchsticks
- ▶ 1 cup blanched green beans or haricots verts (baby green beans)
- ▶ 2 medium Belgian endives, cut in matchsticks
- ▶ 2 Tbsps black nicoise olives
- ▶ 1 Tbsp capers, drained and rinsed
- ▶ 2 Tbsps fresh cilantro leaves, stemmed

Dressing:
- ▶ 1/4 cup extra-virgin olive oil
- ▶ 1 Tbsp fresh lemon juice
- ▶ Salt and freshly ground pepper to taste

1. Heat oven to 400°F.
2. In a small baking dish, toss mushroom caps with vinegar, salt and pepper.
3. Roast 10 minutes.
4. Cool slightly and cut into 1/2-inch slices.
5. In a small bowl, whisk together dressing ingredients.
6. In a large bowl, combine spinach, tomatoes, green beans, endives, olives and capers.
7. Toss with dressing.
8. Divide salad greens on 4 plates; top each with a salmon fillet.
9. Sprinkle with cilantro.

To poach fish:
1. Place in a single layer on skillet.
2. Add salt, a bay leaf and enough water to cover fish.
3. Cook 6 to 8 minutes, covered, over low heat.
4. Let fish stand in water, off the heat, for 5 minutes more before removing with a slotted spoon.

> **TURBOTIPS:**
> "Julienne" is a French word meaning to cut food into matchstick-size pieces.
>
> In this salad, julienne veggies are paired with delicate poached salmon.

ROMAINE & RED PEPPER SALAD
 Serves 4

- ▶ 2 Tbsps red wine vinegar
- ▶ 2 tsps Dijon mustard
- ▶ 1/2 tsp salt
- ▶ 1/4 tsp freshly ground pepper
- ▶ 1/4 cup olive oil
- ▶ 1/4 cup chopped roasted red peppers (jarred)
- ▶ 1/2 shallot, finely chopped
- ▶ 4 cups of Romaine hearts
- ▶ 2 plum tomatoes, cut lengthwise into quarters

1. In a salad bowl, whisk vinegar, mustard, salt and pepper until smooth.
2. Gradually add olive oil, whisking constantly.
3. Fold in roasted red peppers and shallot.
4. Add lettuce and tomatoes to bowl; toss gently to combine ingredients.

Salads

RED & BLACK BEAN SALAD

Serves 4

- 15.5-oz can black beans
- 15.5-oz can kidney beans
- 11-oz can corn with red and green peppers (Mexicorn)
- 3 green onions (1/2 cup chopped)
- 3 Tbsps extra virgin olive oil
- 3 Tbsps red wine vinegar
- 1/2 tsp garlic powder
- 1/2 tsp cumin
- 1/4 tsp salt or to taste
- 1/4 tsp black pepper or to taste

1. Pour both cans of beans into colander to drain.
2. Pour the corn on top of the beans.
3. Rinse the vegetables well with cool tap water.
4. Drain well.
5. Pour the beans and corn into a 3-quart or larger bowl.
6. Finely chop the green onions, using all of the whites or enough green tops to make 1/2 cup.
7. Add them to the bowl.

To make dressing:
1. Pour the olive oil into a 2-cup glass measure.
2. Whisk in the vinegar, garlic powder, cumin and salt and pepper.
3. Pour the dressing over the bean mixture, stir until well coated.
4. Serve at once or chill until ready to serve.

THREE-BEAN SALAD

Serves 4

- 1/3 cup white vinegar
- 3 Tbsps chicken broth
- 1 tsp celery seeds
- 1 clove garlic, minced
- 8-oz can cut waxed beans
- 8-oz can cut green beans
- 8-oz can red kidney beans
- 1/2 cup chopped onions
- 1/2 cup chopped green peppers

1. To make the dressing: Stir together the vinegar, broth, celery seeds and garlic.
2. Drain the beans.
3. In a large bowl combine the waxed beans, green beans, kidney beans, onions and green peppers.
4. Add the dressing.
5. Gently stir until combined.
6. Cover and chill for 4-24 hours to blend the flavors, stirring often.

SALAD NICOISE

Serves 2

- 3 Tbsps white wine vinegar
- 2 Tbsps water
- 1 1/2 tsps Dijon mustard
- 1/2 tsp olive oil
- 1/8 tsp freshly ground pepper
- 1/4 lb fresh green beans
- 2 small round red potatoes
- 2 Tbsps thinly sliced sweet red pepper
- 1 Tbsp chopped purple onion
- 6-oz tuna steak (3/4 inch thick)
- 1/2 tsp olive oil
- Vegetable cooking spinach
- 2 cups torn fresh spinach
- 4 cherry tomatoes, quartered

1. Combine first 5 ingredients in a small jar cover tightly, and shake vigorously.
2. Set aside.
3. Wash beans; trim ends, and remove strings.
4. Arrange beans in a steamer basket over boiling water.
5. Cover and steam 5 minutes or until crisp-tender.
6. Drain.
7. Wash potatoes.
8. Cook in boiling water to cover 20 minutes or just until tender.
9. Drain and cool slightly.
10. Cut into 1/4"-thick slices.
11. Combine green beans, potato, red pepper and onion; toss lightly.
12. Add half of vinegar mixture; toss lightly.
13. Chill 2 hours.
14. Brush tuna steak with 1/2 tsp olive oil.
15. Place on a rack of broiler pan coated with cooking spray.
16. Broil 5 1/2" from heat (with electric oven door partially opened) 3 to 4 minutes on each side or until fish flakes easily when tested with a fork.
17. Flake fish into piece.
18. Place spinach on a serving plate.
19. Arrange green bean mixture, tuna, tomato and olives over spinach.
20. Drizzle remaining vinegar mixture over salad.

Salads

HEARTS OF PALM SALAD

Serves 4

- ▶ 1 small head iceberg lettuce
- ▶ 15.5-oz can (about 8) hearts of palm, chilled
- ▶ 8 black olives
- ▶ 8 cherry tomatoes

1. Wash and sore the lettuce.
2. Reserve 4 large leaves for presentation; shed the remaining lettuce.
3. Slice the hearts of palm in half length-wise.
4. Line 4 chilled plates with large leaves, then top with shredded lettuce and sliced hearts of palm.
5. Garnish with black olives and cherry tomatoes.

SPINACH SALAD

Serves 4

- ▶ 10-oz fresh spinach leaves, stemmed and washed
- ▶ 2 cups sliced fresh mushrooms
- ▶ 4 strips of bacon, cook crisp and crumbled
- ▶ 4 large lettuce leaves
- ▶ 8 thin slices onion
- ▶ 2 Tbsps chopped hard-boiled eggs

1. In a large bowl, toss the spinach, mushrooms and bacon.
2. Line for chilled plates with lettuce leaves, then mound some of the dressed spinach on each leaf.
3. Garnish the salads with onion slices and chopped egg.

GARDEN MARKET SALAD

Serves 4

- ▶ 6 large leaves Romaine lettuce
- ▶ 6 cups chopped Iceberg lettuce
- ▶ 2 cups sliced ripe avocado
- ▶ 3 medium ripe tomatoes, sliced
- ▶ 2 cups red onion, sliced into rings
- ▶ 1 small head cauliflower (to yield 24 florets) blanched in boiling water
- ▶ 1 medium cucumber, sliced

1. In a large bowl, combine ingedients.
2. Toss and enjoy!

BROCCOLI & AVOCADO SALAD

Serves 4

- ▶ 1 1/2 lbs. young, tender broccoli
- ▶ 1 avocado
- ▶ 2 Tbsps fresh lemon juice
- ▶ 1/2 cup chopped pecans
- ▶ 1 Tbsp Dijon mustard
- ▶ Salt to taste
- ▶ 1 Tbsp fresh parsley, finely chopped

1. Remove the broccoli florets from the large stems.
2. In a sauce with boiling salted water add the florets and boil about 3 minutes until almost tender.
3. Drain, cool under running water, drain again.
4. Set aside.
5. Peel, pit and cut avocado into cubes.
6. In a small bowl, coat the avocado with 1 Tbsp of lemon juice to prevent darkening.
7. Place the avocado and broccoli in a salad bowl and add the pecans.
8. In a small bowl stir together the remaining lemon juice, the mustard, parsley and salt to taste until well combined.
9. Pour over the salad.
10. Toss and serve immediately.

CUCUMBER with ONION SALAD

Serves 6

- ▶ 8 cups thinly sliced cucumbers, about 5 cucumbers
- ▶ 1 large onion, thinly sliced
- ▶ 1 1/2 cups white vinegar
- ▶ 3 garlic cloves, minced
- ▶ 1 cup water
- ▶ 1/2 tsp white pepper
- ▶ 3 tsps chopped fresh dill

1. In a large bowl, combine cucumber and onions; set aside.
2. Over a high heat bring the vinegar, garlic, and water to a boil, stirring continuously.
3. Pour the mixture over the cucumber and onions; add the pepper and dill and mix well.
4. Refrigerate for 2 hours.
5. Serve immediately.

Salads

BEAN SALAD

Serves 8

- ▶ 16-oz can kidney beans, undrained
- ▶ 16-oz can garbanzo beans (chick peas), undrained
- ▶ 1/4 cup lemon juice
- ▶ 3 chopped scallions
- ▶ 1 Tbsp chopped red bell pepper
- ▶ 1/2 tsp dried basil
- ▶ 3/4 tsp salt
- ▶ 1/4 tsp black pepper

1. In a medium-sized saucepan place the beans.
2. Boil the beans, then drain.
3. Add remaining ingredients.
4. Refrigerate for 12 hours.
5. Serve immediately.

GREEN BEAN SALAD

Serves 6

- ▶ 1 lb fresh green beans, cut in halves and par-boiled
- ▶ 1/2 small onion, thinly sliced
- ▶ 1/2 cup garbanzo beans rinsed and drained
- ▶ 1 cup halved cherry tomatoes
- ▶ 1 Tbsp red wine vinegar
- ▶ 3 Tbsps water
- ▶ 1 tsp basil leaves, finely chopped
- ▶ 1/4 tsp dry mustard powder
- ▶ Salt and pepper to taste

1. In a bowl, toss the green beans, onion, garbanzo beans and cherry tomatoes.
2. In another bowl, blend the remaining ingredients.
3. Toss the vegetable with the blended dressing.
4. Refrigerate for 2 hours.
5. Serve immediately.

AVOCADO & SHRIMP SALAD

Serves 4

- ▶ 4 avocado, peeled and halved
- ▶ 1 1/2 cups boiled shrimp
- ▶ 1 14-oz can hearts of palm
- ▶ 1 Tbsp lemon juice
- ▶ 1/4 cup onion, finely chopped
- ▶ 1 tsp Dijon mustard
- ▶ 1 1/2 tsp salt
- ▶ 1/4 tsp pepper
- ▶ 1/2 tsp garlic salt
- ▶ 3 Tbsps red wine vinegar

1. Cut the hearts of palm in 1/8 inch rounds.
2. In a bowl combine vinegar, mustard, salt, pepper, garlic salt, onion and lemon juice.
3. To the mixture, add the shrimp and hearts of palm.
4. Fill each avocado shell with mixture.
5. Refrigerate for 1 hour.
6. Serve immediately.

SPINACH & BEANS SALAD

Serves 4

- ▶ 2 cups torn spinach leaves
- ▶ 1/2 cup sliced mushrooms
- ▶ 1/2 cup chopped red onion
- ▶ 2 ounces drained cooked white beans
- ▶ 1 Tbsp imitation bacon bits
- ▶ 1 Tbsp natural ranch salad dressing

1. In medium bowl, combine all the ingredients.
2. Toss and enjoy.

GRILLED SWORDFISH SALAD

Serves 2

- ▶ 1 Tbsp reduced-sodium soy sauce
- ▶ 1 Tbsp fresh lemon juice
- ▶ 1 garlic clove, minced
- ▶ 2 4-oz boneless swordfish steak
- ▶ 1 tsp olive oil
- ▶ 2 tsps red wine or rice wine vinegar
- ▶ 1 cup mixed salad greens
- ▶ 1 cup cucumber slices
- ▶ 1 cup green bell pepper stripes
- ▶ 6 cherry tomatoes

1. Combine first 3 ingredients and stir.
2. Set aside.
3. Brush one swordfish steak with soy sauce mixture; grill or broil, turning once, 8-10 minutes, until fish flakes easily when tested with fork.
4. On plate, arrange mixed salad greens, cucumber slices, green bell pepper, and cherry tomatoes; top with cooked swordfish.
5. Drizzle fish and vegetables with olive oil and red wine or rice wine vinegar.

Salads

SLICED STEAK SALAD

Serves
4

- 2 cups arugula leaves
- 2 cups radicchio leaves
- 2 cups Belgian endive leaves
- 8 ounces lean boneless beef sirloin, thinly sliced

Herb Vinaigrette:
- 1 Tbsp + 1 tsp olive or vegetable oil
- 1 Tbsp + 1 tsp wine or cider vinegar
- 1 Tbsp minced fresh thyme, oregano, marjoram or tarragon leaves or 1 tsp dried
- 1 Tbsp dry white wine
- 1/2 tsp prepared mustard
- Pinch salt
- Freshly ground black pepper, to taste

To prepare salad:
1. Divide arugula, radicchio and Belgian endive evenly among 4 places.
2. Top each with 2 ounces sliced steak.

To prepare dressing:
3. In a small jar with tight-fitting lid or small bowl, combine oil, vinegar, thyme, wine, mustard, salt and pepper, cover and shake well or, with wire whisk, blend until combined.
4. Just before serving, pour one-fourth of dressing over each portion of salad.

THAI BEEF SALAD

Serves
4

- 10 ounces lean boneless beef loin, cut into 1/4 strips
- 1/2 cup finely diced onion
- 3 Tbsps reduced-sodium soy sauce
- 2 Tbsps minced deveined seeded jalapeno pepper (wear gloves to prevent irritation)
- 2 garlic cloves, minced
- 1 tsp minced pared fresh ginger root
- 1 cup bean sprouts
- 1/4 cup minced fresh cilantro
- 2 tsps oriental sesame oil
- 8 cups packed trimmed washed spinach leaves, dried and torn into bite-size pieces

1. Spray large nonstick skillet with nonstick cooking spray; heat.
2. Add beef; cook over medium-high heat, stirring constantly, 30 seconds, until no longer pink.
3. Add onion, soy sauce, jalapeno pepper, garlic and ginger; cook, stirring frequently, 5 minutes, until onion is softened.
4. Remove from heat.
5. Add bean sprouts, cilantro and oil; toss to combine.
6. Divide spinach evenly among 4 bowls; top each portion of spinach with one-fourth of the best mixture.

EASY CORN & RED PEPPER SALAD

Serves 1

- ▶ 1/2 cup cooked corn kernels
- ▶ 1/4 cups diced red bell pepper
- ▶ 1 Tbsp minced fresh flat-leaf parsley
- ▶ 1 Tbsp dressing of your choice

1. Combine corn, red bell peppers, parsley and dressing.
2. Toss and enjoy!

TUNA SALAD NICOISE #2

Serves 2

- ▶ 2 cups shredded Romaine lettuce leaves
- ▶ 1 medium tomato, quartered
- ▶ 1/2 cup cooked cut green beans
- ▶ 2-oz canned water-packed tuna, drained
- ▶ 6 large pitted blacked olives
- ▶ 1 Tbsp each rinsed drained capers
- ▶ Balsalmic dressing

1. Combine ingredients.
2. Toss and enjoy!

SALAD NICOISE

Serves 2

- ▶ 1 cup torn Romaine lettuce leaves
- ▶ 1/2 cup cooked cut green beans
- ▶ 4 ounces cooked potato, diced
- ▶ 6 cherry tomatoes, halved
- ▶ 2-oz canned water-packed tuna, drained
- ▶ 1/2 hard-cooked egg white, chopped
- ▶ 3 large or 5 small pitted black olives, sliced
- ▶ 2 Tbsps red wine vinegar
- ▶ 1 anchovy fillet, rinsed and chopped
- ▶ 1/2 tsp olive oil and freshly ground black pepper, to taste

1. Combine ingredients.
2. Toss and enjoy!

Salads

GREEK GRILLED LAMB SALAD

Serves 1-2

- ▶ 2 Tbsps minced fresh oregano, or 1 tsp dried
- ▶ 1 tsp grated lemon zest
- ▶ 7 Tbsps fresh lemon juice
- ▶ 2 garlic cloves, minced
- ▶ 8 ounces lean boneless loin of lamb
- ▶ 1 Tbsp olive oil
- ▶ 1 Tbsp tomato sauce (no salt added)
- ▶ 1 tsp Dijon-style mustard
- ▶ 1/4 tsp salt
- ▶ Pinch freshly ground black pepper
- ▶ 8 cups torn assorted tender lettuce leaves
- ▶ 2 medium tomatoes, each cut into eight wedges
- ▶ 1 1/2 ounces feta cheese, crumbled
- ▶ 6 large Greek olives, pitted and finely chopped

To prepare lamb:

1. In gallon-size sealable plastic bag, combine oregano, zest, 1/4 cup of the juice and half the garlic; add lamb.
2. Seal bag, squeezing out air; turn to coat lamb.
3. Refrigerate at least 1 hour or overnight, turning bag occasionally.
4. Preheat outdoor barbecue grill according to manufacturer's directions, or preheat broiler and spray rack in broiler pan with nonstick cooking spray.
5. Drain marinade into small saucepan; bring to a boil.
6. Remove from heat.
7. Grill lamb over hot coals or place onto prepared rack in broiler pan and broil 4" from heat, turning once and brushing frequently with marinade, 12 minutes, until cooked through.
8. Transfer lamb to cutting board; slice thinly.
9. Divide lettuce among 4 bowls; top each portion with 4 tomato wedges, one-fourth of the cheese, one-fourth of the olives and 2 ounces of the cooked lamb, then drizzle each portion with one-fourth of the dressing.

To prepare dressing:

1. In small jar with tight-fitting lid or small bowl, combine oil, tomato sauce, mustard, the remaining garlic, the salt, pepper and remaining 3 Tbsps juice.
2. Cover and shake well, or, with wire whisk, blend until combined.

QUICK TUNA VEGETABLE SALAD

Serves 1

- ▶ 1 cup torn iceberg lettuce leaves
- ▶ 6 cherry tomatoes, halved
- ▶ 1/2 cup cucumber slices
- ▶ 4 ounces drained canned water-packed tuna
- ▶ 1 1/2 tsps of olive oil
- ▶ 1/4 tsp red wine vinegar
- ▶ Pepper to taste

1. Combine ingredients.
2. Toss and enjoy!

GRILLED CHICKEN SALAD

Serves 2

- ▶ 1 cup torn spinach leaves
- ▶ 1/2 medium tomato sliced
- ▶ 1/2 medium roasted red boil pepper, sliced
- ▶ 1/2 cup cooked artichoke hearts
- ▶ 3 ounces skinless boneless grilled chicken breast, sliced
- ▶ 2 tsps red wine vinegar
- ▶ 1 tsp olive oil
- ▶ Freshly ground black pepper

1. Combine ingredients.
2. Toss and enjoy!

SPINACH-CHICKPEA SALAD

Serves 1

- ▶ 2 cups torn spinach leaves
- ▶ 4 ounces drained cooked chickpeas
- ▶ 6 cherry tomatoes, halved
- ▶ 1/4 cup diced red onion
- ▶ 1 Tbsp vinaigrette dressing

1. Combine ingredients.
2. Toss and enjoy!

Salads

GRILLED TUNA & VEGETABLE SALAD

 Serves 4

- ▶ 12 eggplant slices, 1/4" thick
- ▶ 1/4 tsp salt
- ▶ 2 Tbsp rice wine vinegar
- ▶ 1 Tbsps + 1 tsp oriental sesame oil
- ▶ 2 tsps sesame seeds
- ▶ 2 garlic cloves, minced
- ▶ 1/4 tsp ground red pepper
- ▶ 2 medium zucchini, cut into thin lengthwise slices
- ▶ 2 medium yellow bell peppers, seeded and quartered
- ▶ 4 5-oz boneless tuna steaks

TURBOTIPS:
This recipe is great with swordfish, too!

1. Place eggplant slices in a single layer onto paper towel; sprinkle evenly with salt.
2. Let stand 15 minutes par dry.
3. In small bowl, combine vinegar, oil, sesame seeds, garlic and ground red pepper; brush over one side of zucchini slices, bell pepper wedges, tuna steaks and dried eggplant slices.
4. Preheat outdoor barbecue grill or indoor stove-top grill according to manufacturer's directions.
5. Grill vegetables over hot coals or on stove-top grill, turning as needed, until tender.
6. Remove vegetables from grill; keep warm.
7. Grill tuna, turning once, 6 minutes, until fish flakes easily when tested with fork.
8. Serve tuna with grilled vegetables.

HEFTY CHEF'S SALAD

 Serves 6

- ▶ 2 small tomatoes, sliced
- ▶ 4 green onions, sliced thin
- ▶ 2 cup lean roast beef, chicken or turkey, cut into strips
- ▶ 1 cucumber diced
- ▶ 3 hard cooked egg whites, chopped
- ▶ 1/4 lb Goat cheese, crumbled
- ▶ 6 radishes, sliced thin

1. Combine all vegetables.
2. Sprinkle with cheese and egg whites.
3. Top with meat strips.
4. Serve with a vinaigrette dressing of your choice.

SWORDFISH & ENDIVE SALAD

Serves 4

- 2 Tbsps olive oil
- 2 tsp grated lemon zest
- 2 Tbsps fresh lemon juice
- 1 Tbsp minced fresh tarragon leaves
- 1 Tbsp finely minced chives
- 12 asparagus spears
- 4 5-oz boneless swordfish steaks
- 1 1/2 cups watercress leaves
- 1 medium Belgian endive, leaves separated

1. In large pot of boiling water, cook asparagus 3 minutes, until just tender.
2. Drain, discarding liquid; set aside.
3. Preheat outdoor barbecue grill or indoor stove-top grill according to manufacturer's directions.
4. Grill swordfish over hot coals or on stove-grill, turning once, 6 minutes, until fish flakes easily when tested with fork.
5. Divide watercress, endive, cooked asparagus and grilled swordfish evenly among 4 places; drizzle evenly with dressing.

To prepare dressing:
1. In small jar with tight-fitting lid or small bowl, combine oil, zest, juice, tarragon, chives and 2 Tbsps water.
2. Cover and shake well or, with wire whisk, blend until combined.

CHEF SALAD

Serves 2

- 1 cup shredded lettuce
- 1 hard-boiled eggs, sliced
- 2 ounces roasted, sliced, skinless turkey or chicken breast
- 2 ounces boiled, sliced ham
- 1/4 cup cucumber, sliced
- 4-6 cherry tomatoes

1. In a large bowl, add all ingredients.
2. Serve immediately.

THREE BEAN SALAD

Serves 4

- ▶ 10 ounces all-purpose potatoes, pared and cut into 1" cubes
- ▶ 2 cups cut green beans (1" pieces)
- ▶ 2 cups julienned carrots (1" pieces)
- ▶ 4 ounces drained cooked chickpeas
- ▶ 4 ounces drained cooked red kidney beans
- ▶ 1/2 cup diced red bell pepper
- ▶ 1/2 cup julienned celery (1" pieces)
- ▶ 1 cup low-sodium mixed vegetables juice
- ▶ 2 Tbsps fresh lemon juice
- ▶ 1 Tbsp + 1 tsp olive oil
- ▶ 3/4 tsp dried oregano leaves
- ▶ 1/2 tsp salt
- ▶ 1/4 tsp freshly ground black pepper
- ▶ 2 cups torn Romaine lettuce leaves

1. Place potatoes into large pot; add water to cover.
2. Bring liquid to a boil; reduce heat to low.
3. Simmer 10-15 minutes, until potatoes are tender.
4. With slotted spoon, transfer potatoes to large bowl; set aside to cool.
5. In same pot of boiling water, cook green beans and carrots 4 minutes, until green beans are bright green and vegetables are just tender; drain; discarding liquid.
6. Transfer vegetables to bowl with potatoes; set aside to cool.
7. Add chickpeas, kidney beans, bell pepper and celery to bowl with cooked potatoes and vegetables. Toss to combine.
8. In medium jar with tight-fitting lid or medium bowl, combine vegetable and lemon juices, oil, oregano, salt and black pepper; cover and shake well or, with wire whisk, blend until combined.
9. Pour over potato-mixture; toss to combine.
10. Refrigerate, covered, until chilled.
11. Line each of 4 plates with 1/2 cup lettuce; top each portion of lettuce with one-fourth of the potato mixture.

SPINACH-ONION SALAD

Serves 2

- ▶ 2 cups torn spinach leaves
- ▶ 1/4 cup sliced red onion
- ▶ 2 tsps balsamic vinegar
- ▶ 1 tsp each olive oil
- ▶ Imitation bacon bits

1. In a large bowl, add all ingredients.
2. Serve immediately.

GREEK SHRIMP SALAD

Serves 4

- ▶ 15 ounces medium shrimp, peeked and deveined
- ▶ 1 lemon slice
- ▶ 2 Tbsps fresh lemon juice
- ▶ 1 Tbsp olive oil
- ▶ 1 Tbsp minced fresh oregano leaves, or 1/2 tsp dried
- ▶ 2 tsps minced fresh mint leaves
- ▶ 1 garlic clove, minced
- ▶ 1 1/2 cups torn chicory leaves
- ▶ 2 large plum tomatoes, cut into thin wedges
- ▶ 2 Tbsps minced scallions
- ▶ 6 large kalamata olives, pitted and thinly sliced
- ▶ 1 1/2 ounces feta cheese, crumbled

1. In large saucepan, bring 1 quart water to a boil; add shrimp and lemon slice.
2. Bring liquid to a broil; reduce heat to low.
3. Simmer 1-2 minutes, until shrimp turns pink.
4. Drain, discarding liquid and lemon slice; set aside.
5. Prepare dressing.
6. In small jar with tight-fitting lid or small bowl combine juice, oil, oregano, mint, garlic and 1 Tbsp water; cover and shake well or, with wine whisk, blend until combined.
7. Pour 2 Tbsps of the dressing over cooked shrimp; toss to combine.
8. Refrigerate covered, until chilled.
9. To prepare salad, in large bowl, combine chicory, romaine lettuce tomatoes, scallions, olives and chilled shrimp.
10. Pour remaining dressing over salad; toss to coat.
11. Serve sprinkled with cheese.

WALNUT AVOCADO SALAD

Serves 4

- ▶ 1/2 head iceberg lettuce, shredded
- ▶ 1/2 head romaine lettuce, shredded
- ▶ 1 cup chopped walnuts
- ▶ 1 avocado, diced and sprinkled with lemon juice
- ▶ 1/3 cup wine vinegar
- ▶ 2 Tbsps olive or macadamia oil
- ▶ 2 garlic cloves, minced
- ▶ 1/4 tsp freshly ground pepper

1. Combine lettuce, nuts and avocado in salad bowl.
2. Chill thoroughly.
3. Combine remaining ingredients in bowl, or jar with tight-fitting lid and blend well.
4. Refrigerate.
5. Toss with chilled vegetables just before serving.

Salads

BLACK BEAN, CORN & QUINOA SALAD

Serves
8

- ▶ 1 cup water or vegetable broth
- ▶ 1/2 cup quinoa, well rinsed
- ▶ 1 tsp olive oil
- ▶ 3 tsps lime juice
- ▶ 1/4 tsp ground cumin
- ▶ 1/8 tsp cayenne pepper
- ▶ 1 Tbsp minced scallions
- ▶ 1 Tbsp chopped fresh cilantro
- ▶ 1/4 cup chopped green onions
- ▶ 15-oz no-salt black beans, rinsed and drained
- ▶ 1 ear fresh corn, cooked and kernels removed (about 1 cup kernels)
- ▶ 1 small tomato, chopped (about 3/4 cup)
- ▶ 3/4 cup chopped bell pepper (red, orange, yellow or a mix)
- ▶ 2 Tbsps canned diced green chilies
- ▶ 1 cup chopped fresh mango or peach
- ▶ Lime wedges

1. In a saucepan, bring water to a boil.
2. Add quinoa, cover and simmer on low heat until water is absorbed (10-15 minutes).
3. Let cool.
4. In a small bowl, combine olive oil, lime juice, cumin, cayenne, scallions and cilantro.
5. In a large bowl, combine cooled quinoa, green onions, beans, corn kernels, tomato, bell pepper, green chilies and mango or peach.
6. Add olive oil mixture and toss gently.
7. Season with salt and pepper.
8. Cover and refrigerate until cool.
9. Serve with lime wedges on a bed of chopped lettuce(s) of choice.

SPINACH MUSHROOM SALAD

Serves
4

- ▶ 1 lb of fresh spinach washed and drained (about 8 cups)
- ▶ 3 cups sliced mushrooms
- ▶ 4 slices of bacon, cooked crispy, crumbled
- ▶ 2 hard-cooked eggs, coarsely chopped
- ▶ 1/3 cup light olive oil
- ▶ 1/4 cup wine vinegar
- ▶ 1 clove garlic, minced
- ▶ 1/4 tsp salt
- ▶ Freshly ground black pepper to taste

1. Whisk together oil, vinegar, salt, pepper and garlic.
2. Toss with spinach and mushrooms.
3. Sprinkle salad with crumbled bacon and chopped eggs.

CHICKEN PESTO SALAD

Serves 4

- ▶ Olive oil cooking spray
- ▶ 4 boneless, skinless chicken breasts (about 6 ounces each)
- ▶ 2 cups packed fresh basil
- ▶ 2 Tbsps freshly grated Parmesan
- ▶ 1 Tbsp pine nuts, toasted 10 minutes in a cast-iron skillet in a 350°F oven
- ▶ 1 clove garlic
- ▶ 1/4 cup reduced-sodium chicken broth
- ▶ 2 Tbsps olive oil
- ▶ 4 cups lettuce chopped (such as frisée)
- ▶ 1 Tbsp fresh lemon juice
- ▶ 1 cup halved cherry tomatoes
- ▶ 1/4 cup cubed part-skim mozzarella

1. Heat oven to 400°F.
2. Coat a baking sheet with cooking spray.
3. Season chicken with salt and pepper, place on sheet and bake until cooked through, 20 to 25 minutes.
4. Cut into 1/2-inch slices.

To make pesto:
1. Pulse basil, Parmesan, pine nuts and garlic in a food processor until finely chopped.
2. With motor on, slowly add broth and oil.
3. Season with salt and pepper.
4. Toss lettuce with lemon juice; coat chicken, tomatoes and mozzarella with pesto.

SOUTHWESTERN QUINOA SALAD

Serves 4

- ▶ 1 cup + 2 Tbsps water
- ▶ 1/4 tsps sea salt
- ▶ 2 tsps salt-free chili powder blend
- ▶ 3/4 cup quinoa, well rinsed
- ▶ 1 1/2 cups frozen, shelled edamame
- ▶ 6-oz jar roasted red bell peppers, drained
- ▶ 2 medium cloves garlic
- ▶ 2 tsps olive oil
- ▶ 2 tsps lime juice, add more to taste
- ▶ 3 Tbsps chopped fresh cilantro
- ▶ 3/4 cup grated carrot

1. Bring water, salt, and chili powder to a boil in a medium saucepan.
2. Stir in quinoa and edamame.
3. Bring to a boil again, then reduce heat to low, cover and simmer for 15 minutes, until all water is absorbed.
4. Let rest, covered and undisturbed, for 5 minutes.
5. Meanwhile, purée peppers, garlic, olive oil, and lime juice in a food processor or blender.
6. Stir pepper sauce, cilantro, and grated carrot into quina mixture.
7. Add extra lime juice and salt to taste if desired.

TURBOTIPS:

Prep tip: Add crumbled quiso cotija or feta cheese for a more indulgent dish.

Serving tips: for best flavor, let the salad come to room temperature before serving.

It's delicious wrapped in butter lettuce leaves.

Salads

SALSA SALAD BOWL

Serves 4

- ▶ 1 can low-sodium black beans, rinsed and drained
- ▶ 1 pint cherry tomatoes, preferably sweet grape, quartered
- ▶ 4-oz Mozzarella cheese, cut into 1/4 inch cubes
- ▶ 1/2 of a medium poblano pepper or green bell pepper, chopped
- ▶ 1/2 cup chopped red onion
- ▶ 1/3 cup chopped fresh cilantro
- ▶ 1/4 cup lime juice (juice of 2 medium limes)
- ▶ 1 Tbsp extra virgin olive oil
- ▶ 1/4 tsp salt
- ▶ 1/8 tsp cayenne pepper

1. In medium mixing bowl, combine beans, tomatoes, cheese, poblano pepper, onion and cilantro.
2. Cover and refrigerate until needed.
3. Combine lime juice, olive oil, salt and cayenne in small container.
4. Cover and refrigerate until needed.
5. To transport individual servings, place equal amounts of salad in 4 quart-size resealable plastic food storage bags or lidded containers.
6. Stir dressing and put about 1 1/2 Tbsp of dressing in each of 4 small resealable plastic food storage bags.
7. Place the smaller bags inside the larger bags.
8. To serve, pour dressing into quart-size bag with salad.
9. Seal bag and toll to coat salad with dressing.

CHERRY TOMATO SALAD

Serves 4

- ▶ 1/3 cup olive oil
- ▶ 1/3 cup red wine vinegar
- ▶ 2 Tbsps chopped fresh parsley
- ▶ 1 1/2 Tbsps Dijon mustard
- ▶ 1 Tbsp fresh lemon juice
- ▶ 1 Tbsp chopped fresh dill
- ▶ 3 green onions, chopped
- ▶ 1 garlic clove
- ▶ Coarse salt and freshly ground pepper
- ▶ 4 cups (2 pints) cherry tomatoes, stemmed and halved
- ▶ 1 hard-cooked egg, grated (garnish)
- ▶ Fresh dill (garnish)

1. Combine first 8 ingredients with salt and pepper to taste in processor or blender and mix well.
2. Place tomatoes in serving bowl, pour sauce over and toss lightly.
3. Cover and chill 1 to 2 hours.
4. Sprinkle with grated egg and additional dill just before serving.

SESAME SPINACH SALAD

- ► 1 Tbsp sesame seed
- ► 2 Tbsps olive oil
- ► 1 Tbsp fresh lemon juice
- ► 1 tsp soy sauce
- ► Dash of hot pepper sauce
- ► Salt and freshly ground pepper
- ► 4 canned water chestnuts, drained and sliced (optional—but add a nice "crunch")
- ► 2 large mushrooms, thinly sliced
- ► 1/2 lb fresh spinach, washed, stemmed and dried

1. Toast sesame seed in small saucepan over medium heat, shaking pan occasionally to prevent burning.
2. Cool.
3. Whisk in next 4 ingredients with salt and pepper to taste.
4. Stir in water chestnuts and mushrooms.
5. Cover and refrigerate until ready to use.
6. To serve, tear spinach into bowl, add chilled mixture and toss.

SPINACH, BACON & APPLE SALAD

- ► 1/4 cup olive oil
- ► 3 Tbsps wine vinegar
- ► 1/2 tsp prepared mustard
- ► Salt and freshly ground pepper
- ► 5 slices bacon
- ► 1/3 cup sliced almonds
- ► 1 lb fresh spinach, washed, stemmed, dried and torn into bites sized pieces
- ► 1 unpeeled red apple, cored and coarsely chopped
- ► 3 green onions, thinly sliced

1. Combine first 3 ingredients with salt and pepper to taste in jar with tight fitting lid and shake well.
2. Refrigerate.
3. Cook bacon slices in large skillet over medium high heat until brown and crisp.
4. Drain well on paper towels.
5. Crumble and set aside.
6. Discard all but 1 Tbsp fat from skillet.
7. Add almonds to skillet and shake pan over medium high heat until nuts are lightly toasted.
8. Remove from heat.
9. Combine spinach with bacon, apple, onion and almonds and toss lightly.
10. Shake dressing, pour over salad and toss again.
11. Serve immediately.

AVOCADO-FROSTED
CAULIFLOWER SALAD

Serves
4

- ▶ 1 head cauliflower
- ▶ Toasted sliced almonds
- ▶ Lettuce leaves
- ▶ Cherry tomatoes

Marinade:
- ▶ 3 Tbsps olive or macadamia nut oil
- ▶ 3 Tbsps distilled white vinegar
- ▶ Salt and freshly ground pepper

Sauce:
- ▶ 3 medium avocadoes
- ▶ 3 Tbsps marinade
- ▶ Dash of freshly ground nutmeg
- ▶ Salt

1. Steam cauliflower until tender but still firm and place in bowl.

To make marinade:
2. Combine all ingredients and pour over cauliflower while still warm.
3. Chill overnight, turning once or twice.

To make sauce:
4. Mash avocados with fork in medium bowl.
5. Add onion, 3 Tbsps marinade, nutmeg and salt to taste; mix well.
6. Frost cauliflower completely with sauce.
7. Cover with toasted almonds.
8. Serve on bed of lettuce and garnish with cherry tomatoes.

SNOW PEA & WHITE CORN SALAD

Serves
6

- ▶ 1 lb fresh snow peas (strings discarded), cut diagonally into 1/4-inch strips
- ▶ 6 small ears of sweet corn (preferably white), scraped and blanched
- ▶ 1 shallot, chopped
- ▶ 2 Tbsps coarsely ground French mustard
- ▶ 2 Tbsps cider vinegar
- ▶ 9 fresh tarragon leaves or 1/8 tsp crumbled dried tarragon
- ▶ 5 fresh mint leaves
- ▶ 2 medium fresh basil leaves or generous pinch of crumbled dried basil
- ▶ 3 Tbsps olive or peanut oil or macadamia nut oil
- ▶ Salt and freshly ground pepper
- ▶ 4-5 whole snow peas (garnish)

1. Place sliced snow peas in colander and pour boiling water over.
2. Drain well; immediately plunge into ice water and drain again.
3. Transfer to container.
4. Mix in corn and set aside.
5. Combine shallot, mustard, vinegar, tarragon, mint and basil in processor or blender and mix until smooth.
6. With machine running, gradually add oil in slow steady stream until mixture is creamy.
7. Season to taste with salt and pepper.
8. Pour over vegetables and mix gently.
9. Cover and refrigerate 4 hours.
10. Garnish with whole peas.

VEGETABLE SALAD WITH FETA CHEESE Serves 6

- ▶ 1 garlic clove, halved
- ▶ 1 head iceberg lettuce, torn into bite-size pieces
- ▶ 3 tomatoes, quartered
- ▶ 1 cucumber, peeled and sliced
- ▶ 1 red onion, chopped
- ▶ 3 celery stalks, diced
- ▶ 1 green bell pepper, seeded and chopped
- ▶ 6 radishes, sliced
- ▶ 1 carrot, shredded
- ▶ 2 Tbsps chopped fresh parsley
- ▶ 1/3 cup olive oil
- ▶ 1/4 cup red wine vinegar
- ▶ 1 1/2 Tbsps fresh lemon juice
- ▶ 1 tsp dried oregano
- ▶ 1/2 tsp freshly ground pepper
- ▶ 1 lb feta cheese
- ▶ 12-14 Kalamata olives

1. Rub interior of large wooden salad bowl with cut side of garlic.
2. Discard garlic.
3. Add lettuce, tomatoes, cucumber, onion, celery, bell pepper, radishes, carrot and parsley to bowl.
4. Toss lightly.
5. Combine oil, vinegar, lemon juice, oregano, salt and pepper in jar with tight-fitting lid and shake well.
6. Pour over salad and toss to coat.
7. Add cheese and olives and toss again.

MARINATED VEGETABLE SALAD Serves 6

- ▶ 1 lb fresh green beans, cut into 3-inch lengths
- ▶ 1 pint cherry tomatoes
- ▶ 6 medium size green onions, sliced into 1/4-inch pieces
- ▶ 1/3 cup olive oil
- ▶ 1 medium garlic clove, minced
- ▶ 1/2 lb small mushrooms
- ▶ 3 Tbsps red wine vinegar
- ▶ 2 Tbsps minced onion
- ▶ 1 Tbsp fresh lemon juice
- ▶ 1 tsp Dijon mustard
- ▶ 1 tsp dried tarragon, crumbled
- ▶ 1/2 tsp dried coriander, crumbled
- ▶ Salt and freshly ground pepper

1. Parboil green beans 5 minutes, drain.
2. Transfer to large bowl and add cherry tomatoes and green onions.
3. Heat oil with garlic in medium skillet over medium low heat until very warm, but not hot.
4. Add mushrooms and stir to coat.
5. Cool to room temperature.
6. Add mushrooms to green beans using slotted spoon.
7. Stir vinegar, onion, lemon juice, mustard, tarragon and coriander into garlic oil.
8. Pour over vegetables and toss to coat.
9. Season with salt and pepper.
10. Cover and refrigerate overnight.
11. Serve chilled.

Salads

LEBANESE SALAD

Serves 4

- ▶ 4 green onions, finely chopped
- ▶ 3 tomatoes, cut into wedges
- ▶ 2 small cucumbers, peeled and thinly sliced
- ▶ 1/2 small green bell pepper, sliced into thin strips
- ▶ 5 fresh parsley springs, coarsely chopped
- ▶ 4 mint springs, coarsely chopped

Dressing:
- ▶ Makes about 1/2 cup
- ▶ 1/4 cup olive oil
- ▶ 1/4 cup fresh lemon juice
- ▶ 1 tsp salt
- ▶ 1 garlic clove, minced
- ▶ Salt and freshly ground pepper

1. Combine all ingredients except dressing in large bowl and toss lightly.
2. Just before serving, pour dressing over and toss.

BIBB & WALNUT SALAD

Serves 4

- ▶ 2 heads Bibb lettuce, washed, dried and torn into bite-sized pieces
- ▶ 2/3 cup coarsely chopped walnuts, toasted
- ▶ 1/4 cup walnut oil, or to taste
- ▶ 3-6 Tbsps wine vinegar
- ▶ Salt and freshly ground pepper

1. Arrange lettuce in salad bowl.
2. Sprinkle with walnuts and toss with walnut oil and vinegar.
3. Season to taste with salt and pepper and serve immediately.

PETITE CHICKEN SALAD

Serves 4

- ▶ 2 hard-cooked egg whites
- ▶ 2 cups diced, cooked chicken
- ▶ 1/4 cup diced jicama
- ▶ 1/2 cup raw zucchini, diced
- ▶ 1/2 cup celery, diced
- ▶ 1/4 cup radishes, sliced thin
- ▶ 1/4 cup chives, chopped

1. Mix all ingredients together with "Mustard Salad Dressing".

THAI CUCUMBER &

RADISH SALAD

Serves 4

- ▶ 1/2 cup rice wine vinegar
- ▶ 3 Tbsps sugar
- ▶ 2 Tbsps light oil, such as canola or safflower
- ▶ 1 lb daikon radish, peeled and thinly sliced
- ▶ 1 English or seedless cucumber, thinly sliced
- ▶ 1 red bell pepper, seeded and very thinly sliced
- ▶ 1 tsp crushed red pepper flakes
- ▶ 20 fresh basil leaves

1. In the bottom of a medium bowl, combine vinegar, sugar, oil.
2. Add daikon, cucumber, bell pepper, pepper flakes.
3. Toss and combine.
4. Cover and chill until ready to serve.
5. When ready to serve, tear basil into pieces and add to salad.
6. Toss salad to incorporate basil and serve.

Vegetarian

FDA TIPS

Fresh, raw fruits and vegetables are simply the original TurboCharging "fast foods." They are always the most healthy food choices.

Follow these tips from the FDA to keep your produce safe, wholesome and delicious!

- ▶ At the store, purchase produce that is not bruised or damaged.
- ▶ Fresh-cut produce should be refrigerated or surrounded by ice. At home, put produce that needs refrigeration away promptly.
- ▶ Fresh produce should be refrigerated within two hours of peeling or cutting.
- ▶ Discard any cut produce if left out at room temperature for more than two hours.
- ▶ Wash hands often with hot soapy water before and after handling fresh produce.
- ▶ Twenty seconds is all it takes for a thorough washing! Always wash fruits and vegetables with cool tap water before cutting, eating raw or cooking.
- ▶ Bagged, pre-washed produce is safe and ready to eat as packaged. Scrub firm or thick-skinned produce thoroughly with a clean produce brush and water.
- ▶ Do not use soap and detergents.
- ▶ One exception to this rule is if the produce has a thick, inedible rind, such as melon.
- ▶ Melons should be cleaned with water and a mild detergent on the outside surface ONLY to prevent any dirt or bacteria on the rind from being transferred to the inside of the melon when it's cut.
- ▶ Wash cutting boards, dishes, utensils and countertops with hot soapy water often.
- ▶ Sanitize plastic cutting boards by using a solution of 1 tsp of chlorine bleach to one quart of water—dip and air dry.
- ▶ Or use the "sanitize" setting on your dishwasher. Don't cross-contaminate! Use clean cutting boards and utensils when handling fresh produce.
- ▶ If possible, keep a separate cutting board just for fresh produce and a separate one for raw meat, poultry and seafood.
- ▶ Do not consume ice that has come in contact with produce or other raw products.

PREPARATION TIPS

▶ To ripen fruits, place them in a paper bag and put it under the counter where it won't be moved frequently. To ripen kiwi, peaches, apricots, plumbs, mango, nectarine and persimmons evenly (instead of near the edge only), place in the same bag as bananas.

▶ If at all possible use fresh fruits and vegetables, however if canned or frozen are occasionally used, they must be placed in a sieve and rinsed under cold water prior to adding to preparation.

▶ Use rice vinegar for a new dimension in cooking or seasoning your vegetables. It is much milder than other vinegars. It is usually found in oriental food stores.

▶ If tomato juice, paste or puree are called for, use salt and sugar free.

▶ Use a cooler with ice or ice gel packs when transporting or storing perishable foods outdoors including cut fresh fruits and vegetables.

▶ Wash your vegetables well before slicing. After slicing don't soak in water or you will lose a lot of nutritional value.

▶ Steam or cook vegetables gently in small amounts of water. Instead of salt and butter, try seasoning and cooking with onion slice, lemon juice, chives, dill or garlic.

▶ Liven up soggy lettuce by soaking it in a mix of a bit of lemon juice and cold water. Also, don't wash lettuce until you use it. Keep the leaves dry until you are ready to add it to a salad.

▶ If your celery has gotten limp, give it a drink by standing it upright in a glass of cold water and refrigerate.

▶ To quickly bake or grill a potato, boil first for 10 to 15 minutes. Then bake or grill.

▶ If you want to make some quick-baked stuffed peppers, sprinkle a little of your favorite cheese over a bowl of frozen or fresh assorted vegetables and stir to distribute the cheese evenly. Then place the peppers upright in lightly oiled or stick-free muffin tins before baking. The peppers won't tip and the juices will stay contained.

▶ Buy mushrooms before they "open." When stems and caps are attached firmly, the mushrooms are fresh.

THE BEST WAY TO COOK VEGETABLES

The best way to cook vegetables is to steam them in a small amount of water. Doing so, you avoid losing vitamins and minerals in the water, as happens when you boil vegetables. Steaming works especially well for broccoli, string beans, carrots and Brussels sprouts, for example. Greens, however, like kale, collards or mustard, are better boiled or sauteed. Steaming seems to make them tough and bitter and strips their color to a drab olive green.

To boil greens, simply place in water to cover them completely, and boil uncovered for 10-15 minutes. They will be sweet, delicious and an appetizing bright green. To saute', place in a saucepan with a small amount of water or broth, cover and cook 5-10 minutes. This will boil away some vitamins and minerals, but the greens are so high in nutrients to begin with (a cup of kale provides a total daily requirement for vitamin A!) a little leeway here is fine.

SPAGHETTI SQUASH

Serves 6

- 3 lbs spaghetti squash
- 3/4 cup freshly grated Parmesan cheese
- 2 tsps olive oil
- 1 cup diagonally sliced carrot
- 1/2 cup diagonally sliced celery
- 1 cup preshredded cabbage
- 1 small zucchini, cut into thin strips
- 16-oz can kidney beans, rinsed and drained
- 14.5-oz can no-salt-added whole tomatoes, drained and chopped
- 3 tsps water
- 1 tsp dried thyme
- 1 tsp dried parsley flakes
- 1/2 tsp garlic power
- 1/8 tsp pepper

1. Cut squash in half lengthwise; remove and discard seeds.
2. Place squash, cut side down, in a Dutch oven; add water to depth of 2".
3. Bring to boil; cover reduce heat, and simmer 20 to 25 minutes or until tender.
4. Drain.
5. Using a fork, remove 3 cups spaghetti-like strands from squash; reserve remaining squash for another use.
6. Discard squash shells.
7. Combine strands and cheese; toss.
8. Set aside; keep warm.
9. Coat a nonstick skillet with cooking spray; add oil.
10. Place over medium heat until hot.
11. Add carrot and celery; sauté 5 minutes.
12. Add cabbage and zucchini; sauté 5 minutes.
13. Add beans and remaining 6 ingredients.
14. Cook over medium heat 5 minutes, stirring often.
15. Place 1/2 cup squash mixture on each plate.
16. Top evenly with vegetables.

HERBED CORN ON THE COB

Serves 4

- 1 Tbsp dried dill weed
- 1 Tbsp dried thyme
- 1 Tbsp water
- 1 clove garlic, minced
- 4 medium ears frozen corn

1. Combine first 4 ingredients in a small bowl; stir well.
2. Spread over corn.
3. Place each ear on a piece of heavy-duty aluminum foil; wrap tightly.
4. Bake at 450°F for 25 minutes, turning occasionally.
5. This can also be prepared the same way and cooked on a grill until firmly tender.

Vegetarian

CHINESE VEGETABLE STIR-FRY

Serves 4

- ▶ 1/4 cup fresh lemon juice
- ▶ 1/4 cup low-sodium soy sauce
- ▶ 1 Tbsp peeled, grated gingerroot
- ▶ 2 cloves garlic, minced
- ▶ 1 cup chopped onion
- ▶ 10-oz package firm tofu, drained and cubed*
- ▶ 2 cups shredded Chinese cabbage
- ▶ 1 cup fresh bean sprouts
- ▶ 1 cup diced sweet red pepper
- ▶ 1 cup sliced fresh mushrooms
- ▶ 1/4 cup sliced green onions

1. Combine first 4 ingredients.
2. Add onion and tofu.
3. Cover and marinate in refrigerator 2 to 3 hours.
4. Drain, reserving marinade.
5. Lightly oil around top of wok, coating sides.
6. No excess oil should remain.
7. Heat at medium (350°F) until hot.
8. Add tofu mixture; stir-fry 5 minutes or until tofu starts to brown and onion is tender.
9. Remove from wok; set aside; and keep warm.
10. Add cabbage and next 4 ingredients to wok; stir-fry 2 to 3 minutes or until crisp-tender.
11. Combine reserved marinade stirring well.
12. Add marinade mixture to vegetables; stir-fry 3 minutes.
13. Add tofu mixture, and stir-fry 30 seconds or until thoroughly heated.

TURBOTIPS:
*Tofu is really not an ideal Turbo-Charged food. It is too highly processed. However, this recipe is included for those who like it. See www.turbocharged.us.com for more details.

SUMMER SWEET CORN

Serves 12

- ▶ 6 cups fresh corn cut from cob (about 12 ears)
- ▶ 1 1/2 cups water
- ▶ 1/2 cup chopped green onions
- ▶ 1/4 cup chopped green pepper
- ▶ 2 Tbsps chopped fresh basil
- ▶ 2 Tbsps white wine vinegar
- ▶ 1/4 tsp salt
- ▶ 1/4 tsp ground white pepper
- ▶ 1/4 tsp hot sauce
- ▶ Fresh basil sprigs (optional)

1. Combine first 4 ingredients in a medium saucepan.
2. Bring to a boil; reduce heat, and simmer, uncovered, 20 minutes.
3. Add chopped basil and next 4 ingredients; cook 10 minutes or until corn is tender.
4. Transfer to a serving bowl; serve with a slotted spoon.
5. Garnish with basil sprigs if desired.

TURBOTIPS:
If you don't have fresh corn, use 6 cups frozen whole kernel corn.

Vegetarian

GARLIC-ROASTED NEW POTATOES

Serves
2

- ▶ 1 1/2 cups torn Boston lettuce
- ▶ 1 1/2 cups torn red leaf lettuce
- ▶ 1/2 lb jicama, peeled and cut into very thin strips
- ▶ 1 1/2 cups sliced celery
- ▶ 1 large pink grapefruit, peeled and sectioned

1. Coat potato halves with cooking spray.
2. Coat a 9" cast-iron skillet with cooking spray; add oil.
3. Place skillet over medium heat until hot; add potato, bay leaves, garlic, and rosemary, stirring lightly.
4. Sprinkle with ground pepper and salt.
5. Bake at 450°F for 40 minutes or until potato is browned, stirring twice.
6. Remove and discard bay leaves and rosemary.

ROSEMARY POTATOES

Serves
4

TURBOTIPS:
If you don't have fresh rosemary, substitute 1/4 tsp of dried rosemary.

- ▶ 2 Baking potatoes
- ▶ 3 Tbsps water
- ▶ 1 tsp fresh rosemary, crushed
- ▶ 1/4 tsp paprika
- ▶ 1/8 tsp pepper

1. Cut potatoes in half lengthwise; slice each half into 4 wedges.
2. Combine water and next 4 ingredients in a bowl; add potato wedges, and spray with canned olive oil.
3. Place in an 11x 7x1 1/2 " baking dish lined with aluminum foil.
4. Bake at 400°F for 35 minutes or until wedges are tender.

ROASTED ASPARAGUS

Serves
2

- ▶ 1 lb fresh asparagus
- ▶ Olive oil-flavored vegetable cooking spray

1. Snap off tough ends of asparagus.
2. Remove scales from stalks with a knife or vegetable peeler, if desired.
3. Coat asparagus with olive oil-flavored cooking spray, and bake at 450°F for 10 minutes or until tender.

GARLIC POTATO STICKS

Serves 4

- ▶ 2 medium baking potatoes (about 1 lb)
- ▶ Vegetable cooking spray
- ▶ 2 cloves garlic, minced
- ▶ 1/8 tsp salt
- ▶ 1/8 tsp ground red pepper
- ▶ 1/8 tsp paprika

1. Cut potatoes into 2x 1/4 -inch strips, place strips in a large bowl of ice water until slicing is complete.
2. Drain potato strips; press between paper towels to remove excess moisture.
3. Coat a nonstick skillet with cooking spray.
4. Place over medium heat until hot.
5. Add potato strips, lightly spray with oil and cook 10 minutes.
6. Add garlic, and cook 10 to 15 additional minutes or until potato strips are lightly browned and tender, stirring frequently.
7. Sprinkle with salt, pepper, and paprika.

PEASANT-STYLE GREEN BEANS

Serves 7

- ▶ 1 lb fresh green beans
- ▶ 1 Tbsp water
- ▶ 1 cup chopped onion
- ▶ 2 cloves garlic, crushed
- ▶ 14.5-oz can no-salt-added whole tomatoes, drained and chopped
- ▶ 1/3 cup dry red wine
- ▶ 1/2 tsp dried oregano
- ▶ 1/2 tsp pepper

1. Wash beans; trim ends, and remove strings.
2. Arrange beans in a vegetable steamer over boiling water.
3. Cover and steam 5 minutes or until crisp-tender.
4. Set aside,and keep warm.
5. Heat water in a large nonstick skillet over medium-high heat until hot.
6. Add onion and garlic; cook over low heat 15 minutes, stirring occasionally.
7. Remove from heat; and beans, tossing well to combine.

> TURBOTIPS:
> This goes well with broiled chicken.

Vegetarian

SAVORY ITALIAN ASPARAGUS

Serves
4

- ▶ 1 lb fresh asparagus
- ▶ 1 medium tomato, seeded and chopped
- ▶ 2 Tbsps chopped green onions
- ▶ 1/8 tsp dried oregano
- ▶ 1/8 tsp dried thyme
- ▶ 1/8 tsp pepper
- ▶ 2 tsps freshly grated Parmesan cheese

1. Snap off tough ends of asparagus.
2. Remove scales with a knife or vegetable peeler, if desired.
3. Arrange asparagus in a vegetable steamer over boiling water.
4. Cover and steam 4 minutes or until crisp-tender.
5. Drain; arrange on a serving platter, and keep warm.
6. Combine tomato and next 4 ingredients in a small bowl; stir well.
7. Spoon tomato mixture over asparagus; sprinkle with cheese.

Microwave Instructions:
1. To microwave asparagus, snap off tough ends and remove scales with a vegetable peeler, if desired.
2. Arrange spears in an 11x7x1 1/2" baking dish with stem ends toward outside of dish; add 1/4 cup water.
3. Cover with heavy-duty plastic wrap, and vent.
4. Microwave at HIGH 6 to 7 minutes or until crisp-tender.
5. Let stand, cover, 1 minute or until crisp-tender.
6. Let stand, covered, 1 minute; drain.
7. Proceed with recipe as directed.

ZUCCHINI STICKS

Serves
4

- ▶ Vegetable cooking spray
- ▶ 1 tsp olive oil
- ▶ 2 medium zucchini, sliced lengthwise into strips

1. Coat a nonstick skillet with cooking spray; add olive oil, and place over medium-high heat until hot.
2. Add zucchini, and sauté 4 minutes or until crisp-tender.

ITALIANO EGGPLANT & SQUASH

Serves 8

- ► Vegetable cooking spray
- ► 1 tsp olive oil
- ► 1/2 cup chopped onion
- ► 8-oz package fresh mushrooms
- ► 2 14.5-oz cans no-salt-added whole tomatoes, undrained and chopped
- ► 1 medium eggplant, cubed
- ► 1 medium-size green pepper, seeded and cut into pieces
- ► 1 cloves garlic, minced
- ► 1/2 tsp dried Italian seasoning
- ► 1/8 tsp salt
- ► 10-oz package frozen sliced yellow squash, thawed and drained
- ► 8 ripe olives, halved
- ► 1 Tbsp red wine vinegar
- ► 2 tsps dried parsley flakes

1. Coat a Dutch oven with cooking spray; add olive oil.
2. Place over medium-high heat until hot.
3. Add onion and mushrooms; sauté 5 minutes or until vegetables are tender
4. Add tomato and next 6 ingredients.
5. Bring to a boil.
6. Reduce heat and simmer 5 minutes; add squash and simmer 15 additional minutes or until vegetables are tender.
7. Stir in olives, vinegar, and parsley.
8. Cook until thoroughly heated.

GRILLED ANTIPASTO

Serves 4

- ► 1 medium-size sweet red pepper
- ► 1 small eggplant (about 1/2 lb)
- ► 1 small zucchini
- ► 1 small yellow squash
- ► 2 Tbsps red wine vinegar
- ► 1/2 tsp dried oregano
- ► 1/8 tsp pepper
- ► Vegetable cooking spray

1. Cut red pepper lengthwise into quarters.
2. Remove and discard membranes and seeds.
3. Cut eggplant into 1/2"-thick slices.
4. Cut zucchini and squash lengthwise into quarters.
5. Combine vinegar and next 2 ingredients in a small bowl; stir well with a wire whisk.
6. Brush vegetables with oil mixture.
7. Coat grill rack with cooking spray; place on grill over medium-hot coals (350° to 400°F).
8. Place vegetables on rack, and grill, uncovered, 2 minutes or until crisp-tender, turning occasionally.

Vegetarian

OKRA-TOMATO-ZUCCHINI MEDLEY

- ▶ 1 small zucchini
- ▶ Vegetable cooking spray
- ▶ 1 1/2 cups sliced fresh okra
- ▶ 2 Tbsps chopped onion
- ▶ 1 cup seeded, chopped tomato
- ▶ 1/8 tsp dried basil
- ▶ 1/8 tsp dried thyme
- ▶ Dash of freshly ground pepper

1. Cut zucchini in half lengthwise; cut into 1/4-inch-thick slices.
2. Coat a nonstick skillet with cooking spray; place over medium-high heat until hot.
3. Add zucchini, okra, and onion; sauté 4 minutes.
4. Stir in tomato and remaining ingredients.
5. Cover and cook over low heat 5 minutes or until thoroughly heated, stirring often.

STEWED OKRA & TOMATOES

- ▶ Vegetable cooking spray
- ▶ 1/2 cup finely chopped onion
- ▶ 1/4 cup finely chopped green pepper
- ▶ 2 cups sliced fresh okra
- ▶ 2 cups seeded, coarsely chopped tomato
- ▶ 1 tsp lemon juice
- ▶ 1 tsp dried oregano
- ▶ 1/4 tsp salt
- ▶ 1/4 tsp hot sauce

1. Coat a medium saucepan with cooking spray; place over medium heat until hot.
2. Add onion and green pepper; sauté 2 minutes.
3. Add okra and remaining ingredients.
4. Cover and cook over medium-low heat 15 minutes or until okra is tender, stirring occasionally.

DILLED SPINACH WITH FETA

- ▶ 1 Tbsp water
- ▶ 2 10-oz packages fresh spinach
- ▶ 1/4 cup crumbled feta cheese
- ▶ 2 Tbsps chopped fresh dillweed
- ▶ 1 Tbsp fresh lemon juice
- ▶ 1/8 tsp fresh ground pepper
- ▶ Lemon slice (optional)
- ▶ Fresh dillweed sprigs (optional)

1. Place water and spinach in a Dutch oven.
2. Bring to a boil: cover and cook over medium heat 2 to 3 minutes or just until spinach wilts.
3. Add cheese and next 3 ingredients; toss.
4. If desired, garnish with lemon slices and dillweed sprigs.

Vegetarian

BRUSSELS SPROUTS

Serves 4

- ▶ 3 cups fresh Brussels sprouts
- ▶ 3 Tbsps water
- ▶ 1/2 chopped large onion
- ▶ 1 tsp parsley, finely chopped
- ▶ 1 tsp garlic powder
- ▶ 1/4 tsp salt
- ▶ 1/4 tsp black pepper
- ▶ 1/2 cup chicken broth or stock

1. Cook fresh Brussels sprouts until tender.
2. Heat water in a large non-stick skillet, sauté the onion, parsley, garlic powder, salt, and pepper until a golden brown.
3. Add the chicken broth or stock to the seasoning and cook for 4 minutes until liquid reduces.
4. Add Brussels sprouts, simmer, and serve.

TURBOTIPS:
You can substitute chunks of broccoli, cauliflower or asparagus for the Brussels sprouts.

SAUTE'ED GREEN BEANS

Serves 2

- ▶ 1 lb fresh green beans, washed and trimmed
- ▶ 1 tsp garlic, minced
- ▶ 1 shallot, finely chopped
- ▶ 1 tsp water
- ▶ 1/4 cup sliced fresh mushrooms

1. Steam beans for 5 minutes, then immerse them in ice water to stop cooking, drain and set aside.
2. In a medium-sized heavy skillet, sauté the shallots and garlic for 2 minutes over medium heat; add mushrooms and sauté for 1 additional minute.
3. Stir in the steamed green beans and cook, stirring until thoroughly heated.
4. Serve immediately.

VEGETABLE CONFETTI

Serves 4

- ▶ 1 large onion, cut in 1/4" pieces (1 1/3 cups)
- ▶ 1 tsp minced garlic
- ▶ 1/4 cup water
- ▶ 1/2 cup chopped fresh basil leaves, crumbled
- ▶ 1/4 tsp each salt and pepper
- ▶ 3 cups 1/2" pieces mixed freshly cooked vegetables (such as carrots, yellow summer squash, zucchini and green or red bell pepper)

1. Put onion, garlic and water in a large nonstick skillet over medium heat.
2. Cover; cook 13 to 15 minutes, stirring three times, until onion is tender.
3. Stir in parsley, basil, salt and pepper, then vegetables.
4. Heat thoroughly.

Vegetarian

BASIC SPAGHETTI SQUASH

Serves 4

▸ 1 large squash

1. Bake squash for 10 minutes, or microwave for 2-3 minutes, to soften skin.
2. Cut squash along length and remove seeds.
3. Bake: Place cut side down on pan and bake 45 minutes at 350°F.
4. Turn and bake until tender.
5. Microwave: Cook 5 minutes cut side down in 1/4 cup water in a dish, covered with clear wrap.
6. When done, pull out vegetable strands with fork.
7. Toss with salt and pepper, spices, bacon bits, Parmesan cheese or spaghetti sauce.

EGGPLANT WITH ZUCCHINI

Serves 4

▸ 2 medium eggplants
▸ 2 large zucchini
▸ 4 large onions, sliced
▸ 2 green peppers, cut in strips (seeds removed)
▸ 2 tomatoes, cut in eighths
▸ 1 can mushrooms, drained, butter (if any) rinsed off
▸ 2 Tbsps minced parsley
▸ 1 1/2 tsps garlic salt
▸ 1/2 tsp oregano
▸ 1/2 tsp paprika

1. Cut eggplants into 1/2" slices (do not peel).
2. Scrub zucchini, remove ends, and cut into 1/2" slices (do not peel).
3. Cook onions and peppers together in no-stick skillet until nearly soft (about 10 minutes); turn up heat and brown.
4. Remove.
5. Cook eggplant, zucchini, tomatoes, mushrooms, and parsley together, with seasonings, until just tender.
6. Add onions and peppers, mix, and serve hot or cold.
7. Add more seasoning if desired.

EGGPLANT NICOISE

Serves
4

- 2 medium eggplants
- 1 Tbsp olive oil
- 1 cup chopped onions
- 1 cup chopped green bell pepper
- 2 garlic cloves, minced
- 5 ounces lean ground beef (10% or less fat)
- 3 cups canned whole Italian tomatoes (no salt added), chopped
- 6 large or 10 small black olives, pitted and chopped
- 1 1/2 tsps minced fresh oregano leaves or 1/2 tsp dried
- Freshly ground black pepper, to taste
- 1 Tbsp + 1 tsp freshly grated Parmesan cheese

1. Preheat oven to 400°F.
2. Cut eggplants lengthwise into halves.
3. With serrated spoon, scoop out eggplant pulp, leaving 1/2 shells.
4. Chop pulp; set aside.
5. Place eggplant shells, cut-side down, onto nonstick baking sheet.
6. Bake 10 minutes; turn shells over.
7. Bake 10 minutes longer, until shells are just tender.
8. Remove from oven; set aside.
9. Leave oven on.
10. Meanwhile, in large nonstick skillet, heat oil; add onions, bell pepper and garlic.
11. Cook over medium-high heat, stirring frequently, 5 minutes, until vegetables are softened.
12. Add beef; cook, stirring to break up meat, 3-4 minutes, until no longer pink.
13. Add tomatoes, olives, oregano, black pepper and reserved eggplant pulp; mixture to a boil.
14. Reduce heat to low; simmer, covered, stirring frequently, 25-30 minutes, until mixture is thickened and flavors are blended. Spoon one-fourth of beef mixture into each eggplant shell; sprinkle evenly with cheese.
15. Bake 15 minutes until slightly crispy.
16. Serve warm or at room temperature.

Vegetarian

EGGPLANT PARMIGIANA

Serves
4

- ▶ 5 Tbsps freshly grated Parmesan cheese
- ▶ 2 cups sliced pared eggplant (1/4" slices)
- ▶ 2 egg whites, lightly beaten with 1 Tbsp of water
- ▶ 2 tsps olive oil
- ▶ 1/2 cup minced onion
- ▶ 2 cups crushed tomatoes (no salt added)
- ▶ 2 Tbsps minced fresh basil
- ▶ 1/4 tsp salt
- ▶ 1 Tbsp skim-milk mozzarella cheese, grated

1. Preheat oven to 400°F.
2. Spray nonstick baking sheet with non-stick cooking spray.
3. On sheet of wax paper or paper plate, place 4 Tbsps of the Parmesan cheese.
4. One at a time, dip eggplant slices into egg white mixture, turning to coat evenly.
5. Transfer eggplant to prepared baking sheet; spray lightly with nonstick cooking spray.
6. Bake 10 minutes; turn slices over.
7. Bake 10 minutes longer, until golden brown and crispy.
8. Meanwhile, in large nonstick skillet, heat oil; add onion.
9. Cook over medium-high heat, stirring frequently, 5 minutes, until softened.
10. Add tomatoes, basil and salt; bring liquid to a boil.
11. Reduce heat to low; simmer 5 minutes, until mixture is heated through and flavors are blended.
12. Spoon half of the tomato mixture into 11"x7" baking dish; top with eggplant slices, then remaining tomato mixture.
13. Bake, covered, 10 minutes; uncover.
14. Sprinkle evenly with mozzarella, then remaining 1 Tbsp Parmesan cheese; bake, uncovered, 5 minutes, until cheeses are melted.

EGGPLANT & RED PEPPER ROLLS

Serves 4

- 1 medium eggplant
- 2 Tbsps balsamic vinegar
- 1 cup tomato sauce (no salt added)
- 1/4 cup minced fresh mint leaves
- 1/2 tsp salt
- 1/2 tsp grated orange zest
- 1 cup part whole ricotta cheese
- 4 1/2 Tbsps freshly grated Parmesan cheese
- 1 egg
- 1 cup drained roasted red ball peppers, cut into strips

1. Preheat oven to 325°F.
2. Cut eggplant lengthwise into 1/4" slices.
3. Select the 8 widest slices; wrap remaining slices up in plastic wrap and refrigerate for use at another time.
4. In large shallow bowl, with wire whisk, combine vinegar and oil, add eggplant slices, turning to coat.
5. Place eggplant slices in a single layer onto nonstick baking sheer; bake, covered, 20 minutes, until soft.
6. Meanwhile, in 8" square baking pan, combine tomato sauce, 2 Tbsps of the mint, 1/4 tsp of the salt and the zest; set aside.
7. In medium bowl, combine ricotta and Parmesan cheeses, egg, remaining 2 Tbsps mint and remaining 1/4 tsp salt.
8. Spread each eggplant slice with an equal amount of cheese mixture; top each with an equal amount of bell pepper strips.
9. Starting at shortest end, roll eggplant slices to enclose filling; place eggplant rolls, seam-side down, into tomato sauce mixture.
10. Bake, covered, 20 minutes, until heated through.

ZUCCHINI NOODLES

Serves 4

- 2 pints cherry tomatoes
- 2 tsps dried oregano
- 1 tsp dried rosemary
- 2 Tbsps lemon juice
- 1/2 cup olive oil
- 1 tsp salt
- 2 zucchini, cut into very thin strips

1. Place all ingredients except zucchini in blender or food processor.
2. Blend until smooth.
3. Place zucchini noodles in a serving bowl; pour marinara over and toss gently.

GRILLED SUMMER
VEGETABLE PLATTER

Serves 4

- 24 thin asparagus spears
- 1 medium green bell pepper, seeded and quartered
- 1 medium yellow bell pepper, seeded and quartered
- 1 medium red bell pepper, seeded and quartered
- 4 2-oz zucchini, halved lengthwise
- 4 2-oz eggplants, halved lengthwise
- 4 1-oz leeks, halved lengthwise
- 1 Tbsp olive oil
- 6 ounces smoked mozzarella cheese, diced
- Fresh flat-leaf parsley sprigs, to garnish

1. Preheat outdoor barbecue grill according to manufacturer's directions.
2. Spray grill basket with nonstick spray.
3. Brush asparagus, green, yellow and red bell peppers, zucchini, eggplants and leeks on all sides with oil; arrange in prepared grill basket.
4. Grill vegetables over hot coals, turning once, 5-10 minutes, until lightly browned and heated through.
5. Divide grilled vegetables evenly among 4 plates; serve each portion with 1 1/2 ounces cheese.
6. Garnish with parsley.

OVEN FRIES

Serves 12

- 2 lbs baking potatoes, scrubbed, halved lengthwise and cut into 1/2"-wide wedges (about 5 cups)
- Vegetable cooking spray

1. Heat oven to 375°F.
2. Generously coat a large cookie sheet with vegetable cooking spray.
3. Spread potato wedges on prepared cookie sheet in a single layer; lightly coat with cooking spray.
4. Bake 35 to 40 minutes, turning potatoes over once, until lightly browned.

FRENCH-STYLE ZUCCHINI

Serves 4

- 4 large zucchini, sliced
- 4 tomatoes, peeled and diced
- 1 1/2 tsps garlic powder
- 1/4 tsp thyme
- 1/8 tsp basil

1. Mix all ingredients together in a saucepan and simmer slowly until zucchini is just tender (30 to 40 minutes).

VEGETABLE MEDLEY

Serves 6

- ▶ 6 medium-size green onions, sliced thin (3/4 cup)
- ▶ 1/2 cup grated Parmesan cheese
- ▶ 1/4 tsp each dried basil and oregano leaves, crumbled
- ▶ 1/4 tsp garlic powder
- ▶ 24 medium-size fresh asparagus spears (about 1 lb), trimmed
- ▶ 3 medium-size ripe tomatoes (about 1 lb), quartered
- ▶ 2 Tbsps water

1. Mix green onions, Parmesan cheese, basil, oregano and garlic powder in a small bowl until blended.
2. On a 10 to 12-inch round microwave safe serving plate, arrange asparagus spoke-fashion with stem ends toward edge of plate and tips overlapping in center.
3. Place tomato quarters in a circular pattern 2 inches from edge of plate.
4. Sprinkle vegetables with water, then the green onion mixture.
5. Cover with vented paper towel.
6. Microwave on high 5 to 7 minutes, rotating dish 1/2 turn once, until vegetables are hot.
7. Let stand covered 3 to 5 minutes until crisp-tender.
8. Tilt plate and drain off liquid through vent opening.

CARROT COINS

Serves 4

- ▶ 1 lb medium-size carrots, peeled and cut in 1/4" thick rounds (2 1/4 cups)
- ▶ 3 Tbsps water
- ▶ 2 Tbsps finely chopped fresh parsley or 1 Tbsp dried
- ▶ 1 Tbsp butter or margarine
- ▶ 1/4 tsp ground ginger
- ▶ 1/4 tsp dried tarragon leaves, crumbled
- ▶ 1/8 tsp garlic salt
- ▶ 1/8 tsp pepper, preferably white

1. Mix all ingredients in a 1-quart microwave-safe casserole.
2. Cover with lid or vented plastic wrap.
3. Microwave on high 6 to 8 minutes, stirring twice, until carrots are almost tender.
4. Let stand 3 minutes or until tender.

Vegetarian

GRILLED ROOTS & HERBS

 Serves 4

- ▶ 3/4 lb red-skin potatoes cut in 1-inch cubes
- ▶ 4 ounces of favorite mushrooms
- ▶ 1 medium onion, cut into bite-sized pieces
- ▶ 3 Tbsps olive oil
- ▶ 1 tsp salt
- ▶ 4-6 cloves of garlic, chopped
- ▶ 1 Tbsp fresh rosemary, chopped

1. Use at least three sheets of foil about 2 feet long.
2. Overlap two lengths in a criss-cross pattern to strengthen package.
3. Place the potato cubes and other ingredients in the center of the cross pattern and spread ingredients into a square.
4. Wrap package tightly.
5. Wrap the third piece of foil around the other package to seal it.
6. Cook for about 40 minutes or until potatoes are tender.
7. Some of the potatoes, especially around the edges, will be charred from the heat.
8. Be careful of the steam.

CONFETTI COLESLAW

 Serves 8

- ▶ 1/2 cup mayonnaise
- ▶ 2 Tbsp white wine vinegar
- ▶ 1 1/2 tsps Dijon mustard
- ▶ 1/2 tsp salt
- ▶ 1/4 tsp pepper
- ▶ 4 cups shredded green cabbage
- ▶ 2 cups shredded red cabbage
- ▶ 1 1/2 cups shredded carrots
- ▶ 1 each red and yellow bell pepper, cut into thin strips
- ▶ 1/2 cup thinly sliced scallions

1. In a large bowl, whisk together mayonnaise, vinegar, mustard, salt and pepper.
2. Add cabbage, carrots, bells pepper, and scallions, tossing to combine.
3. Refrigerate until ready to serve.

SPANISH GREEN BEANS

 Serves 4

- ▶ 4 cups cooked green beans
- ▶ 1 small onion, chopped
- ▶ 1/4 cup water
- ▶ 1/2 cup tomato puree

1. Brown onion in water until golden.
2. Add rest of ingredients.
3. Mix and heat through.

BAKED BUTTERNUT-SQUASH FRIES

Serves 2

- ▶ 2 lbs butternut squash
- ▶ 1/8 tsp coarse salt
- ▶ Nonstick cooking spray

1. Heat oven to 425°F.
2. Using a sharp knife, slice the ends off a 2 lb butternut squash, then cut it in half width-wise.(Squash can be hard to cut, so you'll need to use some muscle!)
3. Peel squash with a vegetable peeler or knife.
4. Cut the round bottom piece in half lengthwise and remove the seeds.
5. Using a crinkle cutter or a knife, cut squash into spears.
6. Pat fries with a paper towel.
7. Sprinkle evenly with salt.
8. Lay spears on a layer of paper towels and let stand for at least 5 minutes, then pat with a paper towel again.
9. Spray baking sheet with nonstick cooking spray, then place spears on it.
10. Bake for 20 minutes, then carefully flip using a spatula.
11. Bake for 20 minutes longer, until crispy on the outside.

NOT REFRIED BEANS

Serves 4

- ▶ 1 large can pinto beans, rinsed under water to remove the no-nos
- ▶ 1 medium onion, diced
- ▶ 1/2 cup water
- ▶ 1/2 cup tomato puree (unsalted)
- ▶ 1 large pinch of cumin
- ▶ 1/4 tsp garlic powder

1. Mix beans thoroughly.
2. Brown onion in water until golden brown.
3. Mix all ingredients together in medium saucepan.
4. Bake in 350°F oven for 1/2 hour.

Vegetarian

OVEN-DRIED TOMATOES

Serves
4

- ▶ 4 lbs ripe plum tomatoes each cut lengthwise in half
- ▶ 2 Tbsps olive oil
- ▶ Salt and pepper
- ▶ 4 springs fresh thyme, torn
- ▶ 5 cloves of garlic, each cut in half

1. Preheat oven to 300°F.
2. Line two 15 1/2 by 10 1/2 jelly-roll pans with parchment paper.
3. In large bowl, combine tomatoes, olive oil, 1/4 tsp salt and 1/4 tsp freshly ground black pepper.
4. Arrange tomatoes, cut sides up, on prepared pans.
5. Scatter garlic cloves and thyme pieces over tomatoes.
6. Bake 4 hours and 30 minutes or until tomatoes have collapsed and begun to brown, rotating pans between racks halfway through baking.
7. Cool tomatoes on parchment on wire rack.
8. Transfer to self-sealing plastic bag and store in refrigerator up to 1 week.
9. For longer storage, transfer tomatoes to jar with tight-fitting lid.
10. Pour in enough oil to cover by 1/4 inch and cover.

TURBOTIPS:
Can be stored in refrigerator up to 1 month.

SWEET POTATO IN ORANGE CUPS

Serves
4

- ▶ 4 oranges
- ▶ 1/2 tsp cinnamon
- ▶ 2 large sweet potatoes, cooked

1. Cut oranges in halves.
2. Remove fruit and reserve for later.
3. Mash potatoes fine and cut fruit from the oranges into very tiny pieces. And add to potatoes, mix well.
4. Pile the mashed potatoes into the orange shells.
5. Sprinkle with cinnamon.
6. Bake in 350°F oven for 15 minutes or until browned on top.

WINTER CANNELLINI

Serves 6

PARMESAN CASSEROLE

- ▶ 2 Tbsps olive oil
- ▶ 1 cup chopped onion
- ▶ 2 tsps minced garlic
- ▶ 1 tsp dried oregano leaves
- ▶ 1/4 tsp black pepper
- ▶ 2 cans onion-and-garlic flavored diced tomatoes, undrained
- ▶ 14-oz jar roasted red peppers, drained and cut into 1/2" squares
- ▶ 2 cans white cannelloni beans or Great Northern beans, rinsed and drained.
- ▶ 1 tsp dried basil leaves or 1 Tbsp chopped fresh basil
- ▶ 3/4 cup grated Parmesan cheese

1. Heat oil in Dutch oven over medium heat until hot.
2. Add onion, garlic, oregano and black pepper; cook and stir 5 minutes or until onion is tender.
3. Increase heat to high.
4. Add tomatoes with juice and red peppers; cover and bring to a boil.
5. Reduce heat to medium.
6. Stir in beans; cover and simmer 5 minutes, stirring occasionally.
7. Stir in basil and sprinkle with cheese.

FRENCH LENTIL SALAD

Serves 4

- ▶ 1/4 cup chopped walnuts
- ▶ 1 1/2 cups dried lentils, sorted, rinsed and drained
- ▶ 4 green onions, finely chopped
- ▶ 3 Tbsps balsamic vinegar
- ▶ 2 Tbsps chopped fresh parsley
- ▶ 1 Tbsp olive oil
- ▶ 3/4 tsp salt
- ▶ 1/2 tsp dried thyme leaves
- ▶ 1/4 tsp black pepper

1. Preheat oven to 375°F.
2. Spread walnuts in even layer on baking sheet.
3. Bake 5 minutes or until lightly browned.
4. Cook completely on baking sheet; set aside.
5. Combine 2 quarts water and lentils in large saucepan; bring to a boil over high heat.
6. Cover; reduce heat to medium-low.
7. Simmer 30 minutes or until lentils are tender, stirring occasionally.
8. Drain lentils; discard liquid.
9. Combine lentils, onions, vinegar, parsley, oil, salt, thyme and pepper in large bowl.
10. Cover; refrigerate 1 hour or until cool.
11. Serve on lettuce leaves, if desired.
12. Top with toasted walnuts before serving.

ZUCCHINI

Serves 4

- ▶ 4 medium zucchini, unpeeled and chopped
- ▶ 2 Tbsps water
- ▶ 1/2 cup sliced or chopped onions
- ▶ 1/4 tsp oregano
- ▶ Dash pepper
- ▶ 10 small mushrooms (optional)

1. Saute zucchini, onions, (mushrooms) in water for 5-10 minutes, stirring frequently.
2. Add seasonings and mix well.
3. Cover and cook a few minutes more or until the tenderness you desire.

Cooking Variation:
4. Follow directions until after seasonings are added, then transfer to baking dish.
5. Add 8-oz can of tomato sauce, sprinkle 2 Tbsps Parmesan cheese over top.
6. Place in 350°F oven and bake 15 minutes.

LEMON & FENNEL
MARINATED VEGETABLES

Serves 4

- ▶ 1 cup water
- ▶ 2 medium carrots, cut diagonally into 1/2" thick slices
- ▶ 1 cup small whole fresh mushrooms
- ▶ 1 small red or green bell pepper, cut into 3/4" pieces
- ▶ 3 Tbsps lemon juice
- ▶ 1 Tbsp olive oil
- ▶ 1 clove garlic, minced
- ▶ 1/2 tsp fennel seeds, crushed
- ▶ 1/2 tsp dried basil leaves, crushed
- ▶ 1/4 tsp black pepper

1. Bring water to a boil in small saucepan.
2. Add carrots; return to a boil.
3. Reduce heat to medium-low, cover and simmer about 5 minutes or until carrots are crisp-tender.
4. Drain and cool.
5. Place carrots, mushrooms and bell pepper in large resealable plastic food storage bag.
6. Combine lemon juice, sugar, oil, garlic, fennel seeds, basil and black pepper in small bowl.
7. Pour over vegetables.
8. Close bag securely; turn to coat.
9. Marinate in refrigerator 8 to 24 hours, turning occasionally.
10. Drain vegetables; discard marinade.
11. Place vegetables in serving dish.
12. Serve with toothpicks.

SPAGHETTI SQUASH
WITH BLACK BEANS

Serves
4

▶ 1 spaghetti squash (about 2 lbs)
▶ 2 zucchini, cut lengthwise into 1/4" thick slices
▶ Nonstick cooking spray
▶ 2 cups chopped seeded tomatoes
▶ 1 can black beans, rinsed and drained
▶ 2 Tbsps chopped fresh basil
▶ 2 Tbsps olive oil
▶ 2 Tbsps red wine vinegar
▶ 1 large clove garlic, minced
▶ 1/2 tsp salt

1. Pierce spaghetti squash in several places with fork.
2. Wrap in large piece of heavy-duty foil, using drugstore wrap technique.
3. Grill squash on covered grill over medium coals 45 minutes to 1 hour or until easily depressed with back of long-handled spoon, turning a quarter turn every 15 minutes.
4. Remove squash from grill and let stand in foil 10 to 15 minutes.
5. Meanwhile, spray both sides of zucchini slices with cooking spray.
6. Grill on uncovered grill over medium coals 4 minutes or until tender, turning once.
7. Remove spaghetti squash from foil and cut in half; scoop out seeds.
8. With two forks, comb strands of pulp from each half and place in large salad bowl.
9. Add tomatoes, beans zucchini and basil.
10. Combine olive oil, vinegar, garlic and salt in small bowl; mix thoroughly.
11. Add to vegetables and toss gently to combine.

Wrap Technique:
1. Place food in the center of an oblong piece of heavy-duty foil, leaving at least a two-inch border around the food.
2. Bring the two oblong sides together above the food; fold down in a series of locked folds, allowing for heat circulation and expansion.
3. Fold short ends up and over again.
4. Press folds firmly to seal the foil pocket.

Vegetarian

MIDDLE EASTERN GRILLED
VEGETABLE WRAPS

Serves
4

- ▶ 1 large eggplant (about 1 lb), cut crosswise into 3/8" slices
- ▶ Nonstick cooking spray
- ▶ 3/4 lb large mushrooms
- ▶ 1 red bell pepper, quartered
- ▶ 1 green bell pepper, quartered
- ▶ 2 green onions, sliced
- ▶ 1/4 cup fresh lemon juice
- ▶ 1/8 tsp black pepper
- ▶ 8 (5") low carb tortillas (net 5 carb max each)
- ▶ 1/2 cup hummus (chickpea spread)
- ▶ 1/3 cup lightly packed fresh cilantro
- ▶ 12 large fresh basil leaves
- ▶ 12 large fresh mint leaves

1. Prepare grill for direct cooking.
2. Lightly spray eggplant with cooking spray.
3. If mushrooms are small, thread onto skewers.
4. Grill peppers, skin-side down, over hot coals until blackened.
5. Place in paper bag; seal.
6. Steam 5 minutes; remove skin.
7. Grill eggplant and mushrooms, covered, over medium coals about 2 minutes on each side or until tender and lightly browned.
8. Cut eggplant and peppers into 1/2 inch strips; cut mushrooms into quarters.
9. Combine grilled vegetables, onions, lemon juice and black pepper in medium bowl.
10. Grill tortillas on both sides about 1 minute or until warmed.
11. Spoon 1/4 of hummus, 1/4 of herbs and 1/4 of vegetables down center of each tortilla.
12. Roll to enclose filling; serve immediately.
13. Makes 4 servings of 2 each or 8 servings as a perfect complement to a hearty vegetable salad.

PARISIAN CARROTS

Serves
4

- ▶ 2 cup cooked carrots, sliced
- ▶ 1 small onion, minced
- ▶ 1 tsp parsley, minced
- ▶ Pepper to taste
- ▶ 1/2 cup water

1. Brown onion in water until golden.
2. Add carrots and pepper.
3. Heat thoroughly.
4. Before serving, sprinkle with parsley.

BROCCOLI & CAULIFLOWER STIR-FRY Serves 2

- ▶ 2 dry-pack sun-dried tomatoes
- ▶ 1 Tbsp + 1 tsp reduced-sodium soy sauce
- ▶ 1 Tbsp rice wine vinegar
- ▶ 1 tsp dark sesame oil
- ▶ 1/8 tsp red pepper flakes
- ▶ 2 1/4 tsps canola oil
- ▶ 1 clove garlic, finely chopped
- ▶ 2 cups cauliflower florets
- ▶ 2 cups broccoli florets
- ▶ 1/3 cup thinly sliced red or green bell pepper

1. Place tomatoes in small bowl; cover with boiling water.
2. Let stand 5 minutes.
3. Drain; coarsely chop.
4. Meanwhile, blend soy sauce, vinegar, sesame oil and red pepper flakes in small bowl.
5. Heat vegetable oil in wok or large non-stick skillet over medium heat until hot.
6. Add garlic; stir-fry 30 seconds.
7. Add cauliflower and broccoli; stir-fry 1 minute or until vegetables are crisp-tender.
8. Add soy sauce mixture; cook and stir until heated through.
9. Serve immediately.

GRILLED PORTOBELLO Serves 4

MUSHROOM STACKS

- ▶ 1 large Portobello mushroom, cleaned and stem removed
- ▶ 1/4 medium green bell pepper, halved
- ▶ 1 thin slice red onion
- ▶ 2 Tbsps balsamic dressing
- ▶ 2 Tbsps mozzarella cheese slice

1. Brush mushroom, bell pepper and onion with dressing.
2. Place vegetables over medium-hot coals and grill for 2 minutes.
3. Turn vegetables over; brush with dressing.
4. Grill 2 minutes or until vegetables are tender.
5. Remove bell pepper and onion from grill.
6. Turn mushroom top side up; brush with any remaining dressing and cover with cheese, if desired.
7. Grill 1 minute or until cheese is melted.
8. Cut pepper into strips.
9. Top mushroom with pepper strips and onion slice.

Vegetarian

COLD LEEKS NICOISE

Serves
4

- ▶ 3-4 large ripe tomatoes
- ▶ 1/4 cup olive oil
- ▶ 2 garlic cloves, minced
- ▶ Fresh parsley
- ▶ 2-3 Tbsps minced fresh basil or 1 tsp dried
- ▶ 1 bay leaf
- ▶ 1/2 tsp thyme
- ▶ Salt and freshly ground pepper
- ▶ 12 leeks, 1/2 to 3/4" thick, trimmed of all but 2 inches of greens
- ▶ 6 black Greek olives (garnish)

1. Immerse tomatoes in boiling water until skins begin to loosen, about 30 seconds.
2. Peel, quarter and set aside.
3. Heat oil in large skillet over low heat.
4. Add garlic and parsley and cook 1 minute.
5. Add tomatoes, basil, bay leaf, thyme and salt and pepper to taste.
6. Cover and cook 5 minutes.
7. With sharp knife, cut small cross into green part of leeks.
8. Rinse thoroughly under cold running water.
9. Add to skillet (they should fit snugly in single layer), cover and braise until tender, about 10 minutes, testing occasionally with sharp knife and removing leeks as they are cooked.
10. Drain well.
11. Arrange on serving platter.
12. Increase heat and cook sauce until thickened; remove bay leaf.
13. Spoon sauce over leeks and garnish with olives.
14. Let stand until slightly cooled before serving.

ITALIAN ASPARAGUS

Serves
4

- ▶ 1 lb fresh cooked asparagus
- ▶ 1 medium can of prepared tomato paste (low or no salt is best)
- ▶ 2 Tbsp chopped green onions
- ▶ 1/8 tsp dried oregano leaves
- ▶ 1/8 dried thyme leaves
- ▶ Fresh ground black pepper to taste
- ▶ 2 Tbsps freshly grated Parmesan cheese

1. While asparagus is cooking, combine all ingredients in a bowl, except the cheese.
2. Mix well.
3. Arrange the cooked asparagus on a serving platter.
4. Spoon tomato mixture over asparagus, sprinkle with the cheese.

GREEN BEANS & SUN-DRIED TOMATOES

Serves 6

- ► 1 lb green beans, trimmed and cut into 1" pieces
- ► 2 Tbsps extra-virgin olive oil
- ► 2 leeks, white and 1" green, thinly sliced
- ► 2 garlic cloves, finely chopped
- ► 1/2 cup white wine
- ► 2 Tbsps sun-dried tomatoes in oil, drained and coarsely chopped
- ► 2 tsps chopped fresh thyme or 3/4 tsp dried
- ► Salt and pepper
- ► 4 ounces soft goat cheese, crumbled

1. Cook green beans in lightly salted boiling water in a large saucepan until crisp-tender, about 5 minutes.
2. Drain and cool.
3. Heat oil in large skillet over medium-high heat.
4. Add leeks and cook 5 minutes, until softened; add garlic and cook 1 minute more.
5. Add wine, tomatoes and thyme.
6. Increase heat to high and bring to a boil.
7. Boil 2 minutes, until most of the wine evaporates.
8. Mix in green beans.
9. Season to taste with salt and pepper.
10. Transfer to a bowl; gently stir in goat cheese.
11. Serve immediately.

ZUCCHINI & CORN SALAD

Serves 6

- ► 1 Tbsp olive oil
- ► 1 small onion, chopped
- ► 1 jalapeno pepper, chopped
- ► 2 lbs zucchini, thinly sliced into 1/2 inch rounds
- ► 1/2 cup corn kernels
- ► 3/4 tsp salt
- ► 1/2 tsp chili powder
- ► 3 to 4 Tbsps water

1. In a large skillet over medium heat, heat oil until it shimmers.
2. Add onion and pepper.
3. Cook 1 to 2 minutes, stirring, until onion is softened.
4. Add zucchini, corn, and chili powder; mix well.
5. Cook 5 minutes or until zucchini is softened.
6. Add 3 to 4 Tbsps water, cover and cook 2 minutes more, until zucchini is soft and tender.

Vegetarian

ASPARAGUS & MUSTARD VINAIGRETTE

Serves 4

- ▶ 1 lb fresh asparagus, trimmed
- ▶ 1/4 small onion, very finely chopped
- ▶ 2 Tbsps white wine vinegar
- ▶ 1 tsp Dijon mustard
- ▶ 1/2 packet sugar substitute, if desired
- ▶ 1/2 tsp salt
- ▶ 1/4 tsp pepper
- ▶ 1/4 cup olive oil
- ▶ 4 cups baby greens (mesclun)
- ▶ 1/4 cup toasted walnuts or almonds

1. Steam asparagus until crisp-tender.
2. Drain, pat dry with paper towels.
3. Set aside.
4. Combine onion, vinegar, mustard, sugar substitute, salt and pepper in a mixing bowl.
5. Gradually whisk in oil.
6. Divide salad mix on plates; arrange asparagus on top and drizzle with vinaigrette.
7. Sprinkle with nuts.

BROILED EGGPLANT

Serves 2

- ▶ 1 medium eggplant
- ▶ 2 cloves garlic, minced
- ▶ 1 tsp grated onion
- ▶ 1/4 tsp sea salt
- ▶ 1/4 cup olive oil or melted butter

1. Peel the eggplant.
2. It is not necessary to drain it.
3. Slice eggplant into 1/2" slices crosswise.
4. Place on a greased baking sheet and brush with oil, season with garlic, onion and salt.
5. Save enough oil to baste eggplant twice more.
6. Broil about 5 inches from heat source about 5 minutes, basting once with oil.
7. Using a pancake turner, turn eggplant slices over.
8. Brush with remaining oil mixture.
9. Broil about 2 minutes longer or until tender.
10. Serve plain or with tomato sauce.
11. Sprinkle with grated cheese if desired.

SAUTEED EGGPLANT

Serves 4

- ▶ 1 eggplant
- ▶ 1 egg, beaten
- ▶ 1 Tbsp chopped fresh parsley
- ▶ 2 Tbsp olive oil
- ▶ 1/2 tsp dried oregano or 1/4 tsp dried basil
- ▶ 1 onion sliced
- ▶ 1 clove garlic, minced

1. Peel eggplant.
2. Slice into 1/2" pieces crosswise.
3. Dip in beaten egg seasoned with parsley and basil or oregano.
4. Saute onion and garlic until onion is translucent.
5. When oil is hot, add eggplant slices.
6. Saute about 4 minutes on a side or until tender.
7. Add oil, if needed.
8. Serve hot.

EGGPLANT WITH ZUCCHINI

Serves 4

- ▶ 2 medium eggplants
- ▶ 2 large zucchini
- ▶ 4 large onions, sliced
- ▶ 2 green peppers, cut in strips (seeds removed)
- ▶ 2 tomatoes, cut in eighths
- ▶ 1 can mushrooms, drained, butter (if any) rinsed off
- ▶ 2 Tbsps minced parsley
- ▶ 1 1/2 tsps garlic salt
- ▶ 1/2 tsp oregano
- ▶ 1/2 tsp paprika

1. Cut eggplants into 1/2" slices (do not peel).
2. Scrub zucchini, remove ends, and cut into 1/2" slices (do not peel).
3. Cook onions and peppers together in no-stick skillet until nearly soft (about 10 minutes); turn up heat and brown.
4. Remove.
5. Cook eggplant, zucchini, tomatoes, mushrooms and parsley together, with seasonings, until just tender.
6. Add onions and peppers, mix and serve hot or cold.
7. Add more seasoning if desired.

Vegetarian

STUFFED EGGPLANT

Serves 4

- 2 lbs eggplant
- 4 brazil nuts or 8 walnuts chopped
- 1 beaten egg
- 1/4 cup chopped mushrooms
- 1 Tbsp butter, diced
- 1/2 cup chicken broth
- 1 tsp minced onion
- 1/2 tsp sea salt
- 1/4 tsp ground black pepper
- 1 Tbsp chopped parsley

1. Slice the top off the eggplant, right under the leafy green cap.
2. Follow the lines of the cap to create a scalloped edge.
3. Save the top for a lid.
4. Scoop out the pulp, leaving a 1/2" shell.
5. Add the pulp to a small quantity of boiling water or stock.
6. Cook until tender and drain.
7. In a large bowl, combine the cooked pulp with the remainder of the ingredients.
8. Preheat oven to 400°F.
9. Fill the shell.
10. Cover with leaf lid.
11. Bake the eggplant until filling is heated (about 45 minutes to an hour).
12. Alternate recipe: Bring kettle of water to a boil.
13. Drop eggplant and boil 15 minutes covered.
14. Remove from water.
15. Drain and slice eggplant in half lengthwise.
16. Carefully remove pulp, leaving a 1/2"-thick shell.
17. Chop the eggplant pulp and add it to the stuffing ingredients above.
18. Fill each eggplant shell half with the stuffing.
19. Place on a greased baking pan.
20. Brush the tops with additional oil and bake at 350°F, about 45 minutes.
21. Serve as is or top with tomato sauce and grated Parmesan or Romano cheese.

VEGETABLE–NUT CASSEROLE

 Serves 4

- ▶ 1/4 medium green cabbage, coarsely chopped
- ▶ 1/4 medium red cabbage, coarsely chopped
- ▶ 1/2 small cauliflower, broken into flowerets
- ▶ 2 medium carrots, thinly sliced
- ▶ 1 large pepper, preferably red, cored and diced
- ▶ 2 medium Jerusalem artichokes, halved and sliced
- ▶ 6 to 8 ounces ground seeds or nuts (optional)

1. Preheat oven to 175°F.
2. Wash all the vegetables, and place them in a large casserole dish and mix the ingredients well.
3. Cover the dish, and place it in the oven.
4. Cook the casserole until it is just tender.
5. This will take about 30 minutes, slightly longer if a deep dish is used.
6. Serve hot.

EGGPLANT PARMIGIANA #2

 Serves 4

- ▶ 2 medium eggplants
- ▶ 8 ounces cashews
- ▶ 3 medium tomatoes
- ▶ 2 stalks celery
- ▶ 1 red (or green) bell pepper

1. Peel the eggplants and slice them 3/4"-thick.
2. Grind the cashews in a blender or nut and seed grinder.
3. Place the ground mix in a bowl, and set it aside.
4. Make fresh tomato sauce or marinara sauce.
5. Slice the tomatoes in circular slices, and dice the celery and bell pepper.
6. Place the eggplant slices in a 9 x 13" casserole dish.
7. Layer on the sliced tomatoes, diced celery and bell pepper and ground cashews.
8. Add another layer of sliced veggies and ground cashews.
9. Cover the parmigiana with foil, and bake at 375°F for 30 minutes.
10. Remove foil, and broil the parmigiana about 5 minutes.

STUFFED EGGPLANT
ITALIAN STYLE

Serves 4

- 2 medium eggplants
- 1 lb fresh mushrooms, sliced, (or 2 6-oz cans mushrooms, drained, butter, rinsed)
- 1 medium onion, chopped
- 2 tsps chopped parsley
- 2 medium tomatoes, cut in eighths
- 1 tsp garlic salt
- 1/2 tsp oregano paprika

1. Wash eggplants and bake in 350°F oven until tender to the touch (about 20 minutes).
2. Remove from oven, cut in halves lengthwise, and carefully remove pulp, reserving shells.
3. Combine pulp with all other ingredients except paprika, and simmer gently on top of stove until tomatoes and mushrooms are soft.
4. Heap mixture into eggplant shells and return to oven for 5 minutes.
5. Sprinkle paprika over tops before serving (try nutmeg if you're adventurous).

SUPER HIGHWAY EGGPLANT

Serves 4

- 2 large firm eggplants, with skin
- Paprika
- 1 tsp parsley flakes
- 3/4 tsp garlic salt
- 1/2 tsp oregano
- 1/8 tsp lemon pepper marinade
- 3 Tbsps tomato juice

1. Wash eggplant, remove ends, and cut lengthwise into 3/4" slices.
2. Mix seasonings together and rub well on both sides of eggplant slices.
3. Cover bottom of large shallow broiler pan with tomato juice and set eggplant slices in it.
4. Broil 4" from heat in preheated broiler until first side is very brown.
5. Turn with spatula, and broil other side until tender and brown (about 10 minutes).
6. If not cooked through, lower heat and broil a little longer.

EGGPLANT CHIPS

Serves
4

- ▶ 1 eggplant
- ▶ Olive oil spray

1. Turn oven on to 400°F.
2. Wash and dry eggplant.
3. Slice diameter-wise into 1/2" discs.
4. Spray a large 9 x 13" baking pan with olive oil.
5. Lay disks onto pan and lightly spray with olive oil spray again.
6. Bake approximately 10-15 minutes, checking bottom side of eggplant.
7. When browned, flip and cook longer until browned.
8. Be careful not to burn.
9. Serve hot either plain or with a sugar-free tomato sauce for dipping.

EGGPLANT MÉLANGE

Serves
4

- ▶ 1 medium eggplant, peeled and cubed
- ▶ 1 cup chopped onion
- ▶ 1/2 Tbsp olive oil
- ▶ 2 strips green pepper, cut up
- ▶ 1 cup chopped tomatoes (fresh or canned)
- ▶ 1/2 tsp salt
- ▶ 1/4 tsp ground pepper
- ▶ 1/4 tsp oregano

1. Sauté onions in oil.
2. Add green pepper and eggplant; sauté, stirring frequently.
3. Combine tomatoes, salt, pepper and oregano with above.
4. Cook covered for 30 minutes.
5. Add a little water if liquid cooks away.

HERBED GRILLED TOMATOES

Serves
4

- ▶ 4 medium tomatoes
- ▶ 1 Tbsp finely chopped parsley
- ▶ 1/4 tsp tarragon
- ▶ 1/4 tsp salt
- ▶ 1/8 tsp black pepper

1. Cut tomatoes in half across.
2. Mix all other ingredients thoroughly, and sprinkle mixture over cut surfaces of tomatoes in a broiler pan.
3. Place pan about 5" from heat, and broil about 10 minutes, or until tomatoes are tender to the fork.

Vegetarian

ITALIAN ZUCCHINI WITH ONIONS

Serves 4

- 8 medium zucchini, cut in thin slices
- 1 large onion, minced
- 1 clove garlic, crushed
- 4 Tbsps low, no-sodium chicken bouillon
- 2 medium tomatoes, cut in small pieces
- 1 green pepper, minced
- 1 tsp seasoned salt
- 1/4 tsp oregano
- Black pepper

1. Brown onion with garlic in bouillon, using large no-stick skillet (about 5 minutes).
2. Add zucchini slices and cook over medium heat until zucchini slices are golden, turning occasionally with spatula (about 8 minutes).
3. Add tomatoes, green pepper, salt, oregano and black pepper to the zucchini, cover and simmer 20 minutes, stirring once or twice.

HOT CAULIFLOWER

Serves 2

- 2 cups cauliflower, washed and divided into flowerets
- 2 Tbsps olive oil
- 2 cloves garlic
- 2 Tbsps onion
- 1 tsp paprika
- 2 tsps vinegar
- 2 Tbsps water from cauliflower
- 1/4 tsp salt or to taste

1. Boil cauliflower in just enough water to cover for 10 to 15 minutes until tender.
2. In small skillet heat oil and sauté garlic until brown.
3. Remove garlic.
4. Add onion and sauté until soft and transparent.
5. Remove from heat.
6. Add paprika, vinegar, water and salt.
7. Mix well and heat.
8. Pour over drained cauliflower.
9. Cover and simmer for 10 minutes.

HERBED GRILLED TOMATOES #2

Serves 4

- 2 large ripe tomatoes
- 1/2 cup freshly grated Parmesan cheese

1. Preheat oven to 375°F or light a grill.
2. Cut a thin slice off the stem and base ends of the tomatoes, then slice them in half crosswise.
3. Bake on greased baking sheet or grill the tomatoes until soft.
4. Sprinkle with Parmesan cheese, then broil until the cheese melts.

ZUCCHINI TREAT

Serves 4

- ▶ 4 large or 6 small zucchini (or yellow crookneck squash)
- ▶ 1/4 tsp salt
- ▶ 2 medium onions, sliced
- ▶ 4 egg tomatoes, or 3 medium tomatoes, sliced
- ▶ Black pepper

1. Scrub zucchini, cut off ends, and split in halves lengthwise.
2. Arrange in baking dish, open side up, and sprinkle with salt.
3. Distribute sliced onions over zucchini halves; salt.
4. Place slices of tomatoes over onions; sprinkle with salt and pepper.
5. Bake in 350°F preheated oven until vegetables are tender.

ZESTY ZUCCHINI

Serves 4

- ▶ 6 small washed zucchini sliced 1/8" thick
- ▶ 4 cleaned and sliced mushrooms
- ▶ 3 Tbsps olive oil
- ▶ 3 Tbsps diced onion
- ▶ 1/2 cup grated Parmesan cheese
- ▶ 1/2 can tomato sauce
- ▶ 1 clove garlic, minced

1. Preheat oven to 350°F.
2. Cut off ends.
3. Heat olive oil in skillet.
4. Add zucchini, mushrooms and onion.
5. Cover and cook over low heat for 15 minutes, stirring occasionally.
6. Place zucchini mixture in baking dish.
7. Add 1/2 Parmesan cheese, tomato sauce, and garlic.
8. Stir with fork.
9. Sprinkle with remaining cheese.
10. Bake for 30 minutes.

ZUCCHINI ON THE GRILL

Serves 4

- ▶ Medium-sized zucchini sliced 1/4" thick
- ▶ Olive oil
- ▶ Pepper
- ▶ Seasoning salt
- ▶ Garlic powder

1. Wash but do not peel zucchini.
2. Brush both sides with olive oil.
3. Gently sprinkle both sides with pepper, seasoning salt and garlic powder.
4. Place on grill, turning frequently.
5. Each side takes about 3 minutes, but watch carefully so as not to burn them.

Vegetarian

GREEN BEANS OREGANO

Serves
4

- ▶ 2 Tbsps oil
- ▶ 2 Tbsps chopped onion
- ▶ 1 clove garlic
- ▶ 8-oz can sugar-free, low or no-sodium tomato sauce
- ▶ 1/4 cup water
- ▶ 1/4 tsp oregano
- ▶ 9-oz package frozen green beans or 1 lb fresh washed green beans

1. Lightly brown onion in hot oil.
2. Add garlic and sauté for 2 minutes.
3. Add tomato sauce, water, and oregano.
4. Simmer for 10 minutes.
5. Prepare green beans according to directions on package.
6. In last 5 minutes add tomato sauce mixture, cover, and simmer for 10 minutes.

If using fresh beans:

7. Place in saucepan.
8. Add tomato sauce mixture after simmering for 5 minutes.
9. Cover and cook beans slowly for 40 minutes or until tender, and add a little water if necessary.

GRILLED VEGETABLES

Serves
2

- ▶ 4 cups sliced fresh summer squash and/or zucchini
- ▶ 4 cups sliced sweet onions, such as Vidalia
- ▶ 4 Tbsps olive or melted butter
  - ▶ 2 Tbsps red wine vinegar
  - ▶ Salt and pepper to taste

1. Toss all ingredients in a large bowl until vegetables are evenly coated with oil and vinegar.
2. Spray a grill basket with nonstick cooking spray.
3. Place on grill rack over hot coals.
4. Pour vegetables into basket, replace grill lid, and cook 15-25 minutes, until vegetables reach desired doneness, stirring every 4-5 minutes.

TURBOTIPS:
For variety, add or substitute your favorite garden vegetables, especially those that are in season.

PARMESAN-BAKED ASPARAGUS

Serves 4

- ▶ 1 lb fresh asparagus
- ▶ 2 tsps olive oil
- ▶ 1/4 tsp salt
- ▶ 1/4 tsp pepper
- ▶ 1/4 cup grated Parmesan cheese

1. Preheat oven to 425°F.
2. Place asparagus (trimmed and washed) on a non-stick baking sheet.
3. Drizzle with olive oil and sprinkle with salt and pepper.
4. Toss to coat.
5. Bake 10 minutes.
6. Toss again.
7. Sprinkle with cheese.
8. Return to oven and bake until the cheese melts, about 5 minutes longer.
9. Variations: After baking for 10 minutes and tossing again, place asparagus on serving plate and drizzle with 2-3 Tbsps balsamic vinegar.

Grilled Variation:
1. After trimming and washing asparagus, brush stalks with oil.
2. Place on preheated grill, direct medium, for 6-8 minutes or until the stem end jags tender.
3. Turn stalks every 2-3 minutes, being careful not to overcook it. (Remember, the asparagus will continue to cook after leaving the grill.) Arrange on platter.
4. Sprinkle with cheese.

VEGETABLE MEDLEY

Serves 4

- ▶ 1 1/2 cups raw broccoli, cut up
- ▶ 1 1/2 cups raw zucchini, cut up
- ▶ 1/2 cup raw sweet red pepper, cut up
- ▶ 1/4 cup raw onion, cut up
- ▶ 2 Tbsps butter
- ▶ 2 tsps chicken broth

1. Combine ingredients in a microwave-safe dish.
2. Cover and microwave on High for 4 minutes.
3. Let stand for 5 minutes before serving.
4. For variety, substitute other raw vegetables that you prefer.

Vegetarian

CHEESY ZUCCHINI TREAT

Serves 4

- ▶ 2 medium zucchini, divided
- ▶ 1 large sweet or Vidalia onion, divided
- ▶ 2 medium tomatoes, divided
- ▶ 2 green peppers, divided
- ▶ 6 slices cheese of your choice
- ▶ Salt and pepper, optional

1. Slice zucchini diagonally into 1/8"-thick slices.
2. Slice onion and tomatoes into 1/8"-thick slices.
3. Seed and slice green peppers into strips.
4. Layer half the ingredients into a lightly greased 2-quart shallow baking dish.
5. Repeat the layers, using all remaining ingredients.
6. Sprinkle with salt and pepper if you wish.
7. Cover tightly and bake at 375°F for 45 minutes.
8. Layer cheese on top.
9. Bake uncovered 2-5 more minutes or until cheese has melted.

CHOPPED ESCAROLE

Serves 4

- ▶ 2 1/2 lbs escarole
- ▶ 1 clove garlic, chopped
- ▶ 1/2 tsp lemon pepper marinade
- ▶ Water to cover

1. Trim escarole and wash carefully.
2. Place in large saucepan, sprinkle with seasonings, cover with water and boil for 20 to 30 minutes until tender.
3. Drain in colander and squeeze out water.
4. Chop.
5. Sprinkle lightly with salt and pepper, if you wish.

LEMONED ASPARAGUS

Serves 4

- ▶ 2 dozen medium asparagus stalks
- ▶ Water
- ▶ 1 tsp salt
- ▶ 1 Tbsp butter, melted
- ▶ 2 Tbsps lemon juice
- ▶ Seasoned salt
- ▶ Paprika

1. Cut off any tough ends from asparagus stalks and wash thoroughly.
2. In deep saucepan with a close-fitting cover, place about 2 inches of water, add 1 tsp salt, bring to boil.
3. Tie asparagus in a bunch, stand with tips at top in boiling water.
4. Cover, boil rapidly for 15 to 20 minutes until tender (steam will cook the tips).
5. Drain, untie and place asparagus on warmed serving plate.
6. Spoon on mixture of melted margarine, lemon juice and seasoned salt.
7. Sprinkle on paprika to taste.

RATATOUILLE

Serves 4

- ▶ 2 zucchini
- ▶ 1 small eggplant
- ▶ 5 ripe plum tomatoes, chopped
- ▶ 3 cloves garlic, minced
- ▶ 1 large onion, sliced thinly
- ▶ 1/4 cup olive oil
- ▶ 1/2 cup sliced black olives
- ▶ 2 green peppers, seeded and cut in strips
- ▶ 1/2 tsp dried oregano or 1/4 tsp dried basil
- ▶ 1/4 tsp sea salt
- ▶ Black pepper to taste
- ▶ 1 Tbsp capers

1. Slice the zucchini.
2. Peel and cube the eggplant.
3. Drain for 1 hour (see Eggplant TurboTip).
4. Prepare the tomatoes.
5. Use a large skillet with a cover to sautee garlic and onion in the olive oil until onion is translucent.
6. Add the zucchini, eggplant cubes, olives and green pepper to the skillet.
7. Season with basil or oregano, salt and pepper.
8. Cover and cook slowly for an hour.
9. Add the tomatoes.
10. Simmer uncovered until the mixture has thickened.
11. Add capers during the last 15 minutes of cooking.

TURBOTIPS:
Delicious hot as a vegetable side dish or cold as an appetizer.

Eggs

PERFECT BOILED EGGS

1. Place the eggs in a saucepan large enough to hold them in a single layer.
2. Cover the eggs with cold water, coming about an inch above the eggs.
3. Place the pan on the heat and bring to a boil.
4. Just when the water hits a full boil, completely remove the pan from the heat and slap on the lid.
5. Let the eggs sit, covered, for 15 minutes.
6. Then drain immediately, cool under running cold water and get ready to peel.
7. The faster you cool the eggs, the less likely you are to face green yolks.
8. You can even plunge them into a bowl of ice water.

STORAGE

1. Unpeeled hard-cooked eggs will keep in the refrigerator for one week.
2. Seal them in a plastic bag to keep them from picking up off flavors or odors (egg shells are porous), and you can devil at a moment's notice. To peel the egg shells from hard-boiled eggs, rinse them quickly under cold water immediately after boiling.
3. For safety, throw away cracked eggs.
4. Do not use them because they may contain bacteria.

> TURBOTIPS:
> For a perfectly centered egg yolk, put the carton of eggs on its side the night before cooking.

NOT SURE IF AN EGG IS FRESH?

1. Place it in a large bowl of cold water.
2. If it floats, don't use it.

BASIC OMELETTE

Serves 2

- ▶ 4 large eggs
- ▶ 1/8 tsp salt
- ▶ 1/8 tsp black pepper

1. In a small bowl, beat the eggs, salt and pepper with a fork until blended.

2. In a non-stick 8" skillet or omelette pan, pour in the egg mixture and stir briskly.

3. Cook the eggs over low heat; lift the edges of the omelette and shake the pan several times during cooking to keep the eggs from sticking.

4. When the eggs are firm and the bottom is light brown, fold the omelette over and transfer it to a heated plate.

CHEDDAR & HAM OMELLETE

Serves 2

- ▶ 4 large eggs
- ▶ 1/8 tsp salt
- ▶ 1/8 tsp black pepper
- ▶ 3/4 cup diced ham
- ▶ 3/4 cup grated sharp cheddar cheese

1. In a small bowl, beat the eggs, salt and pepper with a fork until blended.

2. In an 8" non-stick skillet or omelette pan, add the egg mixture and ham, stirring briskly.

3. Cook the eggs over low heat; lift the edges of the omelette and shake the pan several times during cooking to keep the eggs from sticking.

4. When the eggs are almost set, fold in the cheese.

5. Cook until the bottom forms a golden crust, then fold the omelette over and transfer it to a heated plate.

Eggs

POACHED EGGS

Serves
4

- ▶ 1 1/2 quarts water
- ▶ 2 cups vinegar
- ▶ 8 large eggs

1. Bring the water and vinegar to a boil in a large saucepan.
2. Crack the eggs one at a time and drop them gently into the boiling water, being careful not to break the yolks.
3. Simmer for 3 to 4 minutes, moving the eggs several times with a spoon to cook them evenly.
4. When firm, remove the eggs from the water with a slotted spoon and place in a pan filled with cold water until serving.

ITALIAN CHEESE FRITTATA

Serves
8

- ▶ 1 pat of butter
- ▶ 8 large eggs, beaten
- ▶ 3/4 cup chopped onion
- ▶ 3/4 cup chopped green pepper
- ▶ 1/4 cup grated sharp cheddar cheese
- ▶ 1/4 tsp salt
- ▶ 1/4 tsp black pepper
- ▶ 1/4 tsp dried oregano
- ▶ 1/4 tsp dried basil
- ▶ Grated Parmesan cheese

1. In a large bowl, mix together all the ingredients except Parmesan cheese.
2. Melt pad of butter in large hot non-stick skillet.
3. Pour in mixture.
4. Turn heat to medium-low, cover and cook 30 minutes until mixture is solid.
5. Invert onto platter and cut into serving size portions.
6. Sprinkle with Parmesan cheese and serve immediately.

ASPARAGUS FRITTATA

Serves 4

- 24 asparagus spears, cut into 1" pieces
- 8 eggs
- 2 1/4 ounces freshly grated Parmesan cheese
- 2 Tbsps minced fresh chives
- 1/4 tsp salt
- 1/4 tsp freshly ground black pepper
- 1 Tbsp + 1 tsp butter

1. Preheat oven to 350°F
2. In large pot of boiling water, cook asparagus 2 minutes, until just tender.
3. Drain, discarding liquid; rinse with cold water.
4. Drain again; set aside.
5. In large bowl, with wire whisk, combine egg white, eggs, cheese, chives, salt and pepper.
6. In large cast-iron skillet, heat butter; add asparagus.
7. Cook over medium-high heat, stirring constantly, until cooked; reduce heat to low.
8. Pour egg mixture into skillet; stir quickly to combine.
9. Cook 5 minutes, until edges are set.
10. Transfer skillet to oven; bake 10 minutes until egg mixture is firm.
11. Cut into 4 wedges.

HUEVOS RANCHEROS

Serves 4

- 2 cups chopped tomatoes
- 8 ounces drained cooked black beans
- 1/2 cup minced red onion
- 1/2 cup thawed frozen corn kernels
- 1/2 cup minced fresh cilantro
- 1 tsp chopped reveined seeded jalapeno pepper (wear gloves to prevent irritation)
- 1/2 tsp salt
- 4 eggs

1. In large skillet, combine tomatoes, beans, onion, corn, cilantro, pepper and salt; bring liquid to a boil.
2. Reduce heat to low; simmer, covered, 10 minutes, until flavors are blended and mixture is heated through.
3. Meanwhile, in another large skillet, poach eggs.
4. Divide tomato mixture evenly into 4 equal portions.
5. Top each portion of tomato mixture with 1 poached egg.

Eggs

ROASTED ASPARAGUS WITH EGGS

Serves 4

- ▶ 48 asparagus spears
- ▶ 3 1/4 ounces freshly grated Parmesan cheese
- ▶ 1 Tbsp + 1 tsp melted butter
- ▶ 5 eggs
- ▶ 1/4 cup minced fresh basil
- ▶ 1/4 cup minced fresh chives
- ▶ 1 cup diced plum tomatoes
- ▶ Pinch salt

1. Preheat oven to 400°F.
2. In large pot of boiling water, cook asparagus 2 minutes, until bright green and just tender.
3. Drain, discarding liquid; transfer to prepared baking pan.
4. Sprinkle asparagus with 3 ounces of the cheese; drizzle evenly with 2 tsps butter.
5. Bake 8 minutes.
6. Meanwhile, in small bowl, combine remaining 3/4 ounce cheese, the eggs, 2 Tbsps of the basil, 2 Tbsps of the chives and 1 Tbsp water.
7. In small cast-iron skillet, heat remaining butter; add egg mixture.
8. Cook over medium-high heat 5 minutes, until edges are set.
9. Transfer skillet to oven alongside pan with asparagus; bake 4 minutes, until egg mixture is firm, asparagus is heated through and cheese topping is crusty.
10. Meanwhile, in small bowl, combine tomatoes, salt, remaining 2 Tbsps basil and remaining 2 Tbsps chives.
11. Cut egg mixture into 4 wedges.
12. Divide asparagus mixture evenly into 4 equal portions; top each portion with 1 wedge of the egg mixture and one-fourth of the tomato mixture.

BEEF & EGGS

Serves 1

- ▶ 1 large egg, well beaten
- ▶ 1 ounce leftover lean beef, diced
- ▶ Salt and pepper to taste
- ▶ Mixed herbs to taste
- ▶ Paprika

1. Combine all ingredients, then cook in no-stick skillet, stirring with wooden spatula until set as you like.
2. Serve and sprinkle top with a little paprika (or chopped parsley).

CORN & TOMATO FRITTATA

Serves 6

- Olive oil cooking spray or a tab of butter
- 1 1/4 cups fresh corn cut from cob (about 3 ears)
- 1/4 cup chopped green onions
- 10 eggs
- 1 1/2 tsps minced fresh basil
- 1/8 tsp salt
- 1/8 tsp pepper
- 2 small tomatoes, each cut into 6 wedges cheddar cheese
- Fresh basil sprigs (optional)

1. Coat a medium nonstick skillet with cooking spray or by melting a pad of butter, and place over medium-high heat until hot.
2. Add corn and green onions; sauté until vegetables are tender.
3. Combine eggs and next 4 ingredients in a bowl and stir well.
4. Pour egg mixture over vegetables in skillet.
5. Cover and cook over medium-low heat 15 minutes or until almost set.
6. Arrange tomato wedges on top of egg mixture and sprinkle with cheese.
7. Cover and cook 5 additional minutes or until cheese melts.
8. Cut into 6 wedges and serve immediately.
9. Garnish with basil sprigs if desired.

GOAT CHEESE & TOMATO OMELET

Serves 4

- 4 eggs
- 1 Tbsp heavy cream
- 1 tsp chopped fresh thyme leaves, or 1/2 tsp dried
- 1/2 tsp salt
- 1/4 tsp pepper
- 1 Tbsp butter
- 2 ounces fresh goat cheese, crumbled
- 1 small tomato, seeded and finely chopped

1. In a bowl, beat eggs, cream, thyme, salt and pepper.
2. Melt butter in a medium skillet over medium heat.
3. Pour in egg mixture.
4. Let set 1 minute, push eggs to one side with spatula, tilt pan and let uncooked eggs slide onto skillet.
5. Sprinkle goat cheese and tomato along set side of eggs.
6. Fold eggs over filling; cook 2 minutes more.
7. Slide onto a serving plate; cut it in two.

Eggs

VEGETABLE SWISS OMELET

Serves
2

- ▶ Vegetable cooking spray
- ▶ 1/3 cup finely chopped zucchini
- ▶ 1/4 cup chopped green onions
- ▶ 1/4 cup peeled, seeded, and chopped tomato
- ▶ Dash of pepper
- ▶ 4 whole eggs
- ▶ 2 Tbsps water
- ▶ 1/4 tsp dried basil
- ▶ 1/4 tsp celery seeds
- ▶ 1/8 tsp salt
- ▶ 1/8 tsp pepper
- ▶ 1/4 cup shredded Swiss cheese

1. Coat a 6-inch heavy skillet with cooking spray; place over medium heat until hot.
2. Add zucchini, green onions and tomato; sauté 2 to 3 minutes or until vegetables are tender.
3. Stir in dash of pepper.
4. Remove vegetables from skillet; set aside and keep warm.
5. Wipe skillet dry with a paper towel.
6. Beat eggs and set aside.
7. Combine next 5 ingredients in a small bowl; stir well.
8. Gently fold egg whites into egg substitute mixture.
9. Coat skillet with cooking spray; place over medium heat until hot enough to sizzle a drop of water.
10. Spread half of egg mixture in skillet.
11. Cover, reduce heat to low and cook 5 minutes or until puffy and golden on bottom, gently lifting omelet at edge to judge color.
12. Turn omelet and cook 3 minutes or until golden.
13. Carefully slide omelet onto a warm plate.
14. Spoon half of vegetable mixture over half of omelet; sprinkle with 2 Tbsps cheese and carefully fold in half.
15. Repeat procedure with remaining egg mixture, vegetable mixture and cheese.

SPINACH, BASIL & TOMATO FRITTATAS

Serves 4

- 6 eggs
- 1 Tbsp of half & half
- Black pepper
- 1/4 tsp salt
- 1/4 cup minced fresh basil
- 10 cherry tomatoes, quartered
- 1/4 cup crumbled feta cheese
- 1 tsp olive oil
- 1 tsp minced garlic
- 2 cups baby spinach leaves

1. Preheat oven to 375°F.
2. Coat four 1-cup ramekins or eight 1/2-cup muffin cups with cooking spray.
3. Break eggs into a large bowl and beat well with a whisk.
4. Add milk, pepper, salt, basil, tomatoes and cheese.
5. In a medium sauté pan, heat olive oil; sauté garlic over medium heat for about 2 minutes.
6. Add spinach and sauté 1-2 minutes until spinach is wilted but still a vibrant green.
7. Add spinach mixture to egg mixture.
8. Ladle into prepared ramekins or cups.
9. Bake for 18-20 minutes, until eggs are cooked thoroughly. They will expand while cooking and will collapse while cooling.
10. When cool, remove from tins.
11. Refrigerate in an airtight container for up to a week.

GOAT CHEESE SCRAMBLED EGGS

Serves 4

- 8 large eggs
- 2 Tbsps chopped chives
- 1/4 tsp salt
- 1/4 tsp ground black pepper
- 2 Tbsps butter
- 4 ounces goat cheese, crumbled

1. In a large bowl whisk together the eggs, 2 Tbsps water, chives, salt and pepper.
2. Melt the butter in a large skillet over medium-high heat.
3. Add the egg mixture and cook, stirring frequently, until almost set.
4. Add the goat cheese and cook, stirring until eggs are just set and the cheese is melted.

Eggs

YELLOW SQUASH & GRUYERE FRITTATA

Serves 4

- ▶ 2 Tbsps butter, divided
- ▶ 2 medium yellow squash, cut into 1/4 inch rounds (2 1/2 cups)
- ▶ 1 packed Tbsp thinly sliced fresh sage or basil leaves
- ▶ 10 large eggs
- ▶ 1/4 cup water
- ▶ 1/2 tsp salt
- ▶ 3/4 cup coarsely shredded Gruyere cheese

1. Melt 1 Tbsp butter in 12" nonstick oven-proof skillet over medium-high heat.
2. Add squash and sauté 8 minutes; stir in sage.
3. Cook just 1 to 2 minutes more until tender and browned in spots.
4. Meanwhile, arrange oven rack 6" from heat source; heat broiler.
5. Whisk eggs, water and salt in a bowl.
6. Melt remaining Tbsp butter in skillet; pour eggs over squash.
7. Reduce heat to medium-low, cover, and cook until set on bottom and edges but the top is still loose, about 3 minutes.
8. Sprinkle Gruyere evenly over the top.
9. Broil frittata until just set, about 1 minute.
10. Cut into wedges to serve.

SPICY MEAT 'N' EGGS

Serves 2

- ▶ 3 eggs
- ▶ 1/2 cup meat in small cubes or pieces (use leftover lean beef, lamb or veal)
- ▶ 1 tsp parsley flakes (or fresh minced parsley)
- ▶ 1 tsp grated onion
- ▶ 3 small stuffed olives chopped or slivered
- ▶ 1 Tbsp chili sauce
- ▶ 1 Tbsp water
- ▶ Paprika

1. Combine eggs, meat and other ingredients in a bowl while heating no-stick skillet, including the special salt to taste.
2. Stir with fork to combine all ingredients, but don't whip.
3. Pour into pan and cook over low heat, stirring thickening mixture occasionally.
4. When almost finished, cover pan, turn off heat and let mixture set for 1 or 2 minutes, then divide into two servings using wooden spatula.
5. Sprinkle with paprika for extra color if desired.

HERBED OMELET

Serves 2

- ▶ 2 large eggs, yolks and whites separated
- ▶ 1/4 tsp salt
- ▶ 1/4 tsp mixed herbs
- ▶ 1/4 tsp parsley flakes
- ▶ 1/4 tsp onion flakes
- ▶ 1 Tbsp water
- ▶ Grated cheese of choice

1. Beat egg yolks with salt, herbs, parsley and onion flakes.
2. Beat egg whites until stiff, then fold into yolks slowly.
3. Put the water in a no-stick skillet, and once warm on low heat, add the egg mixture and cook slowly for about 5 minutes.
4. Place omelet under broiler for about 2 minutes until lightly browned, then sprinkle with a little grated cheese and remove carefully from pan.

TURBOTIPS:
Variation: instead of grated cheese, use 1 cup diced chicken.

ZUCCHINI CANAPÉS

- ▶ 2 medium zucchini squash
- ▶ 2 hard-boiled eggs
- ▶ Salt and pepper
- ▶ Paprika

1. Scrub zucchini, trim off ends, and cut into 1/8" thick round slices, leaving on skin.
2. Slice eggs into circles, place one slice on each zucchini circle.
3. Sprinkle on salt, pepper and paprika to taste.

MUSHROOMS, ONIONS & EGGS

- ▶ 1/2 lb mushrooms, sliced
- ▶ 1 small onion, chopped
- ▶ 4 Tbsps butter
- ▶ Seasoned salt to taste
- ▶ 6 eggs
- ▶ 2 Tbsps heavy cream

1. Sauté mushrooms and onion in butter until well browned.
2. Add salt.
3. Beat eggs with heavy cream.
4. Pour over mushroom mixture and stir until eggs are cooked (about 4 stirs).

Eggs

SCRAMBLED EGGS

Serves 6

- ▶ 12 eggs
- ▶ 1/2 tsp salt
- ▶ 1/8 tsp pepper
- ▶ 2 Tbsps butter
- ▶ 2 Tbsps whipping cream

1. Combine the first three ingredients in a large bowl.
2. Beat until well mixed.
3. Melt butter at medium heat in a skillet, making sure the bottom is covered.
4. Add eggs.
5. Stir constantly until eggs firm up but are not dry.
6. Remove from heat.
7. Stir in the cream.
8. Serve immediately.

MEXICAN EGG CASSEROLE

Serves 2

- ▶ 1 small can chopped green chilies, drained
- ▶ 1/4 cup chopped onion
- ▶ 1 cup your choice of shredded cheese
- ▶ 1 cup Monterey Jack cheese, shredded
- ▶ 4 eggs, beaten frothy

1. Spray an 8 x 8 baking dish with non-stick cooking spray.
2. Spread chilies and onion on bottom of the dish.
3. Cover with cheeses.
4. Pour eggs over top.
5. Bake for 45 minutes at 325°F.
6. Let stand 20 minutes before cutting.

CHEDDAR OMELET

Serves 1

- ▶ Non-stick cooking spray
- ▶ 2 eggs
- ▶ 2 Tbsps shredded cheddar cheese

1. Spray small nonstick skillet with non-stick cooking spray; heat.
2. Crack and stir eggs into skillet, tilting to cover bottom of pan.
3. Cook over medium-high heat until underside is set, lifting edges with spatula to let uncooked egg flow underneath.
4. Sprinkle cheese evenly over one side of omelet; with spatula, fold other side over cheese to enclose.

MEXICAN OMELET

Serves 1

- ▶ 2 large eggs
- ▶ 2 Tbsps water
- ▶ 1 Tbsp butter
- ▶ 1/4 cup salsa, room temperature

1. Beat eggs with a fork in a small mixing bowl.
2. Stir in water.
3. Heat butter in a non-stick (or regular) frying pan.
4. Add eggs and cook to desired doneness.
5. Drain salsa a bit to remove some of the liquid.
6. Then spoon over one-half of the egg.
7. Fold egg over salsa and slide onto dinner plate.

ONION & ZUCCHINI FRITTATA

Serves 1

- ▶ Non-stick cooking spray
- ▶ 1 cup chopped onions
- ▶ 1 cup chopped zucchini
- ▶ 1 egg
- ▶ 1 Tbsp heavy cream or half & half
- ▶ 1/4 tsp salt
- ▶ Pepper

1. Spray medium non-stick skillet with nonstick cooking spray; heat.
2. Add chopped onions and zucchini; cook over medium heat, stirring constantly, until tender.
3. In small bowl, beat egg with heavy cream or Half & Half, salt and a pinch of freshly ground black pepper; stir into vegetable mixture.
4. Cook, covered, until mixture is firm.

SUPER-FAST HERB SCRAMBLE

Serves 1

- ▶ 1 tsp minced fresh flat-leaf
- ▶ 1/4 tsp dried parsley
- ▶ 1/4 tsp dried oregano leaves
- ▶ 1/4 tsp dried basil
- ▶ 2 eggs

1. In small microwaveable bowl, crack and whip eggs.
2. Add parsley, oregano and basil; microwave on Medium-High (70% power), 1-2 minutes, stirring once or twice, until set.

Fish

TIPS FOR PREPARING FISH

- ▶ When using tuna or salmon from a can, it must be rinsed well under cold water and drained.
- ▶ Only use water-packed fish.
- ▶ Lemon juice rubbed on fish before cooking will enhance the flavor and help maintain good color.
- ▶ Fish is best thawed in the refrigerator.
- ▶ Remove from freezer first thing in the morning and let it naturally thaw in the refrigerator to reduce likelihood of bacteria proliferation.

ISLAND SWORDFISH

Serves 4

- ▶ 1/2 cup chopped ripe mango
- ▶ 1/4 cup peeled, seeded and chopped papaya
- ▶ 2 Tbsps finely chopped celery
- ▶ 1 Tbsp minced fresh parsley
- ▶ 1 Tbsp lime juice
- ▶ 2 Tbsps finely chopped purple onion
- ▶ 1 Tbsp grated fresh ginger
- ▶ 1 Tbsp seeded, minced jalapeno
- ▶ 2 Tbsps rice vinegar
- ▶ 2 Tbsps Dijon mustard
- ▶ 1 Tbsp + 1 tsp low-sodium soy sauce
- ▶ 4 4-oz swordfish steaks (3/4 inch thick)
- ▶ Vegetable cooking spray
- ▶ Fresh parsley sprigs (optional)

1. Combine first 8 ingredients in a small bowl, tossing gently.
2. Combine vinegar, mustard, and soy sauce in a small bowl; stir with a wire whisk until well blended.
3. Brush over steaks.
4. Coat a grill rack with cooking spray; place on grill over medium-hot coals (350° to 400°F).
5. Place steaks on rack, and grill, covered, 5 minutes on each side or until fish flakes easily when tested with a fork.
6. Serve with mango mixture.
7. Garnish with parsley sprigs if desired.

FLOUNDER EN PAPILLOTE

 Serves 2

- ► Vegetable cooking spray
- ► 1/4 cup chopped green onions
- ► 2 tsps minced garlic
- ► 2 tsps dry white wine
- ► 2 4-oz flounder fillets
- ► 3/4 cup sliced mushrooms
- ► 1/2 cup chopped plum tomato
- ► 2 tsps chopped fresh oregano
- ► 2 tsps chopped fresh basil
- ► 1/4 tsp salt
- ► 1/4 tsp pepper
- ► 1/4 tsp chopped Serrano chili pepper
- ► 2 bay leaves

1. Coat a medium nonstick skillet with cooking spray; place over medium-high heat until hot.
2. Add green onions and garlic; sauté until tender.
3. Remove skillet from heat; stir in wine.
4. Set aside.
5. Cut two 12" squares of parchment paper; fold each square in half, and trim each into a heart shape.
6. Place parchment hearts on a baking sheet and open out flat.
7. Coat open side of parchment paper with cooking spray.
8. Place 1 fillet on half of each parchment heart near the crease.
9. Spoon mushrooms evenly over fillets; top evenly with tomato.
10. Combine oregano and next 4 ingredients; sprinkle evenly over fillets.
11. Top each fillet with a bay leaf.
12. Spoon onion mixture evenly over fillets.
13. Fold paper edges over to seal securely.
14. Starting with rounded edges of hearts, pleat and crimp edges of parchment to make an airtight seal.
15. Bake at 425°F for 15 minutes or until packets are puffed and lightly browned.
16. Place packets on individual plates; cut an opening in the top of each packet; fold paper back.
17. Serve immediately.

Fish

BLACKENED TUNA

 Serves 6

- ► 1 Tbsp onion powder
- ► 1 Tbsp dried basil
- ► 2 tsps dried thyme
- ► 1/2 tsp ground white pepper
- ► 1/2 tsp black pepper
- ► 1/8 to 1/4 tsp ground red pepper
- ► 6 4-oz tuna steaks (1/2" thick)
- ► Vegetable cooking spray
- ► 1 1/2 Tbsps butter, melted
- ► Fresh thyme sprigs (optional)
- ► Lime wedges (optional)

1. Combine first 6 ingredients in a small bowl, and stir well.
2. Rub tuna steaks with pepper mixture.
3. Coat grill rack with cooking spray; place on grill over medium-hot (350° to 400°F) coals.
4. Place tuna on rack; drizzle with margarine, and grill 4 to 5 minutes on each side or until tuna flakes easily when tested with a fork.
5. If desired, garnish with thyme sprigs and lime wedges (not included in analysis).

SWORDFISH KABOBS

 Serves 2

- ► 1 Tbsp coarse-grained mustard
- ► 1 lb swordfish steaks (3/4" thick)
- ► 1 large zucchini, cut into 8 slices
  - ► 1 large sweet red pepper, seeded and cut into 8 (1/2-inch) cubes
  - ► 2 small purple onions, quartered
  - ► 8 medium-size fresh mushroom caps
  - ► Vegetable cooking spray
  - ► Lemon wedges (optional)

1. Spread mustard over swordfish steaks.
2. Cut steaks into 12 (1/4") pieces.
3. Arrange swordfish, zucchini, pepper, onion, and mushrooms alternately on 4 (12") skewers.
4. Place kabobs on rack of a broiler pan coated with cooking spray.
5. Broil 5 1/2" from heat (with electric oven door partially opened) 10 to 12 minutes or until fish flakes easily when tested with a fork, turning occasionally.
6. Serve kabobs with lemon wedges if desired.

TURBOTIPS:

These can also be made with tuna or mahi-mahi.

To Prepare on Grill: Coat grill rack with cooking spray; place on grill over medium-hot coals (350°F to 400°F). Place kabobs on rack; grill 10 to 12 minutes or until fish flakes easily when tested with fork, turning occasionally.

CHEESE-FLAVORED FILLETS

Serves 4

- ▶ 1 1/2 lbs flounder (or other fish) fillets, fresh or frozen (thawed)
- ▶ 1 Tbsp lemon juice
- ▶ 1 Tbsp grated onion
- ▶ 1/8 tsp lemon pepper marinade
- ▶ 1/8 tsp rosemary
- ▶ 1/8 tsp marjoram
- ▶ 1/2 tsp parsley flakes
- ▶ 1 Tbsp grated Parmesan cheese

1. Arrange fillets side by side on no-stick broiling pan.
2. Sprinkle with lemon juice, onion, pepper and herbs.
3. Broil in preheated oven about 4" from heat 10 to 12 minutes, or until fish flakes easily with a fork.
4. Sprinkle cheese on and broil 2 minutes longer.

GARLIC FLOUNDER

Serves 6

- ▶ 6 4-oz flounder fillets
- ▶ 1/4 cup low-sodium soy sauce
- ▶ 2 tsps minced garlic
- ▶ 1 1/2 Tbsps lemon juice
- ▶ 1 Tbsp mixed peppercorns, crushed
- ▶ Vegetable cooking spray
- ▶ Fresh parsley sprigs (optional)

1. Place fish fillets in a shallow baking dish.
2. Combine soy sauce and next 3 ingredients; pour over fish.
3. Cover and marinate in refrigerator 30 minutes.
4. Remove fish from marinade; discard marinade.
5. Sprinkle fish evenly with crushed peppercorns, gently pressing pepper into fish.
6. Place fish on rack of a broiler pan coated with cooking spray.
7. Broil 51/2" from heat (With electric oven door partially opened) 8 to 10 minutes or until fish flakes easily when tested with a fork.
8. Transfer to a serving platter and garnish with parsley sprigs if desired.

Fish

ITALIAN SCALLOP KABOBS

Serves 6

- ▶ 36 sea scallops (about 1 lb)
- ▶ 5-oz package lean, smoked sliced ham, cut into 36 (1/2"-wide) strips
- ▶ Vegetable cooking spray
- ▶ 2 cloves garlic, minced
- ▶ 1/4 cup lemon juice
- ▶ 2 Tbsps minced fresh parsley
- ▶ 3/4 tsp dried oregano
- ▶ Fresh oregano sprigs (optional)
- ▶ Lemon rind strips (optional)

1. Wrap each scallop with a strip of ham; thread 6 scallops onto each of 6 (12") skewers.
2. Set aside.
3. Coat a small nonstick skillet with cooking spray; place over medium heat until hot.
4. Add garlic; sauté until golden.
5. Remove from heat and stir in lemon juice, parsley and oregano.
6. Coat grill rack with cooking spray; place on grill over medium-hot coals (350° to 400°F).
7. Place kabobs on rack, and grill, uncovered, 9 to 10 minutes or until scallops are opaque, turning and basting often with lemon juice mixture.
8. If desired, garnish with oregano sprigs and lemon rind strips.

MEDITERRANIAN FISH STEW

Serves 6

- ▶ 1 1/4 lbs fish fillets
- ▶ 2 tomatoes, peeled, seeded and diced
- ▶ 1 small chopped pimento
- ▶ 1 chopped green onion
- ▶ Juice of 6 limes
- ▶ 6 Tbsps fresh cilantro, finely chopped
- ▶ Salt and pepper to taste
- ▶ 1 diced avocado
- ▶ 1 tsp dried oregano
- ▶ 10 pitted black olives

1. Cut the fillets into 1/2" squares and place in a large bowl.
2. Cover all the pieces with the lime juice and let stand for 4 hours.
3. Drain the fish and pat dry on paper towels.
4. Put the fish into a large bowl and add tomatoes, pimento, green onion and cilantro.
5. Add salt and pepper.
6. Stir to blend and refrigerate for 4 hours.
7. When serving add the avocado, olives and oregano to the fish mixture.
8. Serve immediately.

SPICY SHRIMP

Serves 6

- ▶ 2 lbs raw jumbo shrimp, peeled
- ▶ 1/4 cup garlic, minced
- ▶ 2 cups red onions, thinly sliced
- ▶ 2 cups white onions, thinly sliced
- ▶ 1/2 cup seeded fresh red chili peppers, diced
- ▶ 8 tomatoes, each cut into 6 wedges
- ▶ Salt and freshly ground black pepper to taste
- ▶ 1/2 cup tomato sauce
- ▶ 1/2 cup water
- ▶ 1/2 cup chopped green onions
- ▶ 1/4 cup chopped parsley
- ▶ 1/4 cup chopped cilantro

1. In a large nonstick pot, add the garlic and onions and sauté for 5 minutes.
2. Stir in the chilies, tomatoes, salt and pepper, and shrimp.
3. Cook, stirring and tossing 5 minutes.
4. Add the tomato sauce, water and green onions and bring the mixture to a simmer.
5. Stir in the parsley and cilantro and cook for 1 minute.
6. Serve immediately.

RED SNAPPER &

ARTICHOKE KABOBS

Serves 4

- ▶ 12 large kalamata olives, pitted and thinly sliced
- ▶ 1/4 cup minced fresh flat-leaf parsley
- ▶ 1 Tbsp + 1 tsp olive oil
- ▶ 1 Tbsp fresh lemon juice
- ▶ 1/2 tsp fennel seeds, crushed
- ▶ 15 ounces red snapper fillets, cut into 1 1/2" cubes
- ▶ 1/4 tsp salt
- ▶ Pinch freshly ground black pepper
- ▶ 1 cup cooked large artichoke hearts, quartered

1. Preheat outdoor barbecue grill according to manufacturer's directions or preheat broiler and spray rack in broiler pan with nonstick cooking spray.
2. In small bowl, combine olives, parsley, oil, juice and fennel seeds; set aside.
3. Sprinkle fish on all sides with salt and pepper, alternating ingredients, onto each of 4 long metal showers, thread one-fourth of the fish and one-fourth of the artichoke hearts.
4. Grill over hot coals or place onto prepared rack on broiler pan and broil 4" from heat 3-4 minutes, until fish flakes easily when tested with fork.
5. Place 1 kabob onto each of 4 plates; carefully remove skewers.
6. Sprinkle evenly with olive mixture.

Fish

GRILLED TUNA with BEAN SALSA

- ▶ 8 ounces drained cooked white kidney (cannellini) beans
- ▶ 2 large plum tomatoes, seeded and diced
- ▶ 2 Tbsps minced fresh basil
- ▶ 2 tsps fresh lemon juice
- ▶ 2 tsps olive oil
- ▶ 2 garlic cloves, minced
- ▶ Pinch crushed red pepper flakes
- ▶ 4 5-oz boneless tuna steaks
- ▶ 2 cups arugula leaves

1. To prepare salsa, in medium bowl, combine beans, tomatoes, basil and juice; refrigerate, covered, until chilled.
2. Meanwhile, in small cup or bowl, combine oil, garlic and red pepper flakes; rub into fish on all sides.
3. Refrigerate, covered, 1 hour.
4. Preheat outdoor barbecue grill or indoor stove-top grill according to manufacturer's directions.
5. Grill tuna over hot coals or on stove-top grill, turning once, 6 minutes, until fish flakes easily when tested with fork.
6. Divide arugula evenly among 4 plates.
7. Top each portion of arugula with 1 grilled tuna steak; top evenly with salsa.

MUSTARD-DILL GLAZED SALMON

- ▶ 4 4-oz salmon fillets, center cut
- ▶ 3 Tbsps mayonnaise
- ▶ 1 Tbsp grainy mustard
- ▶ 1 Tbsp chopped dill
- ▶ 1 1/2 tsps dark brown sugar substitute
- ▶ 1 tsp lemon juice
- ▶ 1/2 tsp salt
- ▶ 1/8 tsp black pepper

1. In a small dish, combine mayonnaise, mustard and dill.
2. 1 1/2 tsps dark brown sugar substitute.
3. 1 tsp lemon juice.
4. Put salmon fillets on a foil-lined baking sheet.
5. Season with salt and black pepper and spread mayonnaise mixture over top of fillets.
6. Roast until just cooked through, 12 to 15 minutes.

Fish

PEPPER MARINADED AHI TUNA

Serves
4

- ▶ 4 tuna steaks
- ▶ 1/4 cup extra virgin olive oil
- ▶ Freshly ground pepper
- ▶ Salt to taste

1. Combine olive oil and pepper with whisk.
2. Add frozen or fresh fillets to glass dish and cover with marinade; allow fish to defrost in the refrigerator for 3 hours or overnight.
3. Turn periodically.
4. Cook according to one of the methods for defrost, allowing a few extra minutes for partially frozen fish.

On the Grill:

5. Heat grill to high.
6. Rub a small amount of olive oil on the fillet; season with salt and pepper.
7. Grill 2 minutes per side for Rare and about 3 minutes per side for Medium-Rare.

Pan Seared:

1. Lightly oil an oven proof-skillet and heat over medium flame.
2. Rub fillets with olive oil and season with salt and pepper.
3. Add to hot skillet.
4. Cook about 2 minutes per side for Rare and about 3 minutes per side for Medium-Rare.

Oven Cooked:

1. Heat oven to 450°F and place rack in center of oven.
2. Rub fillets with olive oil and sprinkle with salt and pepper.
3. Place fish in shallow roasting dish.
4. Cook about 6 minutes for Medium-Rare.
5. Bake 15-18 minutes or until fish is lightly cooked through but still moist.

SWORDFISH ALMONDINE
WITH CAPERS

Serves 8

- ▶ 1 1/2 lbs swordfish steak, about 1 inch thick, skinned and cut in 8 pieces
- ▶ Juice of 1 large lemon (about 3 Tbsps)
- ▶ 1/4 cup dry white wine or apple juice
- ▶ 4 tsps capers, drained
- ▶ 1/3 cup whole, blanched almonds, toasted and chopped

1. Lightly coat an 11 x 17" baking dish with vegetable cooking spray.
2. Arrange swordfish in a single layer in prepared dish.
3. Sprinkle with lemon juice, then wine.
4. Cover and let stand 1 hour at room temperature.
5. Heat oven to 350°F.
6. Spoon 1/2 tsp capers over each piece of fish.
7. Cover baking dish with foil.
8. Bake about 12 minutes until fish is barely opaque when pierced with a fork.
9. Do not overcook.
10. Sprinkle 2 tsps almonds over each serving.
11. NOTE: Stir almonds in a heavy skillet over medium-high heat 3 to 5 minutes until lightly toasted.
12. Cool, then chop.

SAUTEED FILLETS

Serves 4

- ▶ 4 flat fish fillets
- ▶ 1 beaten egg
- ▶ 1 Tbsp olive oil
- ▶ 1/2 sliced onion
- ▶ 1 Tbsp chopped parsley or dill
- ▶ 8 lemon wedges

1. Rub fillets with damp cloth and dry.
2. Dredge in beaten egg.
3. Heat olive oil to hot in a large heavy skillet.
4. Put fish and onions in together, sprinkle with parsley.
5. Saute' fish 1-2 minutes on a side.
6. Serve with lemon wedges.

SWORDFISH PROVENCAL

 Serves 4

- ▶ 1 Tbsp + 1 tsp olive oil
- ▶ 8 large garlic cloves, minced
- ▶ 4 5-oz boneless swordfish steaks
- ▶ 1/2 cup red onion wedges
- ▶ 1/2 tsp fennel seeds
- ▶ 1 1/2 cups canned whole Italian tomatoes (no salt added), chopped
- ▶ 6 large or 10 small Greek olives, pitted and thinly sliced
- ▶ 2 Tbsps silvered fresh basil leaves

1. In small bowl, combine 1 Tbsp of the oil and one-half of the garlic; rub over one side of each swordfish steak.
2. Refrigerate covered, 1 hour.
3. Preheat broiler.
4. Line broiler pan with foil
5. In large nonstick skillet, heat remaining 1 tsp oil; add onion, fennel seeds and remaining garlic.
6. Cook over low heat, stirring frequently, 7-8 minutes, until onion is softened.
7. Stir in tomatoes; bring mixture to a boil.
8. Reduce heat to low; simmer, stirring occasionally, 10 minutes, until slightly thickened.
9. Meanwhile, arrange swordfish steaks in prepared broiler pan, garlic-side up; broil 4" from heat, turning once, 6 minutes, until fish flakes easily when tested with fork.
10. Place 1 swordfish steak on each of 4 plates.
11. Top each steak with one-fourth of the tomato mixture; sprinkle evenly with olives and basil.

MEDITERRANEAN SWORDFISH

 Serves 4

- ▶ 1/4 cup olive oil
- ▶ 2 Tbsps fresh lemon juice
- ▶ 1 tsp dried oregano
- ▶ 1/2 tsp grated lemon rind
- ▶ 1/2 tsp crumbled dried rosemary
- ▶ 1/2 tsp salt
- ▶ 1/2 tsp pepper
- ▶ 4 1" thick swordfish steaks (about 1 1/2 lbs)

1. Mix olive oil, lemon juice, oregano, lemon rind, rosemary, salt and pepper in a resealable plastic bag.
2. Add fish steaks; toss to coat.
3. Marinate at room temperature 30 minutes, turning occasionally.
4. Prepare medium grill or heat broiler.
5. Cook steaks about 5 minutes per side for medium doneness.

Fish

RED TROUT &

VEGETABLES EN PAPILLOTE

Serves
4

- ► 1 cup julienned carrot
- ► 1 cup julienned snow peas
- ► 1/2 cup julienned scallions
- ► 4 4-oz red trout fillets
- ► 2 tsps minced fresh thyme leaves
- ► 1 tsp grated lemon zest
- ► 1 garlic clove, minced
- ► 1/4 tsp salt
- ► Pinch freshly ground black pepper
- ► 2 Tbsps fresh lemon juice
- ► 1 Tbsp + 1 tsp olive oil

1. Preheat oven to 425°F.
2. Spray four 15 x 12" sheets of foil with nonstick cooking spray.
3. Place one-fourth of the carrot, snow peas and scallions onto center of each prepared sheet of foil, top each portion of vegetables with 1 trout fillet.
4. In cup or small bowl, combine thyme, zest, garlic, salt and pepper; sprinkle evenly over fish.
5. Drizzle each portion with 1 1/2 tsps of the juice and 1 tsp of the oil.
6. Enclose fish in foil, making 4 individual packets; crimp edges to seal.
7. Place packets onto baking sheet; bake 10-12 minutes, until fish flakes easily when tested with fork and vegetables are just tender.
8. Open foil packets carefully; transfer contents of each packet to a plate.

SEAFOOD STEAKS

Serves
1

- ► 6-8 ounce steak (salmon, tuna, swordfish)
- ► 1/2 tsp dried dill
- ► 1 Tbsp Mayonnaise
- ► Lemon wedges

1. Sprinkle dill on top side of steak, coat lightly with mayonnaise.
2. Place on broiler pan.
3. Broil 2-3 minutes, 3" from heat source.
4. Turn steaks, coat with dill and mayonnaise.
5. Broil about 3 minutes.
6. Turn heat to medium.
7. Broil a few more minutes until done.
8. When fish is done, it should flake easily.
9. Cooking time depends on thickness of steaks.

GRILLED FIVE-SPICE FISH & GARLIC SPINACH

Serves 4

- 1 1/2 tsps grated lime peel
- 3 Tbsps fresh lime juice
- 4 tsps minced fresh ginger
- 1/2-1 tsp Chinese five-spice powder
- 1/2 tsp sweetener substitute
- 1/2 tsp salt
- 1/8 tsp black pepper
- 2 tsps olive or macadamia nut oil, divided
- 1 lb salmon steaks
- 1/2 lb fresh baby spinach leaves (about 8 cups lightly packed), washed
- 2 large cloves garlic, pressed through garlic press

1. Combine lime peel, lime juice, ginger, 5-spice powder, sweetener, salt, pepper and 1 tsp oil in 2-quart dish.
2. Add salmon; turn to coat.
3. Cover; refrigerate 2 to 3 hours.
4. Combine spinach, garlic and remaining 1 tsp oil in 3 quart microwavable dish; toss.
5. Cover; microwave at HIGH (100% power) 2 minutes or until spinach is wilted.
6. Drain; keep warm.
7. Meanwhile, prepare grill for direct cooking.
8. Remove salmon from marinade and place on oiled grid.
9. Brush salmon with marinade.
10. Grill salmon, covered, over medium-hot coals 4 minutes.
11. Turn salmon; brush with marinade and grill 4 minutes or until salmon begins to flake with fork.
12. Discard remaining marinade.
13. Serve fish over bed of spinach.

> **TURBOTIPS:**
> Chinese five-spice powder is available in Asian markets and many supermarkets.
>
> Use prepackaged and washed baby spinach to save time.

SALMON BURGERS

Serves 4

- 2 salmon fillets, skinned and chopped (about 1 1/2 lbs)
- 2 Tbsps chopped red onion
- 1 egg
- 2 tsps grated lemon rind
- 2 Tbsps fresh lemon juice
- 1/2 tsp pepper
- 1 Tbsp olive oil

1. Combine salmon, red onion, egg, rind, juice and pepper.
2. Form into six 4" patties.
3. Chill at least 2 hours.
4. Heat oil in large nonstick skillet over medium heat.
5. Cook patties 3 minutes per side or until cooked through.

Fish

MAHI-MAHI WITH

Serves
4

FRESH PINEAPPLE SALSA

- ▶ 1 1/2 cups diced fresh pineapple
- ▶ 1/4 cup finely chopped red bell pepper
- ▶ 1/4 cup finely chopped green bell pepper
- ▶ 2 Tbsps chopped fresh cilantro
- ▶ 2 Tbsps fresh lime juice, divided
- ▶ 1/2 tsp red pepper flakes
- ▶ 1/2 tsp grated lime peel
- ▶ Nonstick cooking spray
- ▶ 4 mahi-mahi fillets (4-oz each)
- ▶ 1 Tbsp olive oil
- ▶ 1/2 tsp white pepper

1. To prepare salsa, combine pineapple, red and green peppers, cilantro, 1 Tbsp lime juice, red pepper flakes and lime peel in medium bowl.
2. Set aside.
3. Preheat broiler.
4. Spray rack of broiler pan with cooking spray.
5. Rinse mahi-mahi and pat dry with paper towels.
6. Place mahi-mahi on rack.
7. Combine remaining 1 Tbsp lime juice and olive oil; brush on mahi-mahi.
8. Broil, 4" from heat, 2 minutes.
9. Turn to broil 2 minutes or until mahi-mahi flakes when tested with fork.
10. Serve with pineapple salsa.

TURBOTIPS:
Pineapple Salsa can be prepared 1 to 2 days ahead and refrigerated.

SMOKED SALMON ROSES

Serves
16

- ▶ 1 package cream cheese, softened
- ▶ 1 Tbsp prepared horseradish
- ▶ 1 Tbsp minced fresh dill plus whole springs for garnish
- ▶ 1 Tbsp half-and-half
- ▶ 16 slices (12 to 16 ounces) smoked salmon
- ▶ 1 red bell pepper, cut into thin strips

1. Combine cream cheese, horseradish, minced dill and half-and-half in a bowl.
2. Beat until light.
3. Spread 1 Tbsp cream cheese mixture over each salmon slice.
4. Roll up jelly-roll fashion.
5. Slice each roll in half widthwise.
6. Stand salmon rolls, cut side down, on a serving dish to resemble roses.
7. Garnish each "rose" by tucking 1 pepper strip and 1 dill sprig in center.

SEAFOOD MARINARA

Serves 4

- ▶ 1 1/2 lbs fish of your choice
- ▶ Juice of 1 lemon
- ▶ 1 medium onion, chopped
- ▶ 1 cup fresh parsley chopped
- ▶ 1/4 tsp garlic powder
- ▶ 1 cup tomato puree (salt free)
- ▶ 1/2 cup red or white wine
- ▶ 1/2 tsp dill weed
- ▶ 1/8 tsp oregano
- ▶ 1/8 tsp pepper
- ▶ 1 cup water

1. Place fish in baking dish.
2. Pour lemon juice on both sides of fish.
3. Saute onions, parsely and garlic in 1/2 cup water until golden brown.
4. Add tomato puree, remaining water, wine, dill weed, oregano and pepper to onion mixture.
5. Pour over fish.
6. Bake in 350°F oven for 40 minutes.

TURBOTIPS:
An Italian delight; delicious with spaghetti squash.

BROILED HALIBUT STEAKS

Serves 4

- ▶ 4 halibut steaks
- ▶ Juice of 1 lemon
- ▶ 3/4 cup dry white wine
- ▶ 1/2 tsp dill weed
- ▶ 1/4 cup chopped parsley
- ▶ 1/8 tsp pepper

1. Set halibut aside.
2. Blend all other ingredients in a mixing bowl.
3. Place halibut in a dish.
4. Pour marinade ingredients over halibut.
5. Place in refrigerator for 2 hours.
6. Turn fish after 1 hour.
7. Remove halibut, reserving marinade for later.
8. Place fish on broiler pan under broiler until golden brown on one side.
9. Turn and broil for 5 minutes.
10. Heat marinade and pour over halibut.
11. Serve immediately.

Fish

SALMON FILLETS WITH
CUCUMBER RIBBONS

Serves 4

- 2 small English cucumbers, peeled and halved crosswise
- 1 tsp salt, divided
- 1 Tbsp butter
- 2 1/2 Tbsps olive oil, divided
- 4 2" thick center cut salmon fillets (about 2 lbs)
- 1/2 tsp pepper, divided
- 1/2 packet sugar substitute
- 2 tsps tarragon vinegar

1. With a vegetable peeler, peel ribbons along the length of each cucumber half.
2. Keep going until you reach the center core of seeds; discard core.
3. In a bowl, toss cucumber ribbons with 1/2 tsp salt; set aside.
4. In a large skillet over medium-high heat, melt butter in 1 Tbsp oil.
5. Season fish with 1/2 tsp salt and 1/4 tsp pepper.
6. Place fish flesh side down in skillet.
7. Cook 10 minutes, turning carefully once halfway through cooking time, until golden brown and just cooked through.
8. Remove from skillet and tent with foil.
9. Wipe out skillet with a paper towel.
10. Heat remaining 1 1/2 Tbsps oil over medium-high heat until oil shimmers.
11. Add cucumber to skillet; sprinkle with remaining 1/4 tsp pepper and sugar substitute.
12. Cook about 2 minutes, stirring occasionally, until cucumber is just warmed through.
13. Stir in vinegar.
14. Divide cucumber on individual serving plates; top each with a piece of salmon.

FISH WITH VEGETABLES

Serves 4

- ▶ 3 lb whole fish of choice
- ▶ 1/4 cup oil
- ▶ 1 1/2 cup chopped onion
- ▶ 2-4 cloves minced garlic
- ▶ 5-6 prepared plum tomatoes
- ▶ 1/2 cup chopped fresh parsley or coriander
- ▶ 1/4 cup chopped fresh dill (1 Tbsp dried)
- ▶ Freshly ground black pepper
- ▶ 2 Tbsps lemon or lime juice
- ▶ 1 lb fresh spinach
- ▶ 1/3 cup dry white wine or water

1. In a large skillet, heat oil and sauté onion until translucent.
2. Add garlic, tomatoes, parsley, dill and pepper.
3. Cook 10 minutes on medium heat, uncovered.
4. Sprinkle fish lightly with pepper and lemon juice.
5. Pour tomato mixture in a lightly greased 9" x 13" x 2" baking dish and place fish on top of sauce.
6. Pour wine over the fish.
7. Cover with foil and bake at 350°F for 20 minutes.
8. Uncover and continue baking 10 minutes.
9. Add spinach for the last 5 minutes of baking time.
10. Arrange it in the sauce around the fish.

SEA SCALLOPS

Serves 4

- ▶ 1/2 cup Brazil nuts, sliced fine
- ▶ 3 shallots minced
- ▶ 1 minced garlic clove
- ▶ 1 cup dry white wine or water
- ▶ 6 Tbsps butter, cut into bits
- ▶ 1/4 cup minced fresh parsley or coriander
- ▶ 1/8 tsp sea salt
- ▶ Fresh-ground white pepper to taste
- ▶ 1 1/2 lbs sea scallops

1. In a small saucepan, combine shallots, garlic and wine or water.
2. Bring to a boil over high heat until the wine is reduced by half (5 minutes).
3. Turn heat to low, add 4 Tbsps butter and whisk until it is all melted and mixed.
4. Stir in parsley and seasonings to taste.
5. In a large skillet, heat remaining butter.
6. When it sizzles, add the scallops.
7. Saute about 4 minutes over medium heat until the scallops are translucent.
8. Place scallops on preheated serving dish.
9. Pour sauce over them and garnish with the raw Brazil nuts.

SOUTH-OF-THE
BORDER CERVICHE

Serves
4

- ▶ 1 lb fresh red snapper fillets
- ▶ 3/4 cup fresh lime juice
- ▶ 3 chilies Serrano, seeded and cut into thin strips
- ▶ 1 cup thinly sliced red onion
- ▶ 1/2 tsp sea salt
- ▶ Fresh ground black pepper to taste
- ▶ 2 Tbsps chopped cilantro (or 1 Tbsp dried oregano)

1. Cut the fish into narrow strips (2" x 1/4").
2. Put fish into a glass or ceramic bowl.
3. Add the other ingredients and stir.
4. Marinate for 10 minutes.
5. Drain off excess lime juice.
6. Correct the seasonings to taste.
7. Serve cold or at room temperature as an appetizer or main course.
8. Other types of fish work well here: cod or monkfish, for example, could be substituted.

EASY TUNA SALAD

Serves
2

- ▶ 1 can tuna
- ▶ 1 hard-boiled egg
- ▶ 1 tsp Dijon mustard
- ▶ 1/4 cup mayonnaise
- ▶ 1/2 cup chopped vegetables (onion, garlic, carrot, celery, radish, fresh parsley)
- ▶ 1/2 tsp curry powder
- ▶ 1/2 tsp Mrs. Dash (or other seasoning mix)

1. Mash the egg.
2. Put all ingredients in a bowl and mix and blend well. May be done in food processor.
3. Chop vegetables coarse first, then add remaining ingredients to food processor and pulse 3-4 times for desired consistency.

Chicken or Turkey Salad:
4. Replace tuna with 8 oz leftover chopped chicken or turkey.

SEA BASS CONTINENTAL

Serves 4

- ▶ 1 sea bass
- ▶ 2 lbs (not including head and tail)
- ▶ 1 medium onion, quartered
- ▶ 2 stalks celery, cut in halves
- ▶ 6 medium carrots, peeled and cut in serving portions
- ▶ 3 sprigs parsley
- ▶ 5 whole peppercorns
- ▶ 2 cloves
- ▶ 1/2 bay leaf
- ▶ 2 tsps salt
- ▶ 2 Tbsps lemon juice
- ▶ 2 Tbsps white vinegar

1. In large pot, boil together, uncovered, all ingredients except fish in 2 quarts of water.
2. Lower heat and add the sea bass.
3. Cover and simmer about 20 minutes or until fish is tender.
4. Let stand 10 minutes.
5. Carefully remove fish and carrots and place on serving platter.
6. Discard rest of ingredients.

CURRIED ROCK LOBSTER

Serves 4

- ▶ 4 rock lobster tails
- ▶ 2 tomatoes, peeled and diced small
- ▶ 2 onions, minced
- ▶ 1 Tbsp curry powder
- ▶ 1 bay leaf thoroughly crumbled
- ▶ 1/2 tsp garlic salt
- ▶ 2 dashes cayenne (red pepper)
- ▶ 1 Tbsp chopped parsley
- ▶ 1/4 tsp marjoram
- ▶ 1 Tbsp low sodium bouillon

1. Place frozen lobster tails in boiling salted water, then bring water to boil again and simmer for about 5 minutes.
2. Drain immediately and plunge into cold water.
3. With sharp knife under meat, strip all meat from shells, saving shells for serving.
4. Dice the lobster meat into 1/2" chunks while sautéing the onions in bouillon in no-stick pan.
5. When hot, stir in the tomatoes and all seasonings, mixing well.
6. Simmer slowly for about 20 minutes, then add lobster pieces and heat thoroughly, mixing well occasionally.
7. Place the mixture in the lobster shells, sprinkle with paprika and serve at once.

BROILED FRESH SALMON

Serves
4

- ▶ 2 medium-sized fresh salmon steaks, 1" thick
- ▶ Lime juice
- ▶ Butter
- ▶ Salt
- ▶ Freshly ground black pepper
- ▶ 4 pinches dried tarragon
- ▶ 4 ounces dry white wine

1. Place salmon steaks in shallow, fireproof baking pan and squeeze lime juice over them.
2. Dot steaks liberally with butter, sprinkle with salt and pepper and a pinch (for each steak) of dried tarragon leaves.
3. Pour wine in pan (around steaks--not over them)
4. Place pan under broiler about 4" from flame.
5. Cook for about 10 to 12 minutes, basting carefully during latter part of cooking so herbs are not disturbed.
6. Turn steaks and season as before.
7. Broil for 5 to 6 minutes.
8. Baste after herbs have been "set" by heat.
9. Skin should get crisp.

BROILED LOBSTER

Serves
4

WITH TARRAGON

- ▶ 4 frozen lobster tails
- ▶ 1/2 stick butter
- ▶ 1 Tbsp chopped or dried chives
- ▶ 1 tsp dried tarragon
- ▶ 1/2 tsp dry mustard
- ▶ Seasoned salt

1. Remove soft part of lobster tail with scissors.
2. Hit hard shell slightly with mallet or cleaver to make it lie flat.
3. Melt butter.
4. Add chives, tarragon, mustard and salt.
5. Spoon generously over tails and let stand in marinade for several hours.
6. Remove from marinade.
7. Broil about 4" from heat for 10 to 15 minutes with meaty side up.
8. Baste often.

FAST PARSLEY BUTTERED FISH

Serves 4

- ▶ 2 Tbsps butter
- ▶ 2 Tbsps lemon juice
- ▶ 1 lb white fish fillets
- ▶ 1 Tbsp chopped fresh parsley, or 1 tsp dried salt to taste, optional

1. Place butter and lemon juice together in a microwave-safe, 8" x 12" glass dish.
2. Microwave on HIGH 30-60 seconds, or until butter is melted.
3. Stir.
4. Coat both sides of fillets with butter sauce.
5. Arrange fish in baking dish.
6. Cover with waxed paper.
7. Microwave on HIGH until fish flakes easily, 5–6 minutes.
8. Sprinkle with parsley and salt if you wish before serving.

TILAPIA WITH MANGO

Serves 4

- ▶ 4 6-oz tilapia fillets
- ▶ 2 Tbsps soy sauce
- ▶ 1/8 tsp salt
- ▶ 1/8 tsp pepper, or lemon pepper seasoning
- ▶ 1 Tbsp butter, cut into chunks
- ▶ 1 mango or slices of dried mango

1. Place tilapia fillets in baking pan.
2. Pour soy sauce over top of fish.
3. Sprinkle salt and pepper over fish.
4. Lay butter on top.
5. Peel the mango and cut into lengthwise pieces.
6. Lay around fish.
7. Bake covered at 400°F for 30 minutes.
8. Turn mango slices after 15 minutes of baking.

STIR-FRY SCALLOPS

Serves 4

- ▶ 12–16 large scallops
- ▶ 1/2 tsp chili powder
- ▶ 1/2 tsp dried oregano
- ▶ 2 Tbsps olive oil

1. Rinse scallops and dry with paper towel.
2. Mix seasonings in small bowl.
3. Toss and coat scallops.
4. Stir fry in hot olive oil for about 3-5 minutes, just until opaque.

SEASONED SALMON

Serves 4

- ▶ 1 lb salmon fillet
- ▶ 3 Tbsps lemon juice
- ▶ 2 Tbsps fresh dill, or 2 tsps dried dill weed
- ▶ 2 Tbsps minced garlic, or powdered garlic to taste
- ▶ 3 slices onion on top

1. Line a 9" x 13" baking pan with foil.
2. Spray foil with non-stick spray.
3. Place fish on foil.
4. Sprinkle with lemon juice.
5. Sprinkle with dill and garlic.
6. Place onion slices on top.
7. Cover with second sheet of foil.
8. Bake at 450°F for 15-20 minutes, or until fish flakes easily.
9. Salmon is still pink after being fully cooked.

SIMPLY GRILLED SALMON

Serves 4

- ▶ 2 lbs salmon steaks or fillets
- ▶ 1/2 cup lemon juice
- ▶ 1 1/2 Tbsps butter
- ▶ Seasoned salt

1. Lay salmon on large piece of foil.
2. Pour lemon juice over top.
3. Lay butter in several slivers over top.
4. Sprinkle evenly with seasoned salt to taste.
5. Close foil and wrap again in second layer so lemon juice will not escape.
6. Grill over medium heat for 15 minutes, or until salmon is flakey but not dry.

CILANTRO SHRIMP

Serves 4

- ▶ 1 bunch finely chopped cilantro
- ▶ 3 each fresh juiced limes
- ▶ 1 lb cooked, peeled and deveined shrimp
- ▶ 1 clove finely chopped garlic
- ▶ Salt to taste
- ▶ Black pepper to taste
- ▶ 1/4 cup olive oil

1. In a large bowl mix all ingredients and toss to combine.
2. Place bowl tightly in the refrigerator for at least 3 hours.
3. Serve on top of a chopped bed of iceberg lettuce.

SPICY SHRIMP MARINARA WITH FETA

- 2 tsps olive oil
- 1 Tbsp minced garlic
- 1/4 tsp crushed red-pepper flakes
- 2 Tbsps white wine
- 1 1/2 cups jarred sugar-free marinara sauce
- 1 tsp dried oregano
- 1 lb large shrimp, peeled
- 2 ounces feta (about 1 cup)
- 1 Tbsp chopped parsley

1. Heat oven to 400°F.
2. Heat olive oil in a large ovenproof frying pan or Dutch oven over medium heat.
3. Add garlic and crushed red-pepper flakes.
4. Stir 30 seconds.
5. Add white wine and stir until almost evaporated.
6. Add marinara sauce and dried oregano.
7. Simmer for 5 minutes.
8. Stir in shrimp.
9. Crumble feta over top.
10. Bake until shrimp are just cooked through, about 8 minutes.
11. Sprinkle with 1 Tbsp chopped parsley.

GINGER SALMON SKEWERS
WITH ASIAN SLAW

- 4 6-oz skinless salmon fillets (1" thick)
- 2 Tbsps vegetable oil
- 2 Tbsps minced fresh cilantro
- 2 Tbsps soy sauce
- 1 Tbsp grated fresh ginger
- 1 Tbsp fresh lime juice
- 4 cups shredded Napa cabbage
- 1 cup shredded carrots
- 1/2 cup sliced radishes
- 1 minced shallot
- 1/2 cup chopped fresh cilantro
- Rice vinegar
- Salt and pepper to taste

1. Cut salmon fillets into large cubes and thread on skewers.
2. Whisk vegetable oil, minced fresh cilantro, soy sauce, fresh ginger and fresh lime juice in a medium bowl.
3. Whisk all until well combined; brush over salmon.
4. Cook salmon on a hot stovetop grill pan, 2 to 3 minutes (for medium).
5. In a separate bowl:
6. Toss together cabbage, carrots, radishes, shallots and cilantro.
7. Season with rice vinegar, salt and pepper to taste.

Meats

TIPS FOR PREPARING MEAT

▶ For maximum safety, thaw meat in the refrigerator.

▶ When slicing meat into thin strips, for an easier slice, partially freeze before slicing.

▶ Roasts with bones cook faster than boneless as the bone carries the heat internally. Grilling burgers? Make them more juicy by adding cold water to the beef before grilling (1/2 cup to each pound of meat).

▶ Meatball tip: Meatballs are easy to make and great to freeze. If you want to be able to make a lot, but also be able to pull them out by the mouthful instead of the frozen mound, place them on cookie sheets in your freezer until they are frozen. Then put them in plastic bags. They won't stick together and you can remove as many as you want when you want them.

CORNED BEEF & CABBAGE

Serves
4

▶ 4-5 lbs corned beef
▶ 1 clove garlic
▶ 6 Tbsps sliced onion
▶ 1 small head cabbage (about 4 cups)

1. Wash beef and place in enough cold water to cover meat.
2. Bring water to boil and remove foam from surface with shallow spoon.
3. Add clove garlic and cover.
4. Reduce heat and simmer for about 3 hours or until meat is tender.
5. Add onion and cook for 30 more minutes.
6. Add cabbage, which has been cut into 6 equal portions, and cook for 10 to 15 minutes or until tender.
7. Remove to heated platter.
8. Slice meat and serve with cabbage.

SAUCY MEATBALLS

Serves 4

- 1 lb ground round
- 1 1/2 cup + 2 Tbsps canned no-salt-added beef broth, undiluted and divided
- 2 Tbsps low-sodium Worcestershire sauce
- 1/4 tsp garlic powder
- Vegetable cooking spray
- 1/2 cup frozen small whole onions, thawed
- 1/2 tsp dried thyme
- 1/4 tsp pepper
- 1/8 tsp salt

1. Combine ground round, 2 Tbsps broth, Worcestershire sauce, and garlic powder.
2. Shape into 28 meatballs, using 1 Tbsp meat mixture for each meatball.
3. Place meatballs on rack of a broiler pan coated with cooking spray.
4. Broil 5 1/2" from heat (with electric oven door partially opened) 10 to 12 minutes or until browned, turning occasionally.
5. Drain and pat dry with paper towels; set aside.
6. Coat a large nonstick skillet with cooking spray; place over medium-high heat until hot.
7. Add onions, and sauté 2 minutes or until tender.
8. Stir in meatballs, remaining 1 1/2 cups broth, thyme, pepper and salt.
9. Bring to a boil; cover, reduce heat, and simmer 20 minutes.

STERLING MEATBALLS

Serves 4

- 1 lb lean ground beef
- 5 cloves minced garlic
- Pinch of dried oregano
- Pinch of basil
- 1/2 cup Parmesan cheese
- One egg
- Mozzarella cheese cut into cubes
- 20 grape tomatoes

1. Mix together first 6 ingredients.
2. Roll into 2 inch balls.
3. Take cube of mozzarella cheese and stuff meatball.
4. Make sure cheese is completely covered.
5. Sauté in olive oil.
6. Slice 20 grape tomatoes in half.
7. Sauté tomatoes with 2 cloves garlic.
8. Eat meatballs with dollop of tomato on top for 90/10 split.

TURBOTIPS:
You can substitute turkey or bison if you prefer.

LAMB CHOPS WITH PARSLEY

Serves 4

- ▶ 4 6-oz lean lamb loin chops (1 1/4 inch thick)
- ▶ 1 lemon, cut in half
- ▶ 1/4 tsp garlic powder
- ▶ 1/4 tsp pepper
- ▶ 3/4 cup chopped fresh parsley
- ▶ 3 Tbsps Dijon mustard
- ▶ Vegetable cooking spray
- ▶ Fresh parsley sprigs (optional)
- ▶ Cherry tomatoes (optional)

1. Trim fat from chop.
2. Rub both sides of each chop with lemon, squeezing juice over chops; sprinkle with garlic power and pepper.
3. Combine chopped parsley and mustard; press mixture on all sides of chops.
4. Place chops in an 11 x 7 x 1 1/2" baking dish coated with cooking spray.
5. Bake, uncovered, at 500°F for 4 minutes.
6. Reduce heat to 350°F, and bake 15 additional minutes or to desired degree of doneness.
7. Transfer to a serving platter.
8. If desired, garnish with parsley sprigs and cherry tomatoes.

CHEDDAR-STUFFED BURGERS

Serves 8

- ▶ 4 lbs ground beef
- ▶ 2 Tbsps Worcestershire sauce
- ▶ 6 Tbsps fresh chives, finely chopped
- ▶ 1 Tbsp fresh basil, finely chopped
- ▶ 2 tsps dried oregano
- ▶ 2/3 tsp chili powder
- ▶ 1/2 tsp salt
- ▶ 3/4 tsp freshly ground black pepper
- ▶ 1 lb sharp Cheddar cheese, crumbled

1. Mix all ingredients except the Cheddar cheese and shape into 8 thick patties.
2. Make a pocket in the center of each patty, fill with the Cheddar cheese and cover the cheese with the meat.
3. Broil, grill or fry the meat to desired doneness.
4. Serve immediately.

MEDITERRANEAN LEG OF LAMB

Serves
10

- ▶ 3 1/2 lb leg of lamb, trimmed
- ▶ 5 clovers garlic, thinly sliced and divided
- ▶ 2 tsps dried rosemary, divided
- ▶ 1 tsp freshly ground black pepper, divided
- ▶ Vegetable cooking spray
- ▶ 1 lb fresh mushrooms
- ▶ 12 plum tomatoes, halved
- ▶ 1 small eggplant, peeled and cut into 1-inch cubes
- ▶ 1 medium-size sweet red pepper, cut into 1-inch piece
- ▶ 1 medium-size sweet yellow pepper, cut into 1-inch pieces
- ▶ 1 large purple onion, cut into wedges
- ▶ 1/4 cup canned low-sodium chicken broth
- ▶ 2 Tbsps balsamic vinegar
- ▶ 1 Tbsp olive oil

1. Cut 1" lengthwise slits in meat; insert half of garlic slices into slits, reserving remaining garlic.
2. Rub meat with 1 tsp dried rosemary and 1/2 tsp ground pepper; place on a rack in a large roasting pan coated with cooking spray.
3. Insert meat thermometer into thickest part of meat, if desired.
4. Bake at 325°F for 1 hour.
5. Remove stems from mushrooms; re-serve stems for another use.
6. Add mushroom caps, tomato, eggplant, red pepper, yellow pepper and onion to pan.
7. Combine remaining garlic, 1 tsp dried rosemary, 1/2 tsp ground pepper, chicken broth, vinegar and oil; stir well.
8. Pour broth mixture over vegetables in pan.
9. Bake at 325°F for 50 minutes or until thermometer registers 150°F.
10. Let stand 10 minutes before serving.

LOUISIANA HAMBURGERS

Serves
4

- ▶ 2 lbs ground beef
- ▶ 3 tsps garlic, minced
- ▶ 1 green pepper, finely chopped
- ▶ 1/2 cup green onions, finely chopped
- ▶ 2 tsps ground cumin
- ▶ 2 tsps dried oregano
- ▶ 1 tsp dried thyme
- ▶ 2 tsps paprika
- ▶ 1 Tbsp Tabasco
- ▶ Salt and black pepper to taste

1. Combine all ingredients with the beef.
2. Shape into 6 hamburger patties.
3. Broil or fry the meat to desired done-ness.
4. Serve immediately.

PORK & VEGETABLE PICCATA

Serves 4

- ▶ 1 lb pork tenderloin
- ▶ Vegetable cooking spray
- ▶ 3 cups small fresh broccoli flowerets
- ▶ 3 cups sliced yellow squash
- ▶ 1/4 cup chopped fresh parsley
- ▶ 1/2 tsp ground white pepper
- ▶ 1/8 tsp salt
- ▶ 2 cloves garlic, crushed
- ▶ 1/4 cup fresh lemon juice, divided
- ▶ 1 cup canned low-sodium chicken broth
- ▶ 1 tsp grated lemon rind
- ▶ 2 clovers garlic, crushed
- ▶ 1 Tbsp drained capers
- ▶ 1/2 tsp paprika

1. Trim fat from pork; cut pork into 16 pieces.
2. Place pork between 2 sheets of heavy-duty plastic wrap; flatten to 1/4" thickness.
3. Coat a large nonstick skillet with cooking spray, and place over medium-high heat until hot.
4. Add broccoli and next 5 ingredients; sauté 6 minutes or until crisp-tender.
5. Add 2 Tbsps lemon juice; toss well.
6. Transfer vegetable mixture to a platter; keep warm.
7. Coat skillet with cooking spray; place over medium-high heat until hot.
8. Add one-third of pork; cook 2 minutes on each side or until done.
9. Drain on paper towels; place on platter with vegetables and keep warm.
10. Repeat with remaining pork.
11. Wipe drippings from skillet.
12. Add broth, lemon rind and garlic to skillet; scrape bottom of skillet with a wooden spoon to loosen browned bits.
13. Bring to a boil, cooking 2 1/2 minutes.
14. Remove from heat; stir in remaining 2 Tbsps lemon juice, capers and paprika.
15. Spoon over vegetable and pork.

STEAK AU POIVR

Serves 4

- ▶ 4 9-oz beef filets
- ▶ 4 Tbsps cracked black peppercorns
- ▶ Preheat a grill or broiler

1. With the knife parallel to the work surface, butterfly the beef filets; do not cut all the way through the filets.
2. Open the filets and press peppercorns onto both sides of the meat.
3. Grill or broil until done to preference.

ROAST PORK

Serves 4

- ▶ 2 1/2 lb boneless pork loin roast
- ▶ 1/2 tsp salt
- ▶ 3/4 tsp dried oregano
- ▶ 3/4 tsp dried thyme
- ▶ 1/4 tsp freshly ground black pepper
- ▶ 3 dashes Tabasco
- ▶ 3 cloves garlic, cut into slivers
- ▶ 3 Tbsps Dijon mustard

1. Preheat the oven to 375°F.
2. Cut small slits in the roast.
3. In a small bowl mix together the salt, oregano, thyme and pepper.
4. Coat the garlic slivers with the spice mixture.
5. Insert the garlic slivers into the slits in the roast and rub the remaining mixture over the top of the meat.
6. Combine the mustard Tabasco and baste the meat with half of the mixture.
7. Place the meat in a roasting pan on a rack.
8. Roast uncovered for 1 hour.
9. Baste roast with the remaining mustard mixture.
10. Roast 1 hour more.
11. Serve immediately.

PORK BURGERS WITH ONIONS

Serves 4

- ▶ 10 ounces lean ground pork
- ▶ 1 tsp ground sage
- ▶ 1 tsp salt
- ▶ 1/2 tsp garlic powder
- ▶ 1/2 tsp freshly ground black pepper
- ▶ 2 cups sliced onions

1. In large bowl, combine pork, sage, salt, garlic powder and pepper. Form into 4 equal patties.
2. Spray large skillet with nonstick cooking spray; heat.
3. Add onions; cook over medium-high heat, stirring frequently, until lightly browned.
4. Remove onions from skillet; set aside.
5. In same skillet, cook patties over medium-high heat, turning once, until cooked through. Serve topped with cooked onions.

Meats

GRILLED HAMBURGER

Serves 4

WITH FRESH SALSA

- ▶ 3/4 cup diced tomato
- ▶ 1/4 cup diced red onion
- ▶ 1/4 cup minced fresh cilantro
- ▶ 1 Tbsp fresh lime juice
- ▶ 1 tsp minced deveined seeded jalapeno pepper (wear gloves to prevent irritation)
- ▶ 1/4 tsp freshly ground black pepper
- ▶ 10 ounces extra-lean ground beef (10% or less fat)
- ▶ 1/2 tsp ground cumin
- ▶ 1/2 tsp onion powder
- ▶ 1/2 tsp salt

1. Preheat outdoor barbecue grill according to manufacturer's directions, or preheat broiler and spray rack in broiler pan with nonstick cooking spray.
2. To prepare salsa, in medium bowl, combine tomato, onion, cilantro, juice, jalapeno pepper and black pepper; set aside.
3. In large bowl, combine beef, cumin, onion powder and salt; form into 4 equal patties.
4. Grill patties over hot coals or place onto prepared rack in broiler pan and broil 4" from heat, turning once, 8 minutes, until beef is cooked through.
5. Serve with salsa.

LAMB BURGERS

Serves 4

WITH FETA CHEESE

- ▶ 9 ounces ground lamb
- ▶ 1/2 tsps salt
- ▶ 1/4 tsp garlic powder
  - ▶ 1/4 tsp dried rosemary leaves, crumbled
  - ▶ Pinch freshly ground black pepper
  - ▶ 3/4 ounce feta cheese, crumbled

1. In medium bowl, combine lamb, salt, garlic powder, rosemary and pepper; form into 4 equal patties.
2. In medium nonstick skillet, cook patties 3 minutes; turn over.
3. Top each patty with one-fourth of the cheese; cook, covered, 3 minutes, until cheese is melted and patties are cooked through.

TURBOTIPS:
Lamb burgers are flavorful changes from beef burgers. If you don't see ground lamb at your supermarket, ask the butcher to grind some for you.

BEEF BOURGUIGNONNE

Serves 4

- ▶ 1 Tbsp + 1 tsp olive oil
- ▶ 1 cup chopped onions
- ▶ 2 garlic cloves, minced
- ▶ 13 ounces lean boneless beef round steak, cut into 1 1/2 cubes
- ▶ 1 1/4 lb all-purpose potatoes, pared and cubed
- ▶ 4 cups sliced carrots (1" slices)
- ▶ 1 cup dry red Burgundy wine
- ▶ 1 bay leaf
- ▶ 1 tsp dried thyme leaves
- ▶ 1/4 tsp salt
- ▶ Freshly ground black pepper, to taste
- ▶ 4 cups small whole white mushrooms, woody ends removed
- ▶ 2 cups frozen pearl onions

1. In large saucepan or Dutch oven, heat oil; add chopped onions and garlic.
2. Cook over medium-high heat, stirring frequently, 7 minutes, until lightly browned.
3. Add beef; cook.
4. Stir frequently, 1-2 minutes, until beef is browned on all sides.
5. Add potatoes, carrots, wine, bay leaf, thyme, salt and pepper to beef mixture; bring liquid to a boil.
6. Reduce heat to low; simmer, covered, adding water, a few Tbsps at a time to keep mixture from sticking, 45 minutes, until carrots and potatoes are tender.
7. Add mushrooms and pearl onions to beef mixture; simmer, covered, 15-20 minutes, until onions are tender.
8. Remove and discard bay.

PIZZA BURGERS

Serves 4

- ▶ 10 ounces extra-lean ground beef (10% or less fat)
- ▶ 1/2 tsp salt
- ▶ 1/2 tsps freshly ground black pepper
- ▶ 1/2 tsp dried oregano leaves
- ▶ 1/4 cup tomato sauce (no salt added)
- ▶ 1/4 cup thinly sliced with mushrooms
- ▶ 1 1/2 ounces mozzarella cheese, grated
- ▶ 1 Tbsp minced fresh flat–leaf parsley

1. In large bowl, combine beef, salt, pepper and oregano; form into 4 equal patties.
2. In medium nonstick skillet, cook patties 3 minutes; turn over.
3. Spread each patty with 1 Tbsp tomato sauce; top each with 1 Tbsp mushrooms and one-fourth of the cheese.
4. Cook, covered, 4 minutes, until cheese is melted and patties are cooked through.
5. Serve sprinkled with parsley.

LEMON-MARINATED LAMB CHOPS

Serves 4

- ▶ 1 tsp grated lemon zest
- ▶ 1/4 cup fresh lemon juice
- ▶ 1 tsp Dijon-style mustard
- ▶ 1/4 tsp salt
- ▶ Pinch freshly ground black pepper
- ▶ 4 3-oz loin lamb chops

1. To prepare marinade, in gallon-size sealable plastic bag, combine zest, juice, mustard, rosemary, salt and pepper; add lamb.
2. Seal bag, squeezing out air; turn to coat lamb, Refrigerate 1-3 hours, turning bag occasionally.
3. Preheat broiler.
4. Spray rack to broiler pan with nonstick cooking spray.
5. Drain and discard marinade.
6. Place lamb onto prepared rack; broil 4" from heat, turning once, 4-5 minutes, until cooked through.

OVEN-BRAISED CITRUS

PORK CUBES

Serves 4

- ▶ 1/2 cup chopped onion
- ▶ 1/4 cup fresh orange juice with pulp plus 1/4 cup of water mixed together
- ▶ 2 tsps fresh lemon juice
- ▶ 3 garlic cloves, chopped
- ▶ 1 bay leaf
- ▶ 1/2 tsp dried oregano leaves
- ▶ 1/2 tsp ground cumin
- ▶ 1/2 tsp freshly ground black pepper
- ▶ 15 ounces lean boneless pork loin, cut into into 1 cubes
- ▶ Fresh cilantro sprigs to garnish

1. To prepare marinade, in gallon-size sealable plastic bag, combine onion, orange and lemon juice, garlic, bay leaf, oregano, cumin and pepper; add pork.
2. Seal bag, squeezing out air; turn to coat pork.
3. Refrigerate at least 2 hours or overnight, turning bag occasionally.
4. Preheat oven to 325°F.
5. Spray 1-quart baking dish with nonstick cooking spray.
6. Transfer pork mixture to prepared baking dish; bake, covered, 3 hours, until pork is very tender.
7. Remove and discard bay leaf.
8. Serve pork mixture garnished with cilantro sprigs.

MEDALLIONS OF LAMB
WITH VEGETABLES

Serves 4

- 2 cups thickly sliced carrots
- 1 cup thickly sliced parsnips
- 1 cup cubed butternut squash
- 1 cup cubed beets
- 1 cup pearl onions
- 1/2 tsp salt
- 1/2 tsp freshly ground black pepper
- 10 ounces lean boneless loin of lamb
- 1 garlic clove, minced
- 1/2 tsp dried rosemary leaves

1. Preheat oven to 400°F.
2. Spray large roasting pan with nonstick cooking spray.
3. Spread carrots, parsnips, squash, beets and onions evenly in prepared roasting pan; sprinkle evenly with 1/4 tsp of the pepper.
4. Spray vegetables lightly with nonstick cooking spray; roast 35 minutes until just tender.
5. Remove vegetables from oven; leave oven on.
6. Sprinkle lamb with garlic, rosemary, remaining 1/4 tsp salt and remaining 1/4 tsp pepper.
7. Move vegetables to sides of roasting pan, making a well in center; place lamb into well.
8. Roast, turning lamb once every 20 minutes, until lamb is cooked through and tender and vegetables are golden brown.
9. Transfer lamb to cutting board; slice thinly.
10. Arrange lamb slices on serving platter; surround with roasted vegetables.

Meats

CHILI-STUFFED ACORN SQUASH

- ▶ 2 14-oz acorn squashes
- ▶ 1 Tbsp + 1 tsp olive oil
- ▶ 1/2 cup chopped onion
- ▶ 1/2 cup finely chopped green bell pepper
- ▶ 4 garlic cloves, minced
- ▶ 1/2 minced deveined seeded jalapeno (wear gloves to prevent irritation)
- ▶ 5 ounces lean ground pork
- ▶ 2 bay leaves
- ▶ 1 tsp mild or hot chili powder
- ▶ 1 tsp ground cumin
- ▶ 1 tsp dried oregano leaves
- ▶ 1 lb drained cooked red kidney beans
- ▶ 1 cup low-sodium chicken broth
- ▶ Freshly ground black pepper, to taste
- ▶ Minced fresh cilantro, to garnish

1. Pierce squashes in several places and microwave on HIGH (100% power) for 1 minute.
2. Halve and seed squashes.
3. Place halves on microwave plate; cover with plastic wrap and microwave on HIGH (100% power) for 7 minutes or until tender.
4. Preheat oven to 375°F.
5. In medium nonstick saucepan, heat oil; add onion, bell pepper, garlic and jalapeno pepper.
6. Cook over medium-high heat, stirring frequently, 5 minutes, until vegetables are softened.
7. Add pork; cook, stirring to break up meat, 3-4 minutes, until no longer pink.
8. Add bay leaves, chili powder, cumin and oregano; cook, stirring constantly, 1 minute.
9. Add beans, broth and black pepper to pork mixture; bring liquid to a broil.
10. Reduce heat to low; simmer, stirring occasionally, 30 minutes, until mixture is thickened and flavors are blended.
11. Remove and discard bay leaves.
12. Fill squash cavities with equal amounts of pork mixture; place onto nonstick baking sheet.
13. Bake 10-15 minutes, until heated through and tops are crispy.
14. Serve sprinkled with cilantro.

BEEF WITH ASPARAGUS
& CHERRY TOMATOES

Serves 4

- 24 asparagus spears, cut diagonally into 1/2 pieces
- 10 ounces lean boneless beef sirloin, cut into 1/4 strips
- 1/2 tsp salt
- 1/4 tsps freshly ground black pepper
- 1/2 cup diagonally sliced scallions (1/2 slices)
- 1 garlic clove, very thinly sliced
- 24 cherry tomatoes

1. In large nonstick skillet, combine asparagus and 1/4 cup water; bring liquid to a boil.
2. Reduce heat to low; simmer 2 minutes, until asparagus are just tender and water is evaporated.
3. Sprinkle beef on all sides with salt and pepper; add beef, scallions and garlic to cooked asparagus.
4. Cook, stirring frequently, 4 minutes, until beef is cooked through.
5. Add tomatoes; cook, stirring frequently, 2 minutes, until tomatoes are heated through.

> TURBOTIPS:
> Substitute sugar snap peas or green beans for the asparagus.

QUICK & EASY GRILLED
TERIYAKI STEAK

Serves 2

- 1/4 cup reduced-sodium soy sauce
- 1 Tbsp dry white wine
- 1 Tbsp rice wine vinegar
- 1/2 tsp dry mustard
- 1/2 tsps freshly ground black pepper
- 10 ounces lean boneless beef sirloin

1. Spray rack in broiler pan with nonstick cooking spray.
2. Preheat broiler.
3. In small bowl, combine soy sauce, wine, vinegar, mustard and pepper; brush beef on both sides with some of the soy sauce mixture.
4. Place beef onto prepared rack in broiler pan; broil 4" front heat, turning once and brushing frequently with remaining soy sauce mixture, until cooked through.
5. Transfer beef to cutting board; slice thinly.

Meats

NO-FUSS SLICED STEAK
WITH VEGETABLES

Serves
4

- ▶ 1 cup baby carrots
- ▶ 24 asparagus spears, cut into 2" pieces
- ▶ 1 cup sugar snap peas
- ▶ 1 cup small red radishes, halved
- ▶ 1/4 tsp freshly ground black pepper
- ▶ 1 Tbsp + 1tsp butter
- ▶ 1 Tbsp fresh lemon juice
- ▶ 10 ounces lean boneless beef sirloin

1. Preheat broiler.
2. Spray rack in broiler pan with nonstick cooking spray.
3. In nonstick skillet, bring 1/2 cup water to a boil; add carrots.
4. Reduce heat to medium; cook, covered, 6 minutes, until just tender.
5. Add asparagus, peas and radishes; cook, covered, 4 minutes.
6. Remove cover; cook 2 minutes, until water is evaporated.
7. Sprinkle vegetables with half of the salt and half of the pepper.
8. Add butter and lemon juice; toss until butter is melted and vegetables are coated.
9. Sprinkle beef on both sides with remaining salt and pepper; place onto prepared rack.
10. Broil, turning once, until cooked through.
11. Transfer beef to cutting board; slice thinly.
12. Arrange beef slices on serving platter; surround with vegetable mixture.

VEAL WITH PEPPER

Serves
4

- ▶ 1 1/2 veal rump
- ▶ 1 large onion, sliced
- ▶ 4 large green peppers
- ▶ 1 lb can tomatoes
- ▶ Pepper to taste
- ▶ 2/3 cup dry sauterne wine

1. Cut veal into cubes.
2. Cut peppers and onion into strips and place on top of meat.
3. Add tomatoes and season with ground pepper.
4. Bake in 325°F oven for 1 hour.
5. Add wine and cook another 15 minutes.

PORK BURGERS WITH ONIONS

Serves 4

- ► 10 ounces lean ground pork
- ► 1 tsp ground sage
- ► 1 tsp salt
- ► 1/4 tsp freshly ground black pepper
- ► 2 cups sliced onions

1. In large bowl, combine pork, sage, salt, garlic powder and pepper; form into 4 equal patties.
2. Spray large skillet with nonstick cooking spray; heat.
3. Add onions; cook over medium-high heat, stirring frequently, 7 minutes, until lightly browned.
4. Remove onions from skillet; set aside.
5. In same skillet, cook patties over medium-high heat, turning once.
6. 10 minutes, until cooked through, serve with cooked onions.

EASY STIR-FRIED PORK

Serves 4

- ► 2 tsps olive oil
- ► 1 medium red bull pepper, seeded and cut into 1/4" strips
- ► 1 medium green bell pepper, seeded and cut into 1/4" strips
- ► 1 medium yellow bell pepper, seeded and cut into 1/4" strips
- ► 2 cups sliced Spanish onions (1/4" slices)
- ► 10 ounces lean boneless pork loin, cut into 1/4" strips
- ► 1/2 tsp dried oregano leaves
- ► 1/2 tsp salt
- ► 1/4 tsp freshly ground black pepper
- ► 1 Tbsp white wine vinegar

1. In large skillet, heat oil; add red, green and yellow bell pepper.
2. Cook over medium-high heat, stirring frequently, about 5 minutes, until peppers are softened.
3. Add onions, cook, stirring frequently, another 5 minutes, until onions are softened.
4. Add pork, oregano, salt and black pepper to vegetable mixture; cook, stirring frequently, 5 minutes, until pork is browned on all sides.
5. Add vinegar; cook, stirring frequently, 1 minute, until pork is cooked through.

Meats

STIR-FRIED PORK & VEGETABLES

Serves 4

- ▶ 2 tsps olive oil
- ▶ 2 medium onions, cut into 1/4" slices
- ▶ 2 cups broccoli florets
- ▶ 1 medium red bell pepper, seeded and cut into 1" pieces
- ▶ 1 medium zucchini, halved lengthwise and cut into 1" pieces
- ▶ 1 cup sugar snap peas
- ▶ 10 ounces lean boneless pork loin, cut into 1/4" strips
- ▶ 1 tsp minced fresh thyme leaves or 1/4 tsp if dried
- ▶ 1/4 tsp salt
- ▶ Pinch freshly ground black pepper
- ▶ 1 Tbsp white wine vinegar

1. In large nonstick skillet, heat oil; add onions.
2. Cook over medium-high heat, stirring frequently, 5 minutes, until softened.
3. Add broccoli and 1/4 cup water; cook, covered, 4 minutes, until broccoli is tender.
4. Add bell pepper, zucchini and peas; cook, covered, 2 minutes, until bell pepper is tender. Move vegetables to sides of skillet, making a well in center; place pork, thyme, salt and black pepper into well.
5. Cook pork mixture, stirring frequently, 6 minutes, until pork is browned on all sides.
6. Add vinegar; toss pork mixture and vegetables together.
7. Cook, continuing to toss, 3 minutes, until pork is cooked through.

STIR FRIED PORK & VEGETABLES #2

Serves 4

- ▶ 1 Tbsp olive oil
- ▶ 12 ounces pork tenderloin, trimmed of all visible fat and cut crosswise in thin slices
- ▶ 8-oz package frozen snap peas
- ▶ 14-oz package frozen vegetables (broccoli, mushrooms, water chestnuts, red pepper and peanuts) with Oriental sauce
- ▶ 1/3 cup water
- ▶ Mung bean sprouts

1. Heat oil in a large, heavy skillet over medium-high heat.
2. Add pork and stir-fry until meat is no longer pink.
3. Add vegetables and water.
4. Mix gently.
5. Bring to a boil, cover and simmer 6 to 8 minutes until vegetables are hot.
6. Garnish with sprouts.

Meats

VEAL CHOPS WITH
MUSHROOM STUFFING

Serves 4

- ▶ 1/2 cup diced onion
- ▶ 1 cup sliced mushrooms
- ▶ 1 garlic clove, minced
- ▶ 1/2 tsp dried thyme leaves
- ▶ 2 Tbsps red wine vinegar
- ▶ 4 3-oz loin veal chops, sliced horizontally to form a pocket
- ▶ 1/2 tsp salt
- ▶ 1/4 tsp freshly ground black pepper
- ▶ 2 tsps olive oil
- ▶ 1/2 cup low-sodium beef broth

1. Preheat oven to 400°F.
2. Spray medium nonstick skillet with nonstick cooking spray; heat.
3. Add onion; cook over medium-high heat, stirring frequently, 5 minutes, until softened.
4. Add mushrooms, garlic and thyme; cook, stirring frequently, 5 minutes, until mushrooms are tender.
5. Add 1 Tbsp of the vinegar, cook, stirring constantly, 2 minutes, until flavors are blended.
6. Sprinkle veal with salt and pepper.
7. Stuff each veal pocket with one-fourth of the mushrooms mixture; secure open edge with toothpick.
8. In large cast-iron skillet, heat oil; add stuffed veal.
9. Cook over high heat, turning once, 2 minutes, until veal is browned on both sides.
10. Transfer skillet to oven; bake 15 minutes, until veal is cooked through.
11. Transfer veal to serving platter.
12. Remove and discard toothpicks; keep veal warm.
13. In same skillet, combine broth and remaining 1 Tbsp vinegar; cook over medium-high heat, scraping up browned bits from bottom of skillet, 3 minutes, until heated through and well combined.
14. Pour broth mixture over warm veal.

Meats

ROAST TENDERLOIN

Serves
4

- ▶ 1 tsp ground rosemary
- ▶ 1 1/2 lb tenderloin roast at room temperature
- ▶ 1 Tbsp Dijon mustard

1. Heat oven to 450°F.
2. Coat roasting pan or metal baking pan with cooking spray.
3. Spread rosemary evenly on a plate along with some salt and pepper.
4. Season roast by rolling it in the seasoning plate.
5. Slather with mustard.
6. Put in prepared pan and roast until done to your taste.
7. (For medium-rare, cook 425°F, about 25 to 35 minutes.) Remove to cutting board and let rest at least 15 minutes.
8. The temperature will rise about 10 degrees during resting.
9. Cut into 1/2" slices and serve warm or at room temperature.

BAKED VEAL CHOPS

Serves
4

- ▶ 8 rib eye veal chops
- ▶ 1 tsp onion powder
- ▶ 1/2 tsp garlic powder
- ▶ 1/2 tsp dry mustard
- ▶ 3 stalks celery, diced
- ▶ 1 medium onion, diced
- ▶ 1/4 lb fresh mushrooms, cleaned and sliced
- ▶ 1/2 cup water
- ▶ 1 cup tomato puree (unsalted)
- ▶ 1 cup water (more if necessary)
- ▶ 1/2 cup red or white wine

1. Season chops on both sides with onion and garlic powder and mustard.
2. Place in baking dish.
3. Sauté celery, onion and mushrooms in 1/2 cup water.
4. Add tomato puree and 1/2 cup water to sautéed vegetables.
5. Simmer 10 minutes.
6. Add wine and pour over chops.
7. Cover with aluminum foil.
8. Bake 1 1/2 hours.
9. Uncover and bake 1/2 hour longer in 350°F oven.

Meats

CHEESY FLANK STEAK

Serves 6

- ▶ 1 cup dry red wine
- ▶ 1/4 cup soy sauce
- ▶ 2 garlic cloves, minced
- ▶ 1 large flank steak, 1 1/2-2 lbs
- ▶ 1 cup thawed frozen chopped spinach, squeezed dry
- ▶ 7-oz jar roasted red bell peppers, drained and chopped
- ▶ 1/2 cup crumbled blue cheese
- ▶ Salt and pepper

1. Combine wine, soy sauce and garlic in small bowl.
2. Place steak in large resealable plastic food storage bag; pour marinade over steak.
3. Seal bag and marinate in refrigerator 2 hours.
4. Preheat oven to 350°F.
5. Combine spinach, peppers and cheese in medium bowl.
6. Remove steak from marinade, pat dry and lay on flat surface.
7. Reserve marinade.
8. Spoon spinach and pepper mixture across the length of the steak, covering bottom 2/3 of steak.
9. Roll steak tightly around vegetables, securing with toothpicks or string.
10. Season with salt and pepper and place in roasting pan, seam side down.
11. Bake 30 to 40 minutes for medium-rare, or until desired degree of doneness is reached, basting twice with reserve marinade.
12. Do not baste during last 10 minutes of cooking time.
13. Allow steak to rest about 10 minutes.

LUSCIOUS LAMB

Serves 4

- ▶ 8 lamb chops
- ▶ Garlic powder
- ▶ 2 Tbsps butter
- ▶ 2 Tbsps Worcestershire sauce
- ▶ 2 Tbsps lemon juice
- ▶ 2 Tbsps gin (optional)
- ▶ 1 tsp seasoned salt

1. Rub lamb chops with small amounts of garlic powder.
2. Melt butter and add Worcestershire sauce, lemon juice, gin and salt.
3. Pour liquid over lamb chops.
4. Allow to marinate for 15 minutes.
5. Remove lamb from marinade.
6. Broil to desired doneness.

Meats

ROAST LEG OF LAMB

Serves
10

▶ 3 Tbsps coarse-grained mustard
▶ 2 cloves garlic, minced*
▶ 1 1/2 tsps dried rosemary, crushed
▶ 1/2 tsp black pepper
▶ 1 leg of lamb, well trimmed, boned, rolled and tied (about 4 lbs)

1. Preheat oven to 400°F.
2. Combine mustard, garlic, rosemary and pepper.
3. Rub mustard mixture over lamb.**
4. Place roast on meat rack in shallow, foil-lined roasting pan.
5. Roast 15 minutes.
6. Reduce oven temperature to 325°F; roast about 20 minutes per lb for medium or until internal temperature reached 145°F when tested with meat thermometer inserted into thickest part of the roast.
7. Transfer roast to cutting board; cover with foil.
8. Let stand 10 to 15 minutes before carving.
9. Internal temperature will continue to rise 5 to 10 degrees during standing time.
10. Cut strings from roast; discard.
11. Carve into 20 slices.

TURBOTIPS:

For more intense garlic flavor inside the meat, cut garlic into slivers. Cut small pockets at random intervals throughout roast with tip of sharp knife; insert garlic slivers.

**At this point lamb may be covered and re-frigerated up to 24 hours before roasting.

SIMPLE ROAST LEG OF LAMB

Serves
8

▶ 3 lbs lean half leg of lamb (with bone)
▶ 1 clove garlic, cut into 8 slivers
▶ 1 tsp crushed mint
▶ 1/2 tsp salt
▶ 1/8 tsp pepper

1. Wipe meat with damp cloth.
2. Cut 8 shallow slashes in top and insert a sliver of garlic in each slash.
3. Combine mint, salt and pepper, and rub well into all surfaces of meat.
4. Leave on kitchen counter for about an hour.
5. Roast in 325°F oven for about 1 1/2 hours.

ITALIAN-STYLE STEAK & ZUCCHINI

Serves
4

- ▶ 2 lbs boneless sirloin steak, no more than 1/2 inch thick
- ▶ 2 large garlic cloves
- ▶ 1 1/4 tsps salt, divided
- ▶ 1/2 tsp freshly ground pepper
- ▶ 1 Tbsp + 1 tsp olive oil
- ▶ 1 large zucchini, cut in half lengthwise and sliced into half-moons
- ▶ 1 Tbsp sun-dried tomato pesto

1. Cut steak into 4 even pieces.
2. Pound each with a meat pounder or rolling pin to flatten to about 1/4 inch thick.
3. Finely chop garlic with 1 tsp of the salt on a cutting board to form a paste.
4. Rub paste onto both sides of steaks and sprinkle evenly with pepper.
5. Heat 1 Tbsp of the olive oil in a large nonstick skillet over medium-high heat.
6. Add zucchini and cook 5 to 8 minutes; turn slices as they brown.
7. Sprinkle with the remaining 1/4 tsp salt and fold in pesto; transfer to plate.
8. Wipe out skillet.
9. Heat remaining 1 tsp olive oil in skillet over high heat.
10. Add steaks and cook 1 to 1 1/2 minutes per side, until browned for medium-rare or longer if desired.
11. Serve immediately with zucchini.

STEAK ON SKEWERS

Serves
6

- ▶ 1 1/2 lbs lean flank steak, cut in 1/8-inch to 1/4-inch strips
- ▶ 1/4 cup no-sugar soy sauce
- ▶ 3 Tbsps low or no-sodium bouillon
- ▶ 1/2 tsp ground ginger
- ▶ 1/2 clove garlic, minced
- ▶ 1 tsp parsley flakes
- ▶ Artificial sweetener equal to 1 tsp sugar
- ▶ Salt
- ▶ Pepper

1. Mix all ingredients except salt and pepper in bowl.
2. Marinate the strips of steak in the sauce for 1 or more hours, turning several times.
3. Pierce and twist strips of steak on skewers.
4. Brush with the marinade sauce and sprinkle lightly with salt and pepper.
5. Broil about 4 minutes on each side, about 3 inches from heat, brushing again with the marinade when turning skewers over.
6. Remove and serve.

Meats

PORTERHOUSE WITH
MUSHROOM TOPPING

Serves
4

- ▶ 4 porterhouse steaks
- ▶ 1 tsp salt, divided
- ▶ 1/2 tsp ground pepper, divided
- ▶ 3 Tbsps butter, divided
- ▶ 2 Tbsps olive oil
- ▶ 2 large shallots, chopped
- ▶ 1 lb white mushrooms or oyster, cremini or baby bellas, sliced

1. Heat broiler.
2. Season steaks with 1/2 tsp salt and 1/4 tsp pepper.
3. In large skillet over medium heat, melt 2 Tbsps of the butter in the olive oil.
4. Add the shallots and cook 2 to 3 minutes, stirring until translucent.
5. Add mushrooms and remaining salt and pepper.
6. Cook, stirring occasionally, about 7 minutes, until most of the mushroom liquid has been given off.
7. Add remaining 1 Tbsp butter; stir to combine.
8. Meanwhile, broil steaks 12 minutes, turning once during cooking time for medium-rare doneness.
9. Serve steaks smothered with mushrooms and accumulated juices.

SIMPLE BEEF TENDERLOIN

Serves
4

- ▶ 4 lbs whole beef tenderloin
- ▶ Salt (garlic salt or seasoned salt if preferred)
- ▶ Pepper

1. When buying, have the butcher remove all possible fat and visible connective tissue from a whole 4 lb beef tenderloin.
2. Season it well with salt (or garlic salt or seasoned salt) and pepper, to taste.
3. Place on a rack in a shallow roasting pan.
4. Insert meat thermometer into center of meat.
5. Roast at 325°F to 140°F on thermometer for rare, to 170°F if wanted well done, usually 45 minutes to 1 hour.
6. Cut leftovers into separate amounts for future meals and place in freezer.

STEAK WITH SPINACH & BLUE CHEESE

Serves
8

- 2 large cloves garlic
- 1 tsp salt
- 1/4 tsp pepper
- 2 lbs boneless sirloin steak (about 1 1/2 to 1 3/4 inch thick)
- 1 1/2 tsps olive oil
- 1 Tbsp butter
- 2 10-oz bags of spinach leaves
- 4 ounces Maytag blue cheese, crumbled

1. Heat oven to 425°F.
2. Chop the garlic, salt and pepper together on a board until a paste forms; rub evenly on both sides of steak.
3. Heat oil in a large ovenproof skillet over high heat.
4. Add the steak and cook 3 minutes per side until deeply browned; transfer to oven and roast 15 to 20 minutes for medium-rare or longer for more doneness.
5. Let stand 10 minutes.
6. During stand time, melt butter in a large saucepan over medium heat.
7. Add spinach and cover with a tight-fitting lid.
8. Cook 1 minute until spinach wilts.
9. Add cheese and stir to melt.
10. Divide spinach on plates.
11. Cut steak into 1/4" thick slices; lay slices over spinach and drizzle with drippings.

LAMB CHOPS

Serves
4

- 2 loin or rib chops per person
- Sea salt
- Freshly ground black pepper
- Parsley

1. Pan broil chops less than 1" thick.
2. Remove the outer skin from the chops.
3. Rub the pan with a small piece of the lamb fat.
4. Heat pan to hot.
5. Sear the chops on each side.
6. Turn several times during cooking.
7. Season to taste.
8. Serve hot.
9. Garnish with parsley.
10. Serve with mustard or horseradish.

TENDERLOIN with VEGETABLES

Serves 8

- ▶ 3 Tbsps olive oil
- ▶ 2 Tbsps grated lemon rind
- ▶ 2 tsps dried thyme leaves
- ▶ 1 tsp dried marjoram
- ▶ 1 1/2 tsps salt
- ▶ 1 tsp pepper
- ▶ 4 lbs trimmed beef tenderloin roast
- ▶ 1 small red bell pepper cut into 1" wedges
- ▶ 1 small yellow bell pepper cut into 1" wedges
- ▶ 8 green onions cut into 2 pieces
- ▶ 2 yellow squash cut into 1-inch pieces

1. Heat oven to 425°F.
2. In a bowl, combine olive oil, lemon rind, thyme, marjoram, salt and pepper.
3. Rub half the mixture over tenderloin and toss remaining mixture with the vegetables to coat.
4. Place beef in a large roasting pan.
5. Roast 40 minutes.
6. Add vegetables to pan.
7. Continue cooking until an instant-read (or meat) thermometer inserted in tenderloin registers 135°F for medium-rare or 145°F for medium doneness.
8. Transfer roast to a cutting board.
9. Let rest 5 minutes before slicing.

LONDON BROIL

Serves 4

- ▶ 1 1/4 lbs lean prime beef flank steak or London broil
- ▶ 2 Tbsps bouillon
- ▶ 1 tsp vinegar
- ▶ 1 tsp Worcestershire sauce
- ▶ 1/8 tsp garlic salt
- ▶ Salt and pepper

1. Combine all ingredients except meat and salt and pepper in a bowl and mix thoroughly.
2. Place the meat in a shallow pan and brush thoroughly with all the sauce.
3. Cover and let stand on the kitchen counter for 2 hours, turning and brushing all over with the sauce every half hour.
4. Brush again with the sauce, then place meat on cold rack in broiler pan in preheated oven, about 3" from heat source.
5. Broil for about 4 minutes, then season with salt and pepper.
6. Turn on other side and broil about 5 minutes more until medium-rare (check with partial cut down the middle).
7. Salt and pepper unseasoned side lightly, then cut in thin diagonal slices and serve.

Meats

ROAST LEG OF LAMB

Serves 4

- ▶ 5 lb leg of lamb
- ▶ Garlic sliced (or 1/2 lemon)
- ▶ Rosemary

1. Remove lamb from refrigerator about 1 hour before cooking.
2. Preheat oven to hot, 450° to 500°F.
3. Remove the papery outer covering.
4. Rub the lamb with cut garlic or lemon.
5. Insert slivers of garlic and rosemary under the skin using a sharp knife.
6. Place the meat, fat side up, in an uncovered greased pan.
7. Insert meat thermometer, being careful to avoid the bone.
8. Put in oven.
9. Close the oven door and immediately set oven on slow 325°F.
10. Pink will be at about 160° to165°F.
11. Well done will be at about 175°F.
12. Well-done lamb will require about 30 minutes/lb cooking time.
13. After removing the lamb from the oven, allow it to rest for 10 minutes or more before slicing.
14. Serve with mustard or horseradish.

LAMB CHOP BROIL

Serves 4

- ▶ 4 6-oz loin lamb chops, all possible fat removed
- ▶ 1 clove garlic
- ▶ 1/2 tsp mixed herbs
- ▶ 1/2 tsp parsley flakes
- ▶ 1/2 tsp salt
- ▶ 2 Tbsps herb vinegar

1. The day before cooking chops, add garlic, herbs, parsley flakes and salt to vinegar, mix thoroughly in a covered bowl and place in refrigerator.
2. An hour before cooking, place the trimmed chops in a large shallow bowl, brush with the seasoned vinegar and let marinate.
3. Remove chops from bowl and broil about 3" from heat for about 12 minutes on each side or until done to your liking.

Meats

ITALIAN VEAL

Serves
4

- ▶ 1 1/2 lbs lean veal, all visible fat removed, cut in cubes
- ▶ 3/4 tsp garlic salt
- ▶ 1/4 tsp lemon pepper marinade
- ▶ 3 fresh green peppers cut into thin strips
- ▶ 1 small onion, chopped
- ▶ 3/4 cup tomato juice
- ▶ 6 ounces Italian plum tomatoes (fresh or canned), cut in halves
- ▶ 3 Tbsps minced parsley
- ▶ 1/4 tsp oregano

1. Season veal cubes with garlic salt and lemon pepper marinade; place in shallow pan.
2. Brown under broiler, stirring so all sides brown evenly.
3. Transfer to large no-stick skillet, and add pepper and onion.
4. Cook together for 3 minutes, stirring, then add other ingredients.
5. Cover skillet and cook over low heat for 45 minutes.
6. If more liquid is needed, add a little tomato juice. If fat rises to surface while cooking, skim it off.
7. Serve piping hot.
8. Sprinkle a little grated Italian cheese on top if desired.

TOMATO-TOPPED MEAT LOAF

Serves
6

- ▶ 1 1/2 lbs very lean ground beef
- ▶ 1 cup chopped parsley
- ▶ 1 large onion (or 2 small), chopped
- ▶ 1 1/4 tsps salt
- ▶ 1/4 tsp pepper
- ▶ 1 tsp Worcestershire sauce
- ▶ 1/2 cup tomato juice or water
- ▶ 1 egg
- ▶ 1 small can tomato paste

1. Lightly combine all ingredients except last with fork.
2. Spoon into baking pan and gently shape to form a loaf.
3. Spread tomato paste over entire top.
4. Bake in 325°F oven for about 1 hour.

EGGED VEAL CUTLETS

Serves 4

- ▶ 4 4-oz veal cutlets
- ▶ 2 eggs beaten
- ▶ 1/4 tsp salt
- ▶ Black pepper to taste
- ▶ 2 Tbsps chicken bouillon, double-strength

1. Dip the cutlets in the beaten eggs to which have been added salt and pepper.
2. Coat well on both sides of cutlets.
3. Cover bottom of no-stick baking dish with bouillon, set in the cutlets, pour any remaining egg mixture over cutlets.
4. Place in preheated 350°F oven to bake 20 to 25 minutes.
5. Turn cutlets about every 5 minutes until done through but not dry.

GREEK LOAF

Serves 6

- ▶ 2 10-oz packages frozen chopped spinach
- ▶ 1 1/2 lbs very lean ground beef, all visible fat removed before grinding
- ▶ 2 eggs, slightly beaten (add salt to taste)
- ▶ 1/2 cup onion, finely chopped
- ▶ 1/2 tsp nutmeg
- ▶ 3/4 tsp salt
- ▶ 1/8 tsp freshly ground black pepper

1. Cook frozen spinach following directions on package and drain thoroughly.
2. Mixing with fork, lightly combine spinach with other ingredients.
3. Spoon into loaf pan and bake 1 hour.
4. If desired, pour some heated tomato sauce over before serving.

SWISS BURGERS

Serves 6

- ▶ 2 lbs ground lean beef
- ▶ 1 Tbsp chopped chives
- ▶ 3/4 tsp crumbled tarragon
- ▶ 2 tsps seasoned salt
- ▶ 1/4 cup chopped fresh parsley
- ▶ 1/4 cup chopped scallions
- ▶ 1 egg, beaten
- ▶ 6 slices Swiss (or blue) cheese
- ▶ 3 Tbsps butter, melted

1. Combine beef, chives, tarragon, salt, parsley, scallions and egg.
2. Shape into 12 equal balls.
3. Flatten each ball to pancake shape.
4. Place cheese on top and press edges together to seal, making 6 two-layered patties.
5. Brush each with melted butter and broil to desired doneness, turning once.

Meats

LAMB WITH VEGETABLES

Serves 4

- ▶ 1 1/2 cups leftover lamb, chopped
- ▶ 3 large onions, chopped fine
- ▶ 1/2 Tbsp olive oil
- ▶ 1 package frozen green beans
- ▶ 1/4 cup chicken broth
- ▶ 3 medium tomatoes
- ▶ Salt
- ▶ Pepper
- ▶ Ground nutmeg

1. In non-stick pan, stir onions and lamb in heated oil over medium flame until onions are brown.
2. Add the frozen beans and broth, stirring occasionally with fork, and cook covered until beans are tender (about 10 minutes).
3. Cut tomatoes into thick slices and place them over the beans.
4. Simmer 10 minutes more, covered.
5. Add salt, pepper and nutmeg to taste.

ROAST PORK

Serves 10

- ▶ 5 lb pork roast (loin or shoulder)
- ▶ 1 large clove garlic, minced fine
- ▶ Salt and pepper to taste

1. Preheat oven to 350°F.
2. Wipe meat with damp cloth.
3. Cut off edges and surplus fat.
4. Cut a small incision in meat and insert garlic.
5. Sprinkle with salt and pepper.
6. Place meat fat-side-up in roasting pan.
7. Roast in 350°F oven.
8. Cook for 30 to 45 minutes per lb.
9. The meat should be a grayish white when done.

ROAST LEG OF LAMB

- ▶ 4-5 lb leg of lamb
- ▶ 1 large clove garlic, minced
- ▶ 4 Tbsps prepared mustard
- ▶ Salt and pepper to taste

1. Preheat oven to 450°F.
2. Wipe meat with damp cloth.
3. Lamb usually has a thick coating of fat on the fat side. Ask your butcher to remove it or you could remove it yourself with a sharp knife.
4. Cut small gashes in meat and insert minced garlic.
5. Cover with mustard.
6. Sprinkle with salt and pepper.
7. Place meat fat-side-up in shallow roasting pan.
8. Adjust heat to 325°F.
9. Roast meat 30 minutes per lb (20 minutes per lb if you prefer it rare).
10. Before serving, slice lamb and spoon pan juices over it.

SPICY SPARERIBS

- ▶ 4 lbs spareribs (or beef ribs)
- ▶ 1 Tbsp paprika
- ▶ 2 tsps chili powder
- ▶ 3/4 tsp salt
- ▶ 1/4 tsp dry mustard
- ▶ 1/4 tsp garlic powder
- ▶ 1/8 tsp pepper

1. Preheat oven to 450°F.
2. Place single layer of ribs, meaty side down, in shallow roasting pan.
3. Roast in 450°F oven for 1/2 hour.
4. Drain off fat.
5. Combine rest of ingredients.
6. Place in saltshaker.
7. Sprinkle evenly over ribs.
8. Reduce oven to 350°F.
9. Roast, meaty side up, for spareribs, 1/2 to 1 hour longer; beef ribs will take about 1 hour longer.

Meats

Meats

SOUTHERN ITALIAN POT ROAST

▶ 1/3 cup red wine
▶ 4 Tbsps sliced onion
▶ 5 cloves garlic
▶ 2 tsps basil
▶ 1 tsp oregano
▶ 1 Tbsp parsley
▶ 1/2 cup olive oil
▶ Salt and pepper
▶ 5 lb rump, chuck or round roast
▶ 8-oz can tomato sauce

1. In a bowl combine wine, onion, garlic, basil, oregano, parsley, 1/3 cup olive oil, salt and pepper.
2. Add meat and turn several times in mixture until meat is completely covered with marinade.
3. Cover bowl and keep in refrigerator for 1 day, turning meat twice.
4. Remove meat from marinade and dry well.
5. Boil marinade until it reduces to about half the volume.
6. Brown roast in remaining olive oil.
7. Pour reduced marinade over meat.
8. Cover and simmer for about 2 hours.
9. Add tomato sauce.
10. Simmer for 1/2 hour or until tender when tested with fork.
11. Remove meat from pan.
12. Skim off excess fat and use remaining sauce as gravy. This is done more easily if chilled first, as fat will harden on surface.
13. Slice meat and return to sauce.
14. Warm through and serve.

MEAT LOAF

▶ 3 lbs chopped meat
▶ 2 tsps chili powder
▶ 3 eggs
▶ 1/4 tsp garlic powder
▶ 1 tsp onion powder
▶ 2 Tbsps parsley
▶ 8-oz can tomato sauce
▶ Olive oil

1. Preheat oven to 350°F.
2. In a large bowl thoroughly mix first 6 ingredients.
3. Add 1/2 can tomato sauce and mix well.
4. Shape meat into loaf and place in oiled loaf pan.
5. Bake for 1 hour.
6. Pour remaining tomato sauce on top of meat loaf and bake for 1/2 hour more, basting occasionally.

NOTES

· · · · · · ·

Poultry

TIPS FOR PREPARING CHICKEN

▶ Be sure to get chicken right into the refrigerator when you get it home.

▶ Do not store it for more than two days in the refrigerator and make sure it is in the coldest section.

▶ Freeze it if you aren't planning on using it within a day or two.

▶ Do not defrost chicken at room temperature for more than a couple of hours—or you run the risk of bacteria developing.

▶ If you stew a chicken, cool it in the broth before cutting into chunks and it will absorb the flavors and stay more moist.

▶ Lemon juice rubbed on chicken before cooking will enhance the flavor and help maintain good color.

▶ Keep cooked chicken in the freezer so it's ready when you need to quickly make a recipe.

CHICKEN CACCIATORE

Serves 4

▶ 3 lb chicken, cut into 8 pieces
▶ 28-oz can whole tomatoes
▶ 1 medium sliced onion
▶ 1/2 cup fresh parsley, finely chopped
▶ 1 tsp dried basil
▶ 1 tsp salt
▶ 1 tsp dried rosemary
▶ 1 tsp dried oregano
▶ 1 garlic clove, minced
▶ 1/4 tsp black pepper
▶ 1/8 tsp crushed pepper
▶ 1 cup sliced fresh mushrooms

1. In a large non-stick skillet add the chicken and brown.
2. Remove the chicken and set aside.
3. Add the onion to the drippings and cook until tender.
4. Add remaining ingredients.
5. Put the chicken back in the skillet.
6. Do not cover skillet.
7. Simmer the chicken for 40-45 minutes; turn the chicken every so often.
8. Serve immediately.

ROASTED CHICKEN & VEGETABLES

Serves 6

- ▶ 3-lb broiler-fryer, skinned
- ▶ Vegetable cooking spray
- ▶ 2 cups thinly sliced leek
- ▶ 1 cup sugar snap peas, trimmed
- ▶ 6 small squash, cut into 1" thick slices
- ▶ 6 small zucchini, cut into 1" thick slices
- ▶ 3 heads Belgian endive, sliced lengthwise
- ▶ 1 cup canned low-sodium chicken broth
- ▶ 1/2 tsp pepper
- ▶ 1/2 tsp minced fresh thyme
- ▶ 1/4 cup water
- ▶ Fresh thyme sprigs (optional)

1. Trim fat from chicken.
2. Remove giblets and neck from chicken; reserve for another use.
3. Rinse chicken with cold water; pat dry.
4. Place chicken, breast side up, on a rack in a large roasting pan coated with cooking spray.
5. Insert meat thermometer into meaty part of thigh, making sure it does not touch bone.
6. Bake at 350°F for 1 hour.
7. Add leek and next 4 ingredients.
8. Combine broth and next 3 ingredients; pour over chicken and vegetables.
9. Bake 45 additional minutes or until meat thermometer registers 180°F to 185°F, basting occasionally with pan juices.
10. Transfer chicken and vegetable to a platter.
11. Pour pan juices through a wire-mesh strainer into a saucepan, discarding solids.
12. Serve sauce with chicken and vegetables.
13. Garnish with thyme sprigs if desired.

CHICKEN IN RED WINE

Serves 4

- ▶ 3 lb fryer chicken, cut into serving pieces
- ▶ 3/4 tsp seasoned salt
- ▶ 1/8 tsp black pepper
- ▶ 2 Tbsps low or no sodium chicken broth or water
- ▶ 1/2 tsp dried tarragon
- ▶ 1/4 tsp crushed dried basil
- ▶ 2 Tbsps chopped parsley
- ▶ 1 Tbsp grated onion
- ▶ 3/4 cup dry red wine

1. Sprinkle salt and pepper over chicken pieces and place side by side in narrow baking dish.
2. Mix together bouillon, tarragon, basil, parsley and onion, and spread over chicken.
3. Bake uncovered in 375°F preheated oven for 50 minutes or until chicken is browned and tender.
4. Baste occasionally with juice from bottom of baking dish.

CHICKEN WITH FETA
& GREEK VEGETABLES

Serves
4

- ► 1 bunch asparagus, trimmed and peeled
- ► 1 Tbsp olive oil
- ► 2 whole bone-in, skinless chicken breasts (about 12 oz each), split cross-wise
- ► 1 medium Spanish onion, thinly sliced
- ► 3 cloves garlic, finely chopped
- ► 8 plum tomatoes, quartered
- ► 1 medium eggplant, cut into 1-inch pieces
- ► 2 cups fresh spinach
- ► 1/4 cup crumbled low-fat feta
- ► 2 Tbsp chopped fresh oregano

1. Heat oven to 375°F.
2. Blanch asparagus in boiling salted water until crisp-tender, 2-3 minutes.
3. Drain stalks and plunge in a bowl of ice water.
4. Drain again and pat dry: set aside.
5. Heat oil in a 6-to-8-quart heavy-bottomed ovenproof pot over medium-high heat.
6. Season chicken with salt and pepper and add to pot.
7. Cover and cook, turning once, until slightly brown, 5 to 8 minutes.
8. Stir in onion and garlic; replace lid and cook until soft, 4 minutes.
9. Stir in tomatoes and eggplant.
10. Replace lid and cook until eggplant is tender, about 18 minutes.
11. Remove pot from oven and stir in asparagus and spinach; sprinkle with feta.
12. Replace lid and let rest 15 minutes.
13. Stir in oregano and season with salt and pepper.

GRILLED TERIYAKI TURKEY CUTLET

Serves
1

- ► 3 ounces skinless boneless turkey breast
- ► 1 Tbsp teriyaki sauce

1. In quart-size sealable plastic bag, combine turkey breast and teriyaki sauce.
2. Seal bag squeezing out air; turn to coat.
3. Refrigerate at least 2 hours or overnight, turning bag occasionally.
4. Preheat grill according to manufacturer's directions.
5. Drain turkey, discarding liquid.
6. Grill turkey 6 minutes, turning once, until cooked through.

SOUTHWESTERN TURKEY/CHICKEN

Serves 4

- ▶ Vegetable cooking spray
- ▶ 1 lb (1/4" thick) turkey breast cutlets, cut into 2 1/2 x 1/2" strips (or skinned or boned chicken breasts)
- ▶ 1 1/4 tsps chili powder
- ▶ 1/4 tsp ground cumin
- ▶ 1 tsp water
- ▶ 1 1/4 cups green peppers strips
- ▶ 1 cup thinly sliced onion, separated into rings
- ▶ 1 cup frozen whole kernel corn
- ▶ 3/4 cup thick and chunky salsa

1. Coat a large nonstick skillet with cooking spray; place over high heat until hot.
2. Add turkey; sauté 3 minutes.
3. Stir in chili power and cumin.
4. Remove turkey from skillet and set aside.
5. Add 1 tsp water to skillet; place over medium-high heat.
6. Add pepper strips and onion; sauté 3 minutes.
7. Return turkey to skillet.
8. Stir in corn and salsa; sauté 2 minutes or until thoroughly heated.

GINGER LEMON CHICKEN

Serves 6

- ▶ 6 chicken breast halves, skinned and boned
- ▶ 1 cup lemon juice
- ▶ 2 cloves garlic, minced
- ▶ 1 Tbsp grated fresh ginger
- ▶ 1 Tbsp chopped fresh tarragon
- ▶ 1/2 tsp salt
- ▶ 1/4 tsp freshly ground black pepper

1. In a bowl, stir together the lemon juice, garlic, tarragon, ginger, salt and pepper.
2. Put the chicken breasts in a baking pan and pour the lemon and ginger mixture over them, coating evenly.
3. Refrigerate for 3 hours.
4. Preheat a grill.
5. Remove the chicken from the mixture and dry with paper towels.
6. Reserve the remaining mixture.
7. Place the chicken on a rack, grill, turning 3 times and brushing with reserved mixture for about 15 to 25 minutes or until the chicken is no longer pink in the center.

ROASTED TURKEY BREAST

Serves 10

- 4 1/2 lb turkey breast
- 1/3 cup chopped onion
- 1/3 cup chopped celery
- 2 tsps lemon juice
- 1 Tbsp minced fresh basil
- 2 Tbsps minced fresh oregano
- Vegetable cooking spray
- 1/2 tsp garlic powder
- 1/4 tsp salt
- Fresh basil sprigs (optional)
- Fresh oregano sprigs (optional)
- Fresh rosemary sprigs (optional)

1. Trim fat from turkey.
2. Rinse turkey under cold water and pat dry.
3. Wrap onion and celery in a single layer of wet cheesecloth; place in cavity of turkey.
4. Combine lemon juice, minced basil and minced oregano; set aside.
5. Place turkey on a rack in a roasting pan coated with cooking spray.
6. Insert meat thermometer into meaty part of breast, making sure it does not touch bone.
7. Sprinkle with garlic powder and salt.
8. Bake at 325°F for 2-2 1/2 hours or until meat thermometer registers 170°F, brushing with lemon juice mixture after 1 1/2 hours.
9. Remove and discard onion and celery.
10. Transfer turkey to a serving platter, and if desired, garnish with basil, oregano and rosemary sprigs.
11. Remove skin from turkey slices before serving.
12. Serve with fresh steamed vegetables.

CHICKEN HAWAIIAN STYLE

Serves 10

- 20 pieces chicken, skin removed
- Paprika
- Ginger
- 1/2 cup dried unsulfured apricots, chopped
- 1 small bell pepper, diced
- 1 medium onion, chopped
- 6-oz can tomato paste, diluted with 1 can water

1. Sprinkle paprika and ginger on chicken.
2. Mix remaining ingredients together.
3. Pour over chicken and bake, uncovered, for 1 hour in 350°F oven.

MEXICAN-STYLE ROAST CHICKEN

Serves 8

- ▶ 2 medium poblano chilies, seeded, deveined and cut into chunks
- ▶ 2 medium onions, halved lengthwise
- ▶ 1/2 cup packed fresh cilantro
- ▶ 1/4 cup fresh lime juice
- ▶ 1/2 tsp salt
- ▶ 1/2 tsp freshly ground black peppers
- ▶ 4 1/2 lb roasting chicken

1. Preheat oven to 350°F.
2. In food processor, combine chilies, 3 of the onion halves, the cilantro, juice, 1/4 tsp of the salt and 1/4 tsp of the pepper; process until finely chopped (do not puree).
3. Gently loosen skin from breast and leg portions of chicken; stuff chili mixture evenly under skin.
4. Sprinkle large cavity of chicken with remaining 1/4 tsp salt and 1/4 tsp pepper, then add remaining onion half; truss chicken.
5. Place chicken, breast-side up, onto rack in large roasting pan, roast 2-2 1/4 hours, until chicken is cooked through and juices run clear when pierced with fork or meat thermometer inserted into thicker portion of thigh registers 180°F.
6. Remove from oven; let stand 10 minutes.
7. Remove and discard skin and chili mixture from chicken.
8. Remove onion from cavity and discard.
9. Carve chicken.

CHICKEN CACCIATORE #2

Serves 4

- ▶ 4 chicken breasts
- ▶ 1 Tbsp olive oil
- ▶ 2 medium onions, thinly sliced
- ▶ 1 clove garlic, minced
- ▶ 1/2 tsp oregano
- ▶ 8-oz can tomato sauce
- ▶ Salt and pepper to taste

1. Remove all skin and visible fat from chicken.
2. In a skillet, brown chicken in oil.
3. Add sliced onion and garlic and allow to cook for a few minutes while stirring.
4. Add remaining ingredients, cooking slowly for about 45 minutes or until chicken is tender.

Poultry

LEMON & ROSEMARY ROASTED CHICKEN

Serves 4

- ▶ 6 large cloves garlic, pressed
- ▶ 1/2 tsp sea salt
- ▶ 1 1/2-2 Tbsps finely minced fresh rosemary
- ▶ 3 Tbsps extra-virgin olive oil, divided
- ▶ 4 Tbsps fresh lemon juice, divided
- ▶ 4 5-oz chicken breast halves with skin and bone, rinsed and patted dry
- ▶ 2 cups (about 10 ounces) frozen petite Brussels spouts
- ▶ 2 cups (about 10 ounces) baby carrots

1. Preheat oven to 500°F.
2. Combine garlic, sea salt and rosemary in a small bowl.
3. Press into a paste.
4. Stir in 2 Tbsps olive oil and 2 Tbsps lemon juice.
5. Using a small, sharp knife, carefully lift skin from top of each chicken breast and spread mixture evenly underneath.
6. In a large baking pan, combine Brussels sprouts and carrots.
7. Drizzle with remaining 1 Tbsp oil and salt; toss to coat.
8. Nestle chicken around vegetables and sprinkle with remaining lemon juice and coarse black pepper.
9. Roast for 25 minutes or until cooked through.
10. Serve immediately.

EASY BROILED CHICKEN

Serves 4

TURBOTIPS:

Meats that are broiled will contain less calories than those baked or fried.

Except when broiling, remove skin from chicken before cooking.

It's more economical to buy whole chickens instead of parts. Use the wings, back, etc. for salads or soups.

- ▶ 1/2 medium broiler chicken per person
- ▶ 1 Tbsp each: olive oil and lemon juice
- ▶ Salt and pepper

1. Mix oil, juice and seasoning and brush lightly on both sides of chicken.
2. If a brush isn't handy, put all ingredients into a plastic bag, hold securely closed and shake.
3. In oven broiler: place chicken skin side down
4. Outdoor grill: place chicken skin side up
5. Broil about 25 minutes on first side.
6. Turn and broil about 20 minutes more.
7. Brush several times with basting mixture.
8. Remove skin after broiling.

ROASTED TARRAGON CHICKEN

Serves 4

- ▶ 2 Tbsp unsalted butter, softened
- ▶ 1 Tbsp chopped fresh tarragon leaves
- ▶ 1/2 tsp each kosher salt and freshly ground pepper
- ▶ 3 1/4 lb chicken, quartered, wing tips removed, trimmed of excess fat
- ▶ 1 Tbsp olive oil
- ▶ 1/2 cup reduced sodium chicken broth
- ▶ 2-3 bunches baby carrots (about 16 carrots total) tops trimmed to 1"
- ▶ 2 cups fresh or frozen green peas, thawed if frozen

1. Heat oven to 400°F.
2. Mix butter, tarragon and half of the salt and pepper in a small cup to combine.
3. Smear butter mixture under skin of chicken pieces (and smear skin with any remaining herb butter).
4. Heat oil in a large cast-iron or ovenproof nonstick skillet over medium-high heat.
5. Add chicken, skin side down; cook 6 minutes or until golden brown.
6. Turn pieces; lightly brown second side 2 minutes.
7. Add broth to skillet and place in oven.
8. Roast 30 minutes, or until chicken is cooked through.
9. While chicken cooks, bring 4 cups water to a boil in a medium saucepan; add carrots and blanch 3 minutes until very crisp-tender.
10. Drain; refresh under cold water.
11. Remove chicken to a serving plate; keep warm.
12. Place skillet with drippings on stovetop over medium heat.
13. Stir in carrots and peas and cook, stirring constantly, 2 to 3 minutes, until peas and carrots are crisp-tender.
14. Spoon vegetables onto plates and top with chicken.

Poultry

BROILED CHICKEN WITH
CILANTRO SALSA

Serves 4

- ▶ 4 4-oz boneless skinless chicken breast halves
- ▶ 4 Tbsps lime juice, divided
- ▶ Black pepper
- ▶ 1/2 cup lightly packed fresh cilantro, chopped
  - ▶ 1/3 cup thinly sliced or minced green onions
  - ▶ 1/4 to 1/2 jalapeno pepper,* seeded and minced
  - ▶ 2 Tbsps pine nuts, toasted (optional)

TURBOTIPS:
*Jalapeno peppers can sting and irritate the skin.

Wear rubber gloves when handling peppers and do not touch eyes.

Wash hands after handling.

1. Spray broiler pan or baking sheet with nonstick cooking spray.
2. Brush chicken with 2 Tbsps lime juice.
3. Place on prepared pan.
4. Sprinkle generously with pepper; set aside.
5. Combine remaining 2 Tbsps lime juice, cilantro, onions, jalapeno pepper and pine nuts, if desired, in small bowl; stir to combine.
6. Set aside.
7. Broil chicken 1-2" from heat 8 to 10 minutes or until chicken is no longer pink in center.
8. Serve with cilantro salsa.
9. Garnish with lime slices if desired.

CHICKEN CACCIATORE #3

Serves 4

- ▶ 3 lb fryer, cut up
- ▶ 1/2 tsp herb seasoning
- ▶ 1 medium onion, chopped
- ▶ 1 clove garlic, minced or 1/8 tsp garlic powder
- ▶ 1/2 cup water
- ▶ 1/2 cup chopped celery
- ▶ 1 medium green pepper, chopped
- ▶ 8 fresh tomatoes, peeled and cut up
- ▶ 1/8 tsp pepper
- ▶ 1/2 cup red table wine
- ▶ 1 tsp chopped parsley
- ▶ 1 cup sliced mushrooms

1. Remove skin from chicken and season with herb seasoning.
2. Place in oven casserole.
3. Brown chicken in broiler until golden, turning once.
4. Set aside.
5. In saucepan, sauté onion and garlic in 1/4 cup water until transparent.
6. Add 1/4 cup water, then add celery and green pepper.
7. Saute' 5 minutes on low heat.
8. Stir occasionally.
9. Add tomatoes, pepper, parsley, mushrooms and wine.
10. Pour over chicken and bake in 350°F oven for 1 hour.

MEXICAN CHICKEN

 Serves 8

- ▶ 2 chickens, cut up and skinned
- ▶ 1/4 tsp pepper

Sauce:
- ▶ 1/2 tsp chili salsa
- ▶ 1/2 tsp chili powder
- ▶ 1/2 cup water
- ▶ 1/2 cup chopped bell pepper
- ▶ 1/2 cup chopped celery
- ▶ 1/2 cup chopped green apple
- ▶ 1/2 cup chopped small onion

1. Arrange chicken in single layer in lightly oiled baking dish.
2. Sprinkle with the pepper.
3. Place chicken in baking dish.
4. Cover with sauce and bake in a covered casserole 45 minutes in a 325°F oven.

To make the sauce:
1. Mix all ingredients.
2. Simmer sauce 15 minutes.

CHICKEN RATATOUILLE

 Serves 8

- ▶ 6 zucchini, sliced
- ▶ 2 medium green peppers, sliced
- ▶ 6 fresh tomatoes, quartered
- ▶ 1 large eggplant, peeled and cut into chunks
- ▶ 2 large onions, sliced
- ▶ 8 boneless breasts, skinned and boned
- ▶ 1/4 tsp tarragon
- ▶ 1/4 tsp pepper
- ▶ 1/4 tsp thyme
- ▶ 1/2 cup sherry wine

1. Steam all vegetables for 15 minutes.
2. Dredge boned chicken in seasoning of 1/4 tsp each of thyme, tarragon and pepper.
3. Arrange chicken evenly on top of vegetables and sprinkle with paprika.
4. Bake in 325°F oven, covered, for 1 hour.
5. Last 15 minutes, remove cover; add 1/2 cup sherry wine and bake at 400°F.

SPICY CHICKEN LEGS

Serves 2

- 2 Tbsps olive oil
- 2 tsps paprika
- 1 tsp dried thyme
- 1 tsp chili powder
- 1/2 tsp dried cumin
- 1/2 tsp garlic powder
- 1/2 tsp salt
- 1/2 tsp pepper
- 1/4 tsp ground nutmeg
- 6 chicken legs with thighs, rinsed and patted dry

1. In a small bowl, mix oil and the spices.
2. Rub chicken legs with spice mixture; arrange on a baking sheet.
3. Refrigerate 30 minutes.
4. Heat oven to 350°F.
5. Bake chicken 40 to 45 minutes or until cooked through.

CITRUS-BAKED CHICKEN

Serves 4

- 2 1/2 lb broiler chicken, cut in eighths
- 1/3 cup dry white wine
- Juice of 1 lemon
- Juice of 1 lime
- 1 tsp garlic salt
- 1/4 tsp thyme
- White pepper
- 1 tsp butter, melted
- Paprika (optional)

1. Wash chicken pieces, pat dry with paper towels and arrange in shallow casserole.
2. Mix together all other ingredients except butter and paprika, and pour over chicken pieces.
3. Refrigerate for 2 or 3 hours, turning chicken over occasionally.
4. Pour off marinade (save), rearrange chicken into a single layer in casserole, brush with melted butter and bake in preheated 400°F oven 1 hour, or until tender, basting frequently with marinade.
5. Serve chicken pieces with pan juices poured over them.
6. Sprinkle with paprika if you like.

BAKED CHICKEN

Serves 4

- 1 fryer cut into parts
- Olive oil
- Sea salt
- 1-2 cloves garlic
- Freshly ground black pepper
- 1/2 tsp dried thyme
- Sprig parsley
- 2 slices onion

1. Preheat oven to 350°F.
2. Wash chicken and pat dry.
3. Lightly coat skin with olive oil.
4. Arrange chicken in a roasting pan.
5. Season with salt and pepper if desired.
6. Sprinkle with crushed thyme.
7. Place onion, garlic and parsley in the pan.
8. Cover with aluminum foil.
9. Bake for 1 hour, basting occasionally.
10. During the last 10 minutes of baking, uncover pan to brown skin.

ROSEMARY CHICKEN

Serves 4

- 1 fryer cut into parts
- Olive oil
- Freshly ground black pepper
- 1-2 sprigs fresh rosemary or 1/2 tsp dried rosemary
- Juice of 1 lemon
- 1/4 cup wine vinegar
- 1/2 tsp paprika
- 2 cloves garlic
- 2 slices onion

1. Preheat oven to 350°F.
2. Wash chicken and pat dry.
3. Lightly coat skin with olive oil.
4. Arrange chicken in a roasting pan.
5. Sprinkle chicken with pepper, rosemary and paprika.
6. Add lemon juice, wine vinegar, onion and garlic to pan.
7. Cover with aluminum foil.
8. Bake for 1 hour, basting occasionally.
9. During the last 10 minutes of baking, uncover pan to brown skin.

CHICKEN SALAD DELIGHT

Serves 4

- ▶ 2 chicken breasts
- ▶ 1/4 cup finely chopped Vidalia onions or scallions
- ▶ 1/2 cup chopped celery
- ▶ 2 Tbsp white wine vinegar
- ▶ 1/4 cup olive oil
- ▶ 1/2 Dijon mustard
- ▶ 2/3 cup mayonnaise
- ▶ Salt and pepper
- ▶ Walnuts and chopped apples, optional
- ▶ 2 tsp fresh dill

1. Put 2 chicken breasts in a shallow dish , add 1/4-1/2 cup water with chicken.
2. Cover with plastic wrap opened at end.
3. Cook in microwave on medium for 10 minutes, turning once.
4. Dice the chicken.
5. Mix in onion, vinegar, celery, oil, mustard, mayonnaise and salt and pepper.
6. Sprinkle with parsley.

SPEEDY CHICKEN IN FOIL

Serves 1

- ▶ 6 ounces raw lean chicken breast

Tangy Tropical:
- ▶ 1/4 cup of fruity sugar-free salsa (mango or peach salsas are great)

Easy Italian:
- ▶ 1/2 cup stewed tomatoes
- ▶ 1/2 tsp chopped garlic
- ▶ 1/4 tsp Italian seasoning

Spicy Tex-Mex:
- ▶ 1 tsp fajita seasoning mix
- ▶ 1/2 cup sliced onions
- ▶ 1/2 cup bell peppers
- ▶ 1/2 cup lime juice

1. Heat oven to 375°F.
2. Choose one of three sets of toppings: Tangy Tropical, Easy Italian or Spicy Tex-Mex.
3. Cut a 6-oz raw lean chicken breast into 1/2" slices, season with salt and pepper, cover with your topping of choice and wrap in foil.
4. If you don't eat meat use Portobello mushroom instead.
5. Bake 25 minutes.
6. Allow packet to cook for a few minutes, then cut to release steam before opening it entirely.
7. Careful! The steam will be hot!

COUNTRY CHICKEN

Serves 4

- 2 lbs chicken fryer parts (thighs, drum sticks or breasts)
- 2 Tbsps chicken broth
- Salt to taste
- Pepper
- 1 clove garlic, chopped
- 2 medium onions, cut in eighths
- 4 quartered tomatoes
- 1 medium eggplant, cut into 1" cubes (leave skin on)
- 2 Tbsps chopped parsley
- 1 tsp dried thyme

1. Brush chicken parts with broth or water, sprinkle with salt and pepper, and place in covered saucepan with other ingredients.
2. Cook over low heat on top of stove until chicken is tender (about 45 minutes).

SAGE CHICKEN WITH
BELL PEPPER CURLS

Serves 4

- 4 boneless chicken breast halves, with skin (about 2 lbs)
- 3/4 tsp salt, divided
- 1/2 tsp freshly ground pepper, divided
- 12 fresh whole sage leaves, +1 tsp chopped
- 1 Tbsp butter
- 2 Tbsps olive oil, divided
- 2 bell peppers of any color(s), cut into thin strips
- 1 cup water

1. Sprinkle chicken with 1/2 tsp salt and 1/4 tsp pepper.
2. Use fingers to loosen the skin of each chicken breast, then spread 3 sage leaves under the skin.
3. Heat oven to 200°F.
4. In a large ovenproof skillet over medium-high heat, melt butter in 1 Tbsp oil.
5. Cook chicken 7 to 10 minutes per side, until browned and cooked through.
6. Transfer to a serving platter, tent with foil, and place in warm oven.
7. Wipe out skillet with paper towel.
8. Heat remaining Tbsp oil over medium-high heat until it shimmers.
9. Add bell peppers; sprinkle with remaining salt and pepper.
10. Add 1 cup of water to skillet.
11. Cook peppers, partially covered, 20 minutes, until softened and curled.
12. Stir in chopped sage during last 5 minutes of cooking time.
13. Serve peppers over chicken.

Poultry

CHICKEN LIVERS & MUSHROOMS

Serves
4

▶ 1 1/4 lbs chicken livers
▶ 18 whole mushrooms
▶ Salt
▶ Lemon pepper or other flavored pepper of choice
▶ 1/8 cup white cooking wine

1. Wash chicken livers and cut in halves, removing fat and membrane in centers.
2. Wash mushrooms, cutting off bottoms of stems.
3. Season mushrooms and livers with salt and seasoned pepper and place in shallow, no-stick broiling pan.
4. Brush tops with some of the wine and broil until livers are brown, about 7 minutes.
5. Turn over, brush with wine, and broil again until brown.
6. Serve piping hot, with juice if there is any.

CHICKEN IN SAUCE

Serves
4

▶ 3 lbs chicken for frying, cut into pieces
▶ Salt
▶ 4 Tbsps olive oil
▶ 1/2 lb mushrooms
▶ 2 Tbsps onion, minced
▶ 2 Tbsps tomato sauce
▶ 2 tsps lemon juice
▶ 1/2 cup white wine

1. Sprinkle chicken pieces with salt.
2. Heat oil in skillet, add pieces of chicken and sauté well on all sides.
3. Remove to dish and keep warm.
4. Sauté mushrooms and onion until onion is soft.
5. Add tomato sauce, lemon juice and wine bring to a boil, stirring constantly.
6. Pour sauce over chicken.

LEMON-BASTED ROAST CHICKEN

Serves 4

- ▶ 1 chicken, cut up
- ▶ 1/2 tsp oregano
- ▶ 1/4 tsp garlic powder
- ▶ 1/4 cup butter (1/2 stick)
- ▶ Salt and pepper
- ▶ Juice of 2 lemons (6 to 8 Tbsps)

1. Preheat oven to 400°F.
2. Sprinkle chicken with oregano and garlic powder.
3. Melt butter in roasting pan or casserole.
4. Roll chicken in it.
5. Sprinkle with salt and pepper.
6. Roast chicken skin-side-up, uncovered, in 400°F oven for 30 minutes or until golden brown.
7. Turn pieces over and continue roasting until brown (about 30 more minutes).
8. Reduce heat to 300°F and cook until tender.
9. Squeeze lemon juice over chicken.
10. Cover and let sit in turned-off oven for 15 minutes.
11. Remove to platter and serve.

CHICKEN WITH FETA CHEESE

Serves 4

- ▶ 6 boneless chicken cutlets
- ▶ 2 Tbsps lemon juice, divided
- ▶ 1/2 package (about 3 ounces) feta cheese, crumbled
- ▶ 1 red, yellow, orange or green pepper, chopped

1. Preheat oven to 350°F.
2. Spray 9 x 13" baking pan with non-stick cooking spray.
3. Place chicken cutlets in bottom of pan.
4. Sprinkle with 1 Tbsp of lemon juice.
5. Crumble feta cheese evenly over the cutlets.
6. Top with remaining Tbsp of lemon juice.
7. Bake uncovered for 35 minutes.
8. Sprinkle with chopped pepper before serving.

ITALIAN CHICKEN

Serves 4

- ▶ 4 boneless, skinless chicken breast halves
- ▶ 14.5-oz can diced tomatoes
- ▶ 14.5-oz can tomato sauce
- ▶ 2 tsps Italian seasoning or
- ▶ 1 tsp dried basil and
- ▶ 1 tsp dried oregano
- ▶ 2 cups shredded herb-flavored cheese

1. Place chicken breast halves, frozen, or thawed, into a greased 7 x 11" baking dish in a single layer.
2. In a medium-sized mixing bowl, stir together diced tomatoes and tomato sauce.
3. Pour over chicken.
4. Sprinkle with seasoning.
5. Bake in 350°F over for 30 minutes if chicken is fresh, or for 1 hour if chicken is frozen.
6. Continue baking until juices run clear when meat is pierced with a fork.
7. Remove pan from oven, turn over to broil.
8. Sprinkle chicken with cheese.
9. Broil 5-7 minutes or until cheese melts and bubbles.

LEMON CHICKEN

Serves 4

- ▶ 6 boneless, skinless chicken breast halves
- ▶ 1/4 cup lemon juice
- ▶ 2 tsp dried oregano
- ▶ 1/2 tsp salt or garlic powder
- ▶ 1/4 tsp ground black pepper
- ▶ Olive oil

1. Preheat oven to 375°F.
2. Place chicken breasts in a greased 9 x 13" baking dish.
3. Mix lemon juice, oregano, salt and pepper together in a small bowl.
4. Pour over chicken.
5. Place in oven.
6. Brush with olive oil every 10 minutes, turning chicken pieces over occasionally.
7. Bake for 40-50 minutes or until juices run clear when pricked with a sharp fork.

CHICKEN CACCIATORE #4

Serves 4

- ▶ 1 green pepper, chopped
- ▶ 1 onion, chopped
- ▶ 1 Tbsp water
- ▶ 1 tsp oregano
- ▶ 15.5-oz can diced tomatoes
- ▶ 6 boneless, skinless chicken breast halves

1. Mix the first 4 ingredients in a bowl.
2. Put chicken in a lightly greased 9 x 13" glass baking dish.
3. Spoon sauce over top.
4. Bake uncovered at 350°F for 1 hour.

Desserts

WHEN YOU NEED "SOMETHING SWEET"

Most people who pick up a cookbook readily admit that they flip right to the desserts section first. Well, this is a desserts section that will not flip around on you and get you stressed. We have included a large selection of truly delicious, tried and true desserts.

These desserts are not meant to be eaten as substitutes for other TurboCharging meals, but are to be enjoyed on special occasions and during those times you feel like you "need something sweet." All of the recipes that follow are sweet, healthy and guaranteed to put the kibosh on any craving you might be experiencing.

You will not only feel satiated, but also pleased with yourself that you didn't stall your TurboCharged status by indulging in some sugary, carbohydrate and fat-laden dessert that will overstay its welcome in many ways.

Also, we'd like to add that these are all especially good for athletes and children—as many are a bit higher in calories and fat.

TIPS FOR DESSERTS

▶ Keep strawberries fresh for up to 10 days by refrigerating them (unwashed) in an airtight container between layers of paper towels.

▶ When grating citrus peel, bits of peel can get stuck in the grater. If this happens, use a new toothbrush to brush it off into your recipe or fruit salad.

▶ To core a pear, slice in half lengthwise. Use a melon baller to cut out the central core, using a circular motion. Draw the melon baller to the top of the pear and you will remove the interior stem in the process.

▶ When dicing dried fruit, if the fruit is sticking to the blade, wipe a very fine coating of olive oil on the blade and the sticking will cease.

▶ Fruit salads become easier and pretty if you use an egg slicer to perfectly cut kiwis, strawberries and bananas.

FOUR TWO-SECOND FRUIT DESSERTS

▶ *Fruit Solo or Salad:* Fresh fruit alone or with many other types washed, diced, chilled and sliced are always a scrumptious and crowd-pleasing dessert. Maybe it's just the fact that the work of chopping and cutting is all done. Maybe it's the fact that too often we forget that fruit really is the ultimate perfectly sweet dessert. Whatever the reason, a big bowl of fresh-cut fruit brings lots of color and a tasty end to a meal. To make it a little more festive—consider adding a few simple finely sliced or whole mint leaves. This touch makes any bowl of fruit seem like a spectacular and fancy dessert. For those into bolder flavor combos—consider finely dicing fresh basil leaves!

▶ *Frozen Banana:* Don't forget this one for a tasty snack, filling meal or luscious dessert. Simply peel before placing in a freezer bag. Freeze for 24 hours. Remove and wrap end in a napkin and enjoy! For kids or those in cruise control, you can peel, roll in crushed nuts of your choice and then freeze. Pecans are especially good for this! Also, these are excellent teething foods for babies, and it sets the stage for a TurboCharged life of health.

▶ *Fruit Popsicle:* Blend up some fresh fruit with water at high speed in your blender. Add nothing else. Load into popsicle trays or ice cube trays and freeze. Have one for dessert or an evening snack. Each will contain only about 70 calories—if you're counting.

▶ *Frozen Grapes:* Red grapes are a delicious dessert all by themselves. But if you want to make them extra fun, try this crowd pleaser. Remove all stems, wash and place in lightly closed plastic bags or freezer containers. Freeze for 24 hours. Remove when ready to serve and eat promptly as they thaw fairly quickly.

APPLE SAUCE

 Serves 4

- ▶ 2 1/2 lb apples
- ▶ 1 cup water
- ▶ 1 Tbsp lemon juice
- ▶ 1 cinnamon stick
- ▶ 3 whole cloves
- ▶ Pinch nutmeg

1. Pare the apples.
2. Remove stem and core.
3. Cut in quarters.
4. Put all ingredients in a saucepan with tight-fitting lid.
5. Bring to a boil.
6. Reduce heat.
7. Cover and simmer for 30 minutes.
8. Remove whole spices and mash apple mixture or puree in blender or food processor.
9. Serve warm or cold.

TURBOTIPS:
Lasts several days in the refrigerator.

Use in place of mint jelly or cranberry sauce with lamb or poultry.

CARROTS & BANANAS SUPREME

 Serves 4

- ▶ 6 cooked carrots
- ▶ 2 bananas
  - ▶ 1/2 tsp vanilla
  - ▶ 1/2 tsp nutmeg
  - ▶ 1/2 tsp cinnamon

1. Slice carrots and cook in small amount of water until tender.
2. Mash carrots and bananas; combine with seasonings.
3. Bake in shallow pie plate until brown on top in 350°F oven.

TURBOTIPS:
This is a great warm breakfast or a tasty dessert.

RAW NUTTY BROWNIE ENERGY BITES

 Serves 4

- ▶ 1 cup raw almond meal
- ▶ 1/2 cup raw cacao powder
- ▶ 1/8 tsp sea salt
- ▶ 1/2 cup packed pitted Medjool dates, roughly chopped
- ▶ 2 Tbsps honey
- ▶ 1/4 cup raw walnuts, crushed

1. Place almond meal, cacao powder and salt in a large mixing bowl and mix well.
2. Add dates and honey, and mix well.
3. Add crushed walnuts and mix.
4. Line a loaf or square pan with parchment paper or plastic wrap.
5. Press mixture into bottom of pan.
6. Enjoy immediately or chill for a firmer texture.

MELON & BERRY SALAD

Serves
4

- ▶ 1 small ripe cantaloupe or other sweet melon
- ▶ 1/2 cup fresh blueberries
- ▶ 1/4 cup fresh raspberries
- ▶ 1 orange, freshly squeezed (about 1/3 cup)
- ▶ 1 Tbsp chopped fresh mint
- ▶ 1/4 tsp ground cinnamon

1. Cut melon in two equal halves; remove seeds.
2. Using a melon baller, remove flesh.
3. Or use a knife and chop into 1/2" chunks.
4. Transfer to a large mixing bowl.
5. Save rinds for serving bowls, if desired.
6. Add blueberries, raspberries and orange juice.
7. Mix gently.
8. Pour mixture (with juices) into serving bowls.
9. Sprinkle with mint and cinnamon.
10. Serve immediately.

TURBOTIPS:
Serving tip: For a fun presentation that wows kids of all ages, serve in hollowed-out melon halves (leave about 1/3 inch flesh attached to the rind).

LAYERED FRUIT DESSERT

Serves
6

- ▶ 1 fresh pineapple, peeled and cored
- ▶ 1 medium cantaloupe, peeled, seeded and thinly sliced
- ▶ 4 kiwifruit, peeled and thinly sliced
- ▶ Fresh mint sprigs (optional)

1. Slice pineapple into 1/8" thick slices.
2. Arrange half of pineapple in bottom of an 8" springform pan, covering bottom of pan.
3. Press gently with fingertips.
4. Arrange half of cantaloupe slices over pineapple, covering pineapple.
5. Press gently with fingertips.
6. Arrange half of kiwifruit over cantaloupe, covering cantaloupe.
7. Press gently with fingertips.
8. Repeat layers with remaining pineapple, cantaloupe and kiwifruit slices.
9. Place spring-form pan on a plate.
10. Cover and chill at least 45 minutes.
11. Remove side of pan; transfer to a serving plate.
12. Garnish with mint sprigs if desired.

Desserts

COBBLER CRUMBLE TOPPING

Serves
4

- ▶ 3/4 cup raw pecans
- ▶ 1/8 tsp sea salt
- ▶ 1/2 tsp ground cinnamon
  - ▶ 1 tsp alcohol-free vanilla extract
  - ▶ 2 Tbsps coconut oil, softened
  - ▶ 1/2 cup packed pitted Medjool dates

1. Place pecans, salt and cinnamon into a food processor.
2. Pulse lightly to mix, making sure to leave large chunks of nuts.
3. Add vanilla, coconut oil and dates and pulse into small pieces.
4. Be careful not to overmix into a butter.
5. You want to end up with a chunky texture that resembles that of the crumbles on cooked cobbler.

TURBOTIPS:
This will keep for at least a week in the fridge.

Serving tips: Use this to top your favorite sliced fruit, like peaches, mangoes, nectarines, persimmons or apples.

CHOCOLATE PEANUT

Serves
18

BUTTER TRUFFLES (GLUTEN FREE)

- ▶ 2 1/4 cups peanuts, unsalted if available, divided
- ▶ 1/3 cup raw honey or agave nectar
- ▶ 1/4 cup raw cacao powder
- ▶ 2 Tbsps natural peanut butter, creamy and salted

1. Grind 1/4 cup of the peanuts in food processor with blade attachment just until there are no large pieces.
2. Pour into a separate bowl and set aside.
3. Place two cups peanuts in food processor and process until there are no big pieces.
4. Add cacao powder and mix.
5. Add honey or agave and peanut butter and mix well.
6. Place mixture in the refrigerator for 30 minutes to make it easier to work with.
7. Form mixture into small balls, about the size of a walnut.
8. Use a melon baller if you would like a uniform size.
9. Roll the balls between your palms until smooth and set aside until all are shaped.
10. Sprinkle with ground peanuts and serve.
11. Refrigerate leftovers in sealed container.

CHERRY WALNUT BITES

Serves 12

- 1 cup dried sour cherries
- 4 Medjool dates
- 1/3 cup walnut pieces
- 1 Tbsp fresh orange juice
- 1/4 tsp ground cinnamon
- 3 Tbsps dark cacao nibs
- 2 Tbsps unsweetened shredded coconut

1. Finely chop dried cherries, dates and walnuts and combine in a large mixing bowl.
2. Add orange juice, cinnamon, chocolate chips and coconut.
3. Mix together with hands, working into a mass.
4. Mixture should be sticky and hold together; if necessary, add another chopped date or a little more juice.
5. With clean, slightly wet hands, roll mixture into walnut-size balls.
6. Gently place into an airtight container and refrigerate.
7. They will become firmer as they cool.

PEACH FLUFF

Serves 4

- 3 egg whites
- 1/4 cup stevia or splenda
- 1/4 tsp cream of tartar
- 1 tsp vanilla
- 6 peach halves

1. Beat egg whites with cream of tartar until foamy.
2. Gradually add stevia or splenda and continue beating until stiff.
3. Fold in vanilla.
4. Divide half the mixture into six portions on a greased cookie sheet.
5. Nestle one peach half in each mound and cover with remaining egg white.
6. Bake at 325°F for 30 minutes.
7. Cool.
8. Serve chilled and on the same day.

Desserts

FRUIT NUT BONBONS

Serves
15

- ▶ 1 cup dried presoaked currants
- ▶ 1/2 cup fresh or presoaked figs
- ▶ 1/2 cup pitted dates
- ▶ 1 cup walnuts, chopped small
- ▶ 1 cup grated coconut

1. Combine the first four ingredients in a blender and grind together.
2. Put in bowl and mix in walnut thoroughly with your hands.
3. Shape into small balls (about the size of walnuts).
4. Roll in coconut.
5. Store in refrigerator.

COCONUT MACAROONS

Serves
4

- ▶ 8 ounces unsweetened shredded coconut
- ▶ 8 ounces almond flour (any nut flour can be used)
- ▶ 4 Tbsps macadamia nut oil
- ▶ 1 Tbsp sugar substitute

1. Combine all ingredients in a stainless steel bowl until well mixed.
2. For each cookie, spoon a Tbspful of the mixture onto a cookie sheet.
3. Bake in a preheated 325°F oven for about 6 minutes or until the cookies just start to get browned.
4. Remove from heat and allow to cool on a wire rack.

COCONUT CREAM PIE ICE

Serves
4

TURBOTIPS:

Lemon Cream
Ice Variation:
Use the same
recipe and add
juice from 1
lemon or 1 lime.

This version
might be too
tangy for some
and may require
a tsp of stevia.

- ▶ 1 cup heavy whipping cream
- ▶ 1 cup unsweetened, shredded coconut
- ▶ 2 cups ice

1. Combine all the ingredients in a blender until well liquefied.
2. Pour into parfait cups and freeze.

STUFFED BAKED APPLES

Serves 4

- ▶ 4 apples
- ▶ 1 cup raisins
- ▶ 4 tsp orange juice concentrate
- ▶ 1/2 cup water

1. Core apples and fill with raisins.
2. Spoon 1 tsp frozen orange juice concentrate into each apple.
3. Place apples in Pyrex dish with 1/2 cup water.
4. Bake, covered, until apples are soft.
5. To make a fancier apple, peel and core.

DATE-STUFFED APPLES

Serves 4

- ▶ 4 apples
- ▶ 8 dates
- ▶ 4 tsp frozen orange juice concentrate
- ▶ 1 tsp cinnamon
- ▶ 1/4 cup water

1. Core apples and fill with 2 mashed dates each and a spoon of frozen orange juice concentrate.
2. Sprinkle with cinnamon.
3. Bake in covered casserole in 1/4 cup water until soft, but watch carefully.
4. Bake 1/2 hour in a 400°F oven.

PINA COLADA CRÈME FRUIT TOPPING

Serves 4

- ▶ 2 cups coconut crème
- ▶ 1 pineapple
- ▶ Fruit salad

1. Blend coconut crème with the fruit from the pineapple until smooth.
2. Serve over fruit salad.

Desserts

COCONUT DROPS

Serves 4

- ▶ 1 cup shredded unsweetened coconut
- ▶ 1 Tbsps crème de cacao
- ▶ 3 egg whites at room temperature
- ▶ 1 Tbsp-equivalent brown sugar substitute

1. Preheat oven to 400°F.
2. Place coconut in bowl.
3. Sprinkle crème de cacao over it and mix well. Drop onto baking sheet and cook until golden.

PEANUT BUTTER DREAMS

Serves 4

- ▶ 1 egg, well beaten
- ▶ 1/3 cup chunk-style peanut butter
- ▶ 1 Tbsp soft sweet butter
- ▶ 1 tsp vanilla
- ▶ 1 Tbsp-equivalent brown sugar substitute
- ▶ 3/4 cup finely chopped walnuts

1. Mix all ingredients except nuts together well.
2. Shape into small balls.
3. Roll in chopped nuts.
4. Refrigerate until firm.

MOCK CHOCOLATE
COFFEE CREAM

Serves 4

- ▶ 3 cups ricotta cheese
- ▶ 1 Tbsp instant coffee
- ▶ 1 Tbsp cognac or brandy (if desired)
- ▶ 2 Tbsp-equivalents sugar substitute
- ▶ 4 Tbsps heavy cream vanilla

1. Combine all ingredients.
2. Beat until smooth.
3. Chill for 1 hour.
4. Serve.

MERINGUE MUNCHIES

Serves
4

- ▶ 2 egg whites
- ▶ 1/4 tsp sea salt
- ▶ 1/4 cup pecans (crushed in blender)

1. Preheat oven to 250°F.
2. Beat egg whites with salt until very stiff.
3. Fold in pecans.
4. Be very careful not to break down stiff egg whites.
5. Grease cookie sheet.
6. Drop egg white mixture by Tbsps onto cookie sheet.
7. Bake in 250°F oven for 1 hour.
8. Turn off oven and allow to sit for 1/2 hour.

MERINGUE SHELL

Serves
4

- ▶ 4 egg whites
- ▶ Pinch of salt
- ▶ 4 tsps crème de cacao
- ▶ Strawberries

1. Preheat oven to 250°F.
2. Place egg whites and salt in bowl.
3. Beat together until frothy.
4. Gradually add crème de cacao.
5. Continue beating until whites are stiff, glossy and stand in stiff peaks.
6. Grease 6 muffin tins.
7. Fill cups with meringue, hollowing out top with back of spoon.
8. Bake in 250°F oven for 1 hour.
9. Top with fresh, rinsed, dried and diced strawberries or other berry of choice.

Desserts

NO-ATMEAL

Serves 4

- ▶ 1 small handful of walnuts
- ▶ 1 small handful of pecans
- ▶ 2 Tbsps ground flax seed
- ▶ 1/2 - 1 tsp ground cinnamon
- ▶ 1 pinch of ground nutmeg
- ▶ 1 pinch of ground ginger
- ▶ 1 Tbsp almond butter
- ▶ 1 banana, mashed
- ▶ 2 eggs
- ▶ 1/4 cup unsweetened almond milk (add more if you prefer it a little runny)
- ▶ 2 tsps pumpkin seeds
- ▶ 1 handful of goji berries or fresh berries

1. Add walnuts, pecans, flax seed and spices to a food processor and pulse it down to a coarse grain, making sure to stop before it's totally ground into a powder.
2. Set aside.
3. Whisk together eggs and almond milk until the consistency thickens a little bit into a loose custard.
4. Thoroughly blend together the mashed banana and almond butter and add it to the custard, mixing well.
5. Stir in the nut mixture.
6. Microwave or gently warm on the stove until the "no-atmeal" reaches your desired consistency; this should only take a few minutes.
7. In both cases, stir the mixture frequently as it cooks.
8. Sprinkle pumpkin seeds and berries on top.
9. Add more almond milk if you want.
10. Lick the bowl clean!

TURBOTIPS:
Pronounced "note-meal" (as in, no oatmeal), this is for all you ex-cereal lovers out there and for anyone who needs a warm bowl of comforting goodness on a cold winter morning.

BLUEBERRY WHIP

Serves 4

- ▶ 1 cup fresh or frozen unsweetened blueberries
- ▶ 4 tsp-equivalents sugar substitute
- ▶ 2 egg whites
- ▶ 1/8 tsp salt

1. Mash blueberries slightly with 3 tsps of sugar substitute.
2. Beat egg whites with salt and 1 tsp sugar substitute.
3. Allow them to get stiff but not dry.
4. Fold berries into egg whites; pile into compote dishes.
5. Serve immediately.

LEARN MORE ABOUT TURBOCHARGED®

Every other diet to date is destined to deliver loss of lean muscle mass, more fat, moodiness, disappointment and failure. Instead, TurboCharged provides an exciting new roadmap using a unique 8-step program that has been called the "Holy Grail of Fat Loss" and even the "Fountain of Youth." Building on an exotic car metaphor, the system requires no strenuous exercise, supplements or special equipment. It shows readers how to get on the road to eliminate excess body fat fast and forever. Within 3 days the program promises to: begin training your body to use excess body fat for energy; show everyday activities that will quickly accelerate fatloss; teach mini-exercises requiring only 3-5 minutes each day that will trigger fatburning while strengthening muscle; explain the ideal foods and how to eat them to burn your body fat fast; eliminate any related diet anxiety or moodiness; prove that you are truly getting younger; and provide easy ways to maintain your new lean and healthy body with minimal effort for life.

"TurboCharged doesn't bog down the reader with lots of science. Instead, it tells you what to do, when to do it, and if you follow the very simple guidelines, you too will be dropping fat fast, leaning out and attaining your goal of a lower body-fat percentage, decreases in inches and a younger metabolic age. TurboCharged is a system designed with genetics in mind and based on sound science. With a combination like that, you can't fail."

-Fred Pescatore, MD, MPH, CCN

Author of The Hamptons Diet

TURBOCHARGED ONLINE

Log on to www.turbocharged.us.com to read up-to-the minute health commentary, find out about TurboCharged events in your area, communicate with the authors or learn more about the TurboCharged experience.

See www.facebook.com/turbochargedUS to enjoy daily chat and read more commentary from Dian and Tom Griesel regarding current trends and news.

Follow us at www.twitter.com/diangriesel. We aggregate a broad compilation of articles and videos regarding health, wellness, stress management, happiness and general wellbeing.

TURBOCHARGED RETREATS, SEMINARS
& TRAINING PROGRAMS

TurboCharged training programs are specifically designed to provide tools and techniques that increase the understanding of how the body works, the requirements of health and how to keep a body lean with the most nutritious, energizing and effective methods. The tools and techniques—designed for practical use in situations characterized by information overload, time pressure and stress—result in greater long-term success, reduce frustration, fight diet burnout and ameliorate physical symptoms of stress and negative moods so often associated with traditional dieting and life in general.

TurboCharged, via its publisher/parent company, The Business School of Happiness Inc., provides lectures, retreats, seminars and both on and off-site programs to help individuals and organizations discover and sustain the use of the TurboCharged solution. The flagship organizational program has a modular design that can be customized to fit an organization's specific healthy business and time objectives.

For more information on training and seminars, call 860-619-0177 or write to:

TurboCharged
c/o The Business School of Happiness
PO Box 302
Washington Depot, CT 06794

You can also email info@turbocharged.us.com to learn more.

BUSINESS SCHOOL OF HAPPINESS BOOKS,
TAPES & LEARNING PROGRAMS

TurboCharged®, developed by Dian Griesel, Ph.D. and Tom Griesel, provides simple, proven strategies with no supplements, gimmicks or special equipment—that result in rapid loss of excess body fat while improving overall health. This eight-step program incorporates highly nutritious and natural foods and utilizes a wonderful understanding of human nature and natural, common sense to produce greater health, leaner bodies, greater levels of peace and relaxation and a distinct sense of better wellbeing.

Explore and experience the depth of the TurboCharged program with additional books, music, book downloads, hypnosis downloads and advanced learning programs.

The TurboCharged program and products can be used by individuals, small groups or organizations to learn and sustain the necessary skills to maintain a lean healthy body and better physical and mental health.

For a free catalog of our complete TurboCharged product line or information on volume discounts, call 860-619-0177, email info@turbocharged.us.com, or write:

TurboCharged
c/o The Business School of Happiness
PO Box 302
Washington Depot, CT 06794

Also visit our online store at: www.turbocharged.us.com to see our current product offerings.

TURBOCHARGED BOOKS, DOWNLOADS,
VISUALS & MORE

The entire TurboCharged® Series is designed to work with your busy, hectic, time-crunched lifestyle.

Other books include:

TurboCharged: Accelerate Your Fat Burning Metabolism, Get Lean Fast and Leave Diet and Exercise Rules in the Dust

The TurboCharged Mind: Eliminate Bad Habits with Hypnosis

Self-Hypnosis Download Series includes:

TurboCharged® Beginner Meditation—free!

TurboCharged® Fat Loss

Relieve Stress and Relax the TurboCharged® Way

TurboCharged® Energy

Visualizing Your TurboCharged® Body

TurboCharged® Goals and Time Management

TurboCharged® Sleep

TurboCharged® to Quit Smoking Now

TurboCharged® to Success

Coming soon, three new books...

365 TurboCharged® Days!

The Science Behind TurboCharged®

TurboCharged® Success Log

TURBOCHARGED® REFRIGERATOR MAGNET

Go to the store at www.turbocharged.us.com and order your TurboCharged magnet to stick on your refrigerator or wherever it is most helpful. It says…

STOP!

Are You Really Hungry
or
Just Thirsty?

Have a Big Drink of Water.

Make it a *TurboCharged®* Day!

WRITE TO THE AUTHORS

Although we cannot guarantee that every letter written to Dian Griesel, Ph.D. and Tom Griesel will be individually answered, all will be forwarded. They appreciate hearing from readers and learning about successes, thoughts and benefits from the TurboCharged program.

You can contact Dian and Tom at www.turbocharged.us.com or by sending a letter to:

Dian Griesel, Ph.D. or Tom Griesel
c/o The Business School of Happiness
PO Box 302
Washington Depot, CT 06794

You can also email them at: info@turbocharged.us.com.

SEND FOR IMPORTANT FREE TURBOCHARGED UPDATES

Let TurboCharged send you, your relatives and friends the latest TurboCharged News Bulletins on health and nutrition discoveries. Periodically, you'll get recipes, cutting-edge science information about health, rapid fat loss, exercise, stress management and longevity, new ways to accelerate your metabolism and more.

Send us your email address or your full address. Please neatly print each address.

Mail to:

TurboCharged

c/o Business School of Happiness
PO Box 302
Washington Depot, CT 06794

Or, log onto www.turbocharged.us.com and sign up yourself and others.

Name:_____

Address:_____

City:_____ State:_____ Zip Code:_____

Email:_____

Made in the USA
Coppell, TX
17 March 2021

51861424R00149